IMAGES
of America

TRUMBULL REVISITED

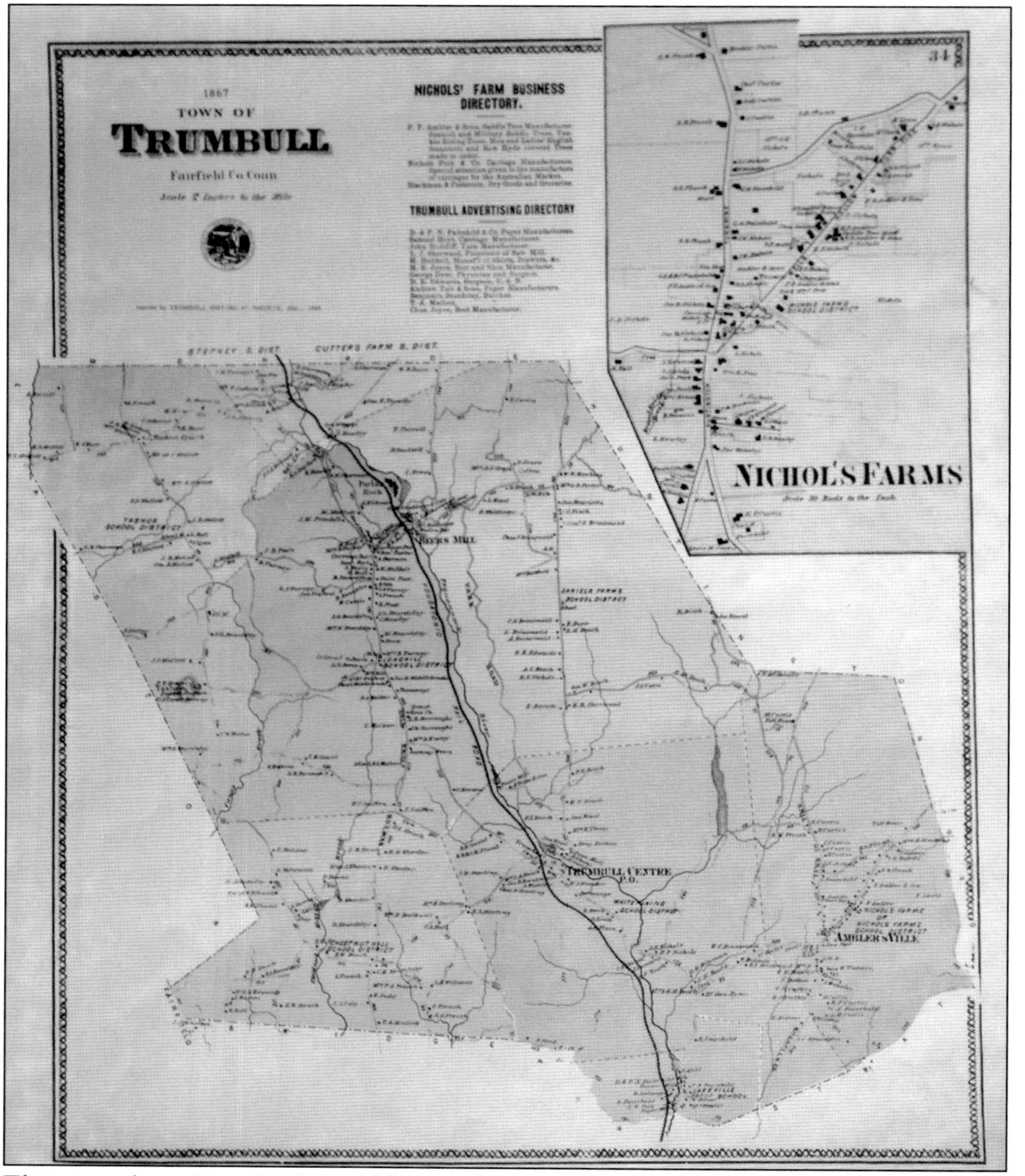

This map shows Trumbull's neighborhoods as they existed in 1867. (Courtesy Trumbull Historical Society.)

ON THE COVER: For more than 50 years, Kurtz's store in Trumbull Center was the place to go for farm feed, groceries, appliances, tools, and homespun advice. Standing outside the store in 1925 are Emmanuel Kurtz and his sons Charlie (left) and John (right). (Courtesy Trumbull Historical Society.)

IMAGES
of America

TRUMBULL REVISITED

Trumbull Historical Society

ARCADIA
PUBLISHING

ISBN 978-1-4671-2240-5

Published by Arcadia Publishing
Charleston, South Carolina

Printed in the United States of America

Library of Congress Control Number: 2014933920

For all general information, please contact Arcadia Publishing:
Telephone 843-853-2070
Fax 843-853-0044
E-mail sales@arcadiapublishing.com
For customer service and orders:
Toll-Free 1-888-313-2665

Visit us on the Internet at www.arcadiapublishing.com

To all of those Trumbull residents who had the foresight to capture their town in photographs and to their families, who had the generosity to share those priceless images.

Contents

ACKNOWLEDGMENTS

A small group of residents formed the Trumbull Historical Society 50 years ago. Concerned that the town's rapid growth threatened the treasures of its past, they embarked on a mission of preservation and historical research, without which this book would not have been possible. Today, we draw so much of what we know about Trumbull's past from the writings of those first guardians of history. The books of E. Merrill Beach and Dorothy Seeley, in particular, were priceless resources. Information on these books and others are included in the bibliography on page 127.

Expanding on that research were volunteers John Lauria, Jennifer Winschel, and Alicia Preusch, who wrote the introductions and captions in this book. All who read this book are indebted to them for stepping up to the plate. So too are we indebted to those who filled in the gaps with their memories and their personal photographs. They include Rick Henrietta, Phil and Ray Kollar, Paul Kurtz, Cindy Hall Arendt, Frances Kleitz, and Ruth and Bill Wakeley.

Without Lois Levine's diligence and hard work, we would have no photograph collection at Trumbull Historical Society. Lois, let me assure you here that despite the pillaging of your files resulting from this book, your years of hard work will not be undone. My immediate next project is to return all the photographs used in this book to their designated files.

Of course, this project also could not have been accomplished without the support and guidance of the Trumbull Historical Society Board of Directors: Ken Martin, Christine El Eris, Samantha Klain, Mallory Huron, Jennifer Winschel, Lois Levine, Gregory Fuimara, Karen Zmijewski, Barry Zmijewski, and treasurer Wayne Sakal. Their tireless efforts to protect and celebrate Trumbull's past could not possibly fit between two covers.

Unless otherwise noted, all images in this book appear courtesy of the Trumbull Historical Society

In closing, I would also like to thank our editor at Arcadia Publishing, Caitrin Cunningham, for her guidance—and most of all her patience—in making this book a reality.

—Debra Judge Silber
Trumbull Historical Society
March 2014

INTRODUCTION

The fascinating thing about the history of a place is that it reveals itself in small ways every day, despite the veil of suburban development. The town of Trumbull, Connecticut, founded in 1797, is no exception. The community's origin as a loose collection of farms, factories, and villages remains ready to be rediscovered by anyone with an interest in exploring the past that lies just beneath the surface. If you are one of those people, we hope this book will help you on your quest.

Conceived as a companion to Images of America: *Trumbull*, published in 1997, *Trumbull Revisited* celebrates the settlements and farms that united to form Trumbull. Although the landscape has changed, their names live on: Nichols, Long Hill, Tashua, Chestnut Hill, Daniels Farm, and Trumbull Center, encompassing the White Plains. Each is celebrated with a chapter in this book, organized roughly in the order in which the area was settled, or, in the case of Daniels Farm and Chestnut Hill, the time period in which that area saw its most marked development. The ruggedly beautiful Pequonnock Valley, the site of much of the town's industry in the 19th century, stands apart today as the town's most precious natural resource. As such, it is the focus of its own chapter.

Many of these areas, now considered neighborhoods, developed more or less simultaneously. More than 100 years before its official incorporation, settlers from the coastal town of Stratford (originally called Cupheag) began surveying the forests to the north. Obtaining lands from the native Paugussett tribes, they established farms there. Abraham Nichols is credited with the first permanent settlement in 1690 in the area that bears his name.

By 1705, families were settling in Trumbull Center, and in 1725, they officially established the parish of Unity. Their first church, Unity Congregational Church, was built in 1730 near what is now the intersection of Unity and White Plains Roads.

At the same time, families were establishing themselves to the west in a place called Long Hill. In 1744, Long Hill and Unity joined together and became the Society of North Stratford. Mills were established along the Pequonnock River, land was cleared for farms, and homes and taverns built. It was not until after the American Revolution, however, that residents would petition for the establishment of a new town. On October 12, 1797, Trumbull—named for the family of the state's colonial governor—was officially recognized by the state's general assembly.

The new town, encompassing just over 23 square miles, got off to a modest start. In 1800, its population stood just shy of 1,300. Over the next 100 years, the population would grow by a mere 300 more residents. Yet the town was changing. Although farms made up much of the area, more mills and small factories appeared, churning out paper, carriages, glove linings, and cigars. Schoolhouses were built. A railroad was laid through the Pequonnock Valley, and beside it, railroad operators built Parlor Rock Amusement Park. Operating from 1878 to 1898, the park's lakes, picnic areas, and other attractions drew as many as 3,000 visitors a day.

The 20th century brought greater changes. A flood in 1905 wiped out the last of the old mills, and by 1932, the railroad was abandoned. Within a few years, the Merritt Parkway would cut a swath through the southern part of town, bisecting old neighborhoods while at the same time creating a demand for new ones. As wartime industries flourished in nearby cities and, later, as servicemen returned home to start families, Trumbull's open spaces beckoned. Between 1940 and 1970, the town's population increased nearly sixfold. Farms and fields folded into housing developments, a regional shopping mall was built, and a new generation of modern schools opened their doors to Trumbull's newest natives.

In the middle of all this progress, the Trumbull Historical Society was founded in 1964. These individuals recognized the danger the town's rapid growth presented to Trumbull's heritage. While the photographs in this book stand as a testament to the many changes the town has undergone, there were, nonetheless, some victories in the name of preservation. Standing out among them is the joint purchase in 1989 of the Pequonnock River Valley by the Town of Trumbull and the state Department of Environmental Protection as an open-space park. Another is the continued vitality of the Trumbull Historical Society, which continues its mission of celebrating Trumbull's history through exhibits, education, and events geared to young and old.

Bringing Trumbull's past alive for all those wishing to understand it is the mission of this book. It has been a daunting project, for recreating the history of a place through photographs—there are more than 200 in this book—is as difficult as it is intriguing. Many of the photographs passed hand to hand (and often generation to generation) before ending up in our collection have arrived unidentified, misidentified, and partially identified. In this book, we have done our best to confirm the identities of the people and places depicted in the photographs we have chosen. Where that was not possible, we have supplied bits of local lore and general information about the subject of those photographs and how they fit into the unfolding story of our town. Mysteries like these make compiling a book of this type frustrating but also fascinating. Most of all, it causes us to look at the ordinary scenery of our town with a new, more perceptive eye. It enables us to see things that more casual viewers do not, to become invested at an entirely different level. It reminds us of how lucky we are to live here.

In 1998, shortly after our first photograph book, Images of America: *Trumbull*, was released, we received a surprising letter. It was from Peter Wyton of Gloucestershire, England, a Royal Air Force retiree who had set foot in the United States but once—visiting an air base in Nebraska. Lamenting that this single visit to our country did not allow him to experience "small town" America, he had taken up that first book of photographs of our town. Without the remotest connection to Trumbull or its families, he was moved to pen this verse, which he enclosed with his letter:

I'd like to go to Trumbull
though I don't suppose I will
by the Housatonic Railroad
via Bridgeport and Long Hill,
where the Berkshire line took tourists
in old-fashioned rolling stock
to promenade and picnic
in the woods at Parlor Rock.

Ride on Campyon Cutter's bus
and hear the Reverend Morgan preach,
buy a shirt from Harvey Hubbel,
eat clam-bake with Agur Beach
get some gas from Walter's garage,
smoke a Gabler's "Judge" cigar,
as I drive down Beardsley Parkway
in an elegant motor car.

Nice trick if you can do it,
travel back a hundred years,
meet the Radcliffes and the Middlebrooks,
the Walkers and the Freers,
crowd the porch around the homestead,
sing, read poetry and play
guitar with pleasant folks in
Trumbull's long-lost yesterday.

While we cannot presume that the photographs chosen for this book will stir our readers to poetry, we do hope they engender a similar feeling of connection to our town. Whether you have grown up in Trumbull, recently moved here, or, like Peter Wyton, never walked our tree-lined streets, we hope these photographs will bring Trumbull home to you.

One

Nichols

The area known as Nichols lies in the southeastern corner of Trumbull. The area also includes the Nichols Farms Historic District, which is listed in the National Register of Historic Places. Nichols was settled in the late 1600s, when settlers were given permission by the village of Stratford to venture further inland to cultivate new farmland. Abraham Nichols, one of the first landowners to establish a farm in Nichols, purchased a large plot of land sometime around 1700. The family maintained large farms in the area for many centuries, giving the village its name. The Trumbull Historical Society Museum, in Abraham Nichols Park, is located on the site of the original Nichols farm. The names of other prominent Nichols families—such as Curtiss, Plumb, Hawley, and Fairchild—can be found on the plaques outside many of the antique homes and on the street signs and buildings.

Before the village of Nichols was established, the area was home to the Paugussett Indian Nation. Today, Nichols is home to the smallest and one of the oldest Native American reservations in the country, a quarter acre of land located on Shelton Road.

Nichols is known for several landmarks, including the green in front of the Nichols Methodist Church, the Bunny Fountain, and the Starkweather House. All three are included in the private trust known as the Nichols Improvement Association. The Nichols area is also home to the former Pine Brook Club, a popular 1930s resort later reestablished as the Pinewood Lake Association. The village is also home to the Trumbull Senior Center, Nichols Fire Department, and the Fairchild Library, the only branch of the Trumbull Public Library still in operation.

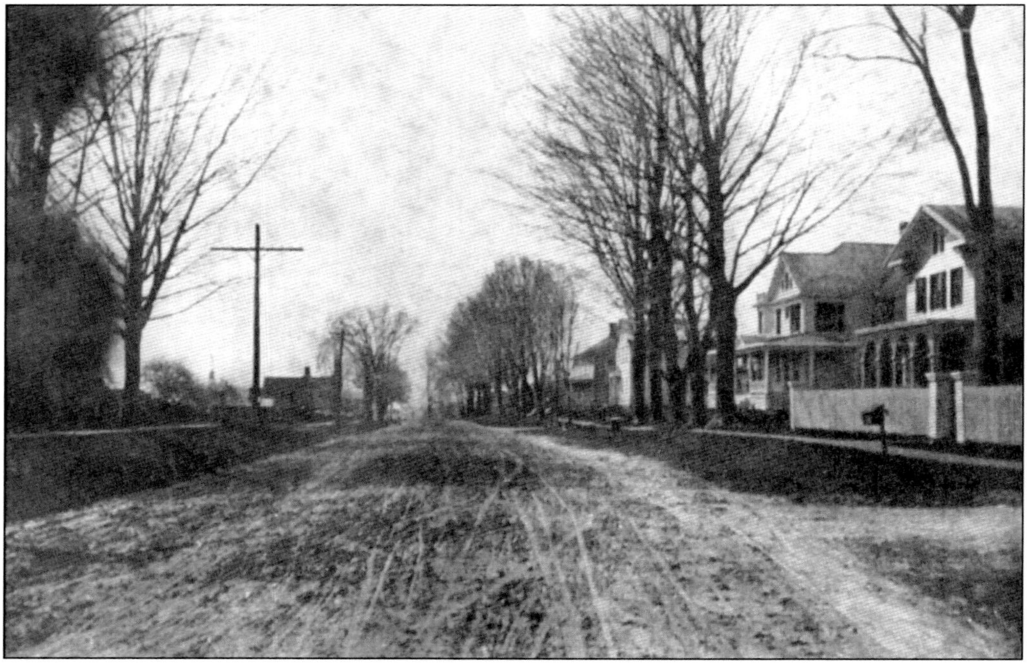

Above, a postcard shows South Main Street (now Huntington Turnpike) in Nichols. Laid out in 1696, the "Farm Highway" connected farms and mills in Nichols to its mother settlement of Stratford. To this day, many of Trumbull's finest old homes line this prominent thoroughfare. Below, a similar photograph taken in 1909 shows the road looking north. The house on the right at 1856 Huntington Turnpike is now the Trumbull Historical Society Museum.

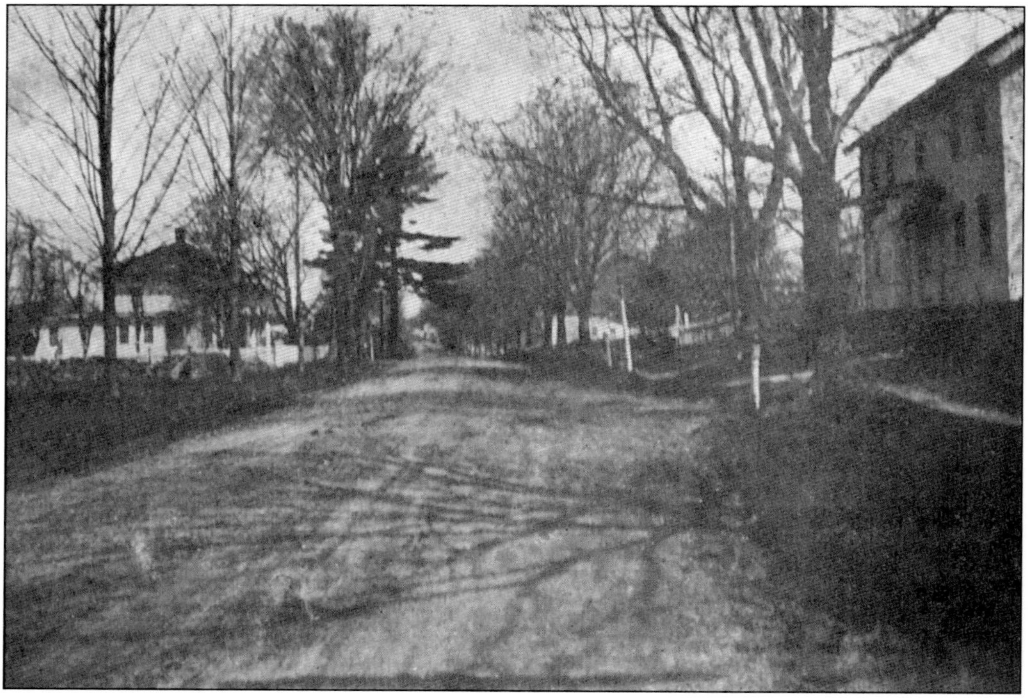

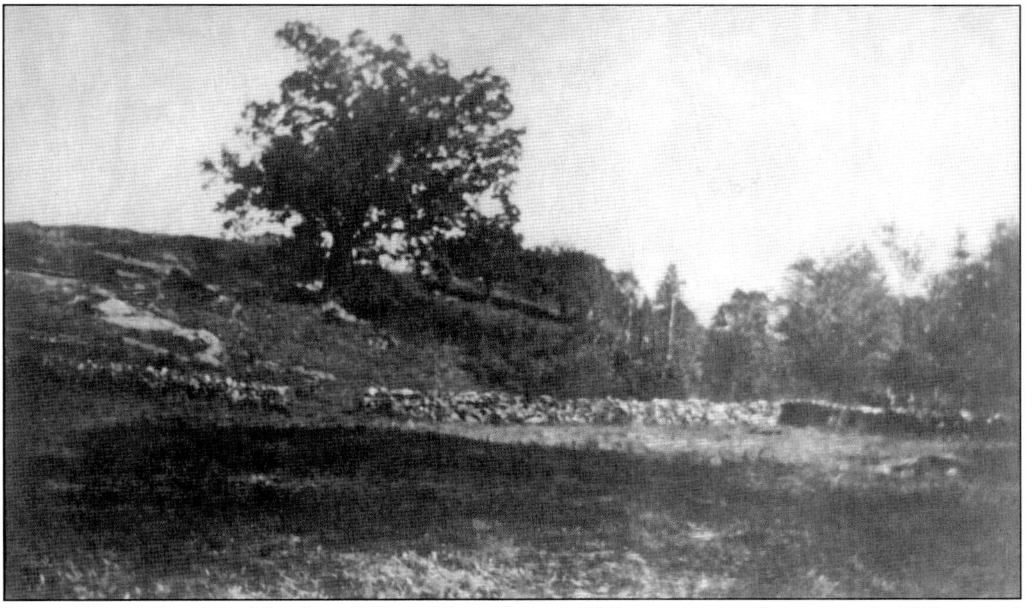

Legend has it that this old oak at the top of Mountain Hill, located behind the Trumbull Historical Society in Abraham Nichols Park, was climbed by Revolutionary soldiers to watch for British ships in Long Island Sound. Though few details are known, reports exist that a contingent of troops under the Comte de Rochambeau, en route to assist Washington, camped in the area. French coins have been recovered on the hill, lending further credence to the story.

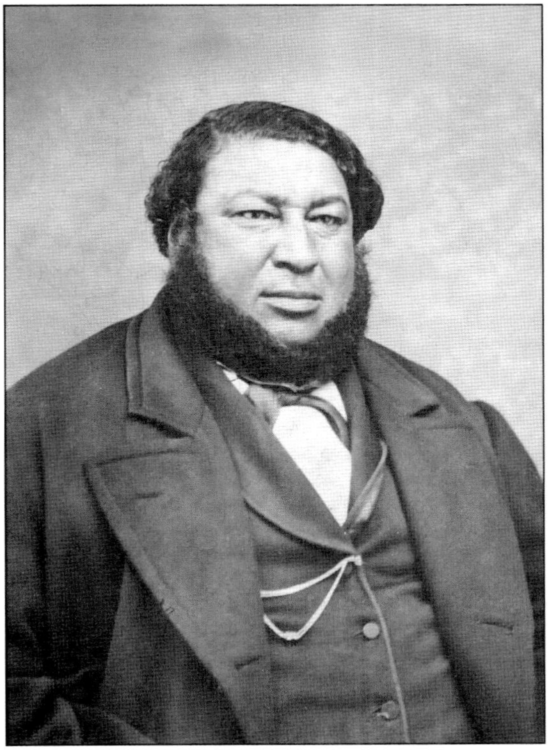

Born in 1825, William Sherman was a member of the Golden Hill Paugussett tribe. His family was among the last of the tribe to remain in Trumbull. In 1875, two years after this photograph was taken, Sherman used money he had saved as a day laborer to purchase for his people a quarter-acre parcel on Shelton Road. Known as the Golden Hill Reservation, it remains one of the oldest and the smallest Native American reservations in the country.

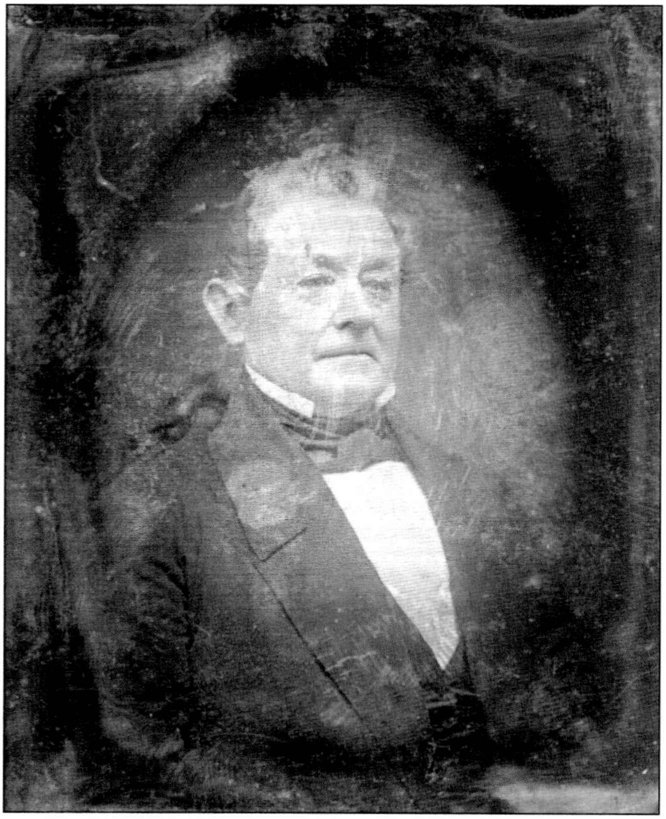

A 19th-century tintype captures the likeness of Franklin P. Ambler, born in 1797, the same year Trumbull was incorporated. In the 19th century, Ambler and his family were involved in the production of carriages and saddletrees (the frame upon which a saddle is built) in Nichols. The family's presence was so prominent that for a time, the area became known as Amblersville.

In addition to Ambler's carriage shop, 19th-century Nichols was home to several businesses. E.L. Hitt operated a blacksmith's shop on what was then called Center Street (now Center Road) in Nichols. The building pictured here was the second one on the site.

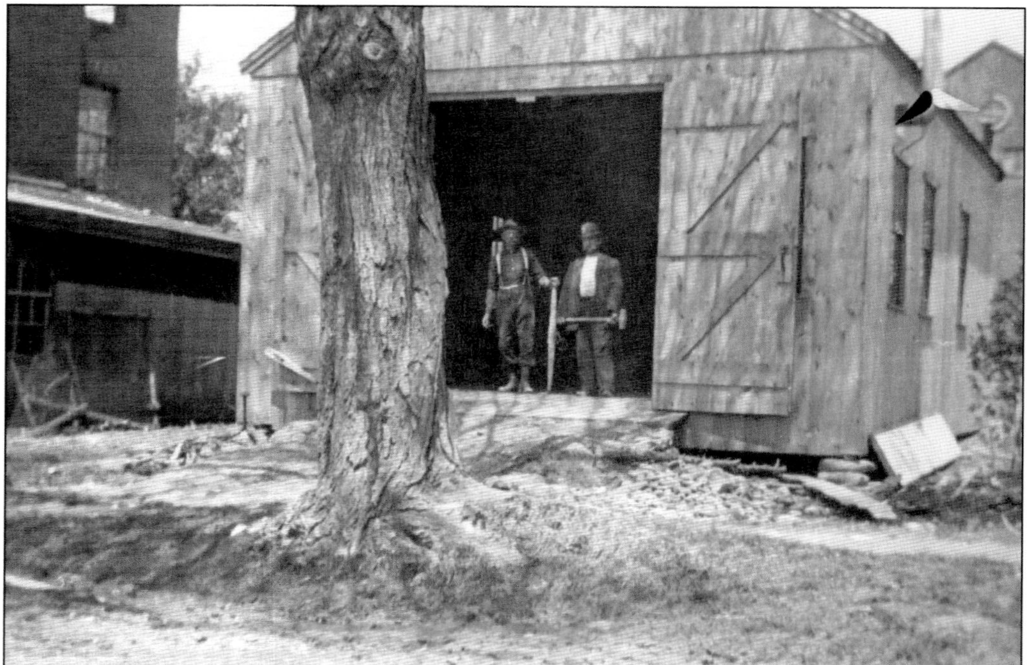

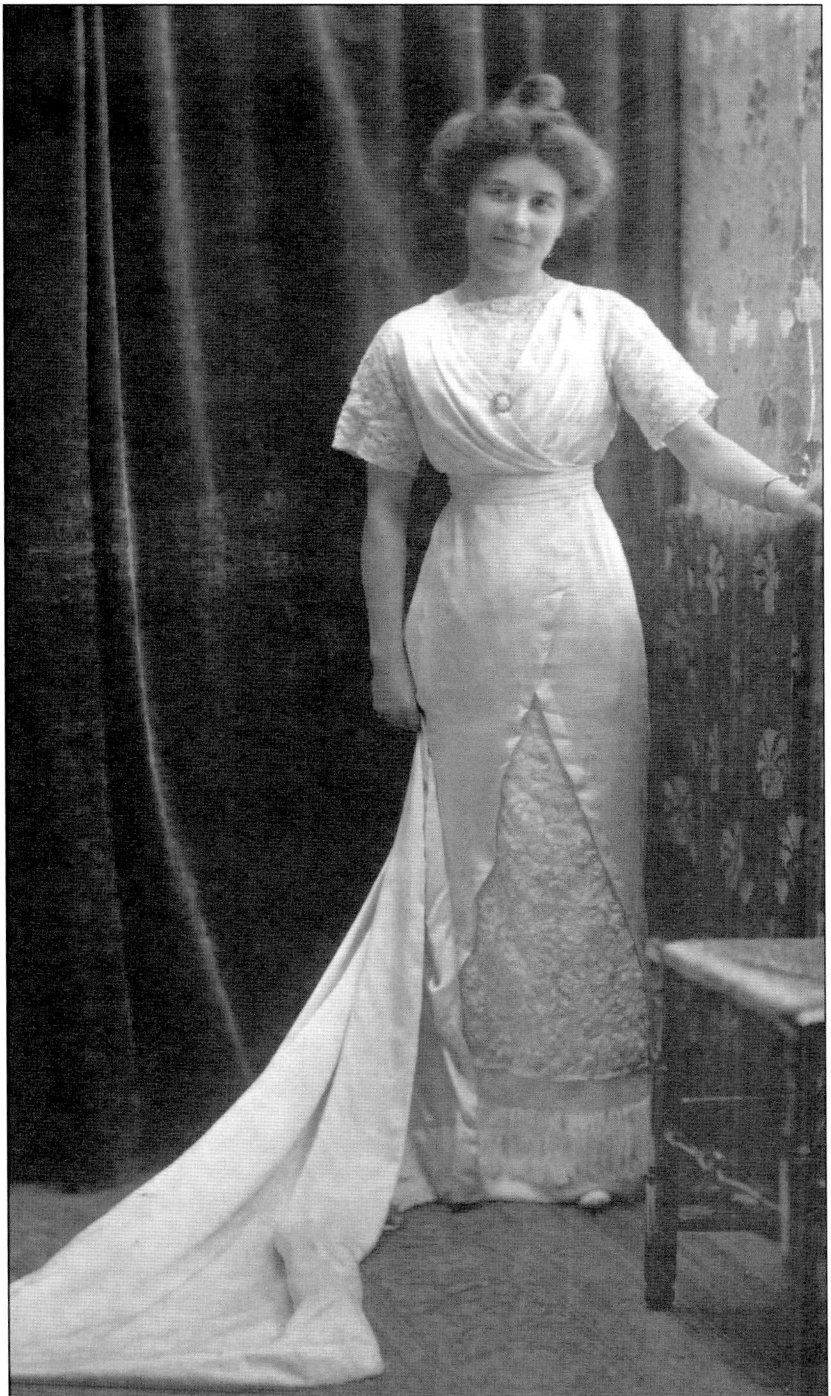

Edith Plumb Nothnagle stands in her wedding dress at the age of 22. Both the Plumbs and the Nothnagles were prominent families of the time in Trumbull. The Nothnagle family owned a large furniture store in Bridgeport, and a small park in Nichols is also named for them.

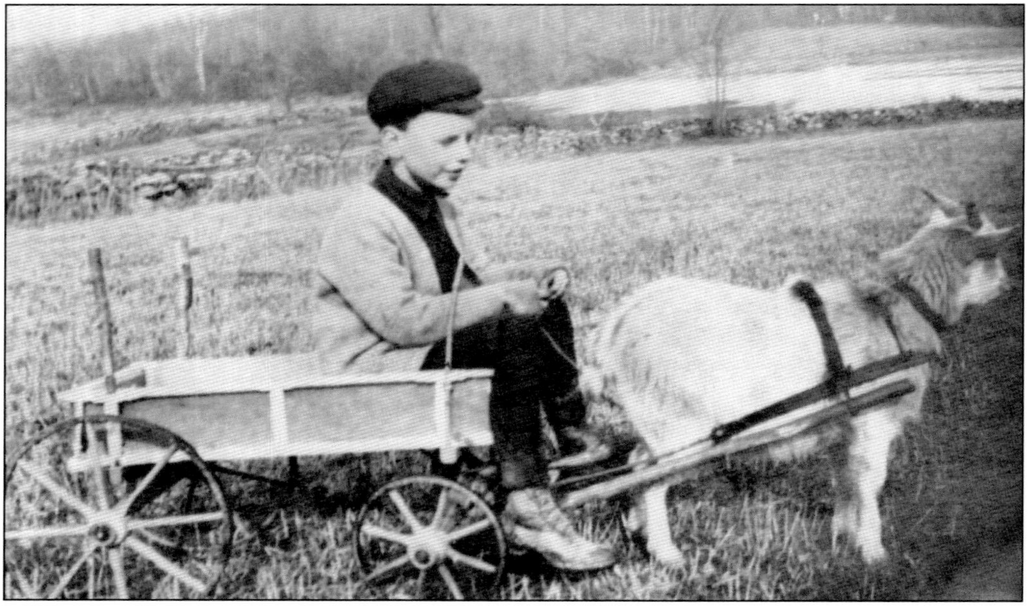

Ray Curtis was just seven years old when this photograph was taken in 1911. Curtis, who lived at 2050 Huntington Turnpike, would often drive his pet goat on the unpaved road up to Fairchild's Feed Store to pick up chicken feed. The store was located on the east side of the road, where Erwin Street now enters Huntington Turnpike.

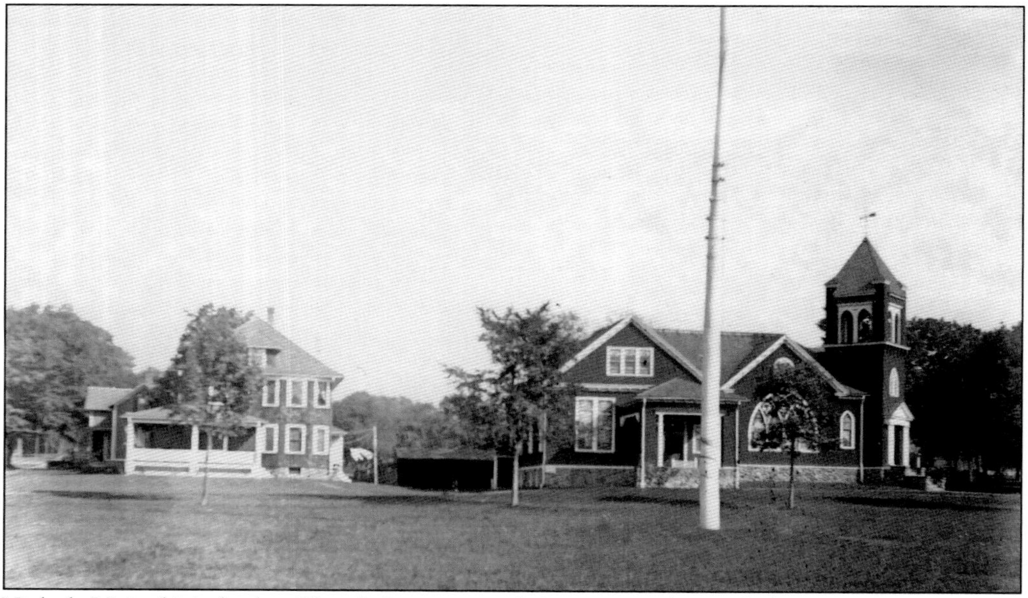

Nichols United Methodist Church has occupied this site on the Nichols Green for more than 150 years. Still located at the triangle formed by Huntington Turnpike and Shelton Road, the green was a popular place for residents to gather and enjoy baseball games and picnics. Erected in 1892, the flagpole was the tallest in the state at the time. Young Nichols boys would take turns trying to climb the flagpole. The green is now owned and maintained by the Nichols Improvement Association.

John Peet ran a successful real estate business in New York but spent his summers in Nichols, where he was born in 1849. He and his wife, Antoinette Edwards, are most fondly remembered for the landmark Bunny Fountain on the corner of Unity Road and Huntington Turnpike. The fountain, which provided drinking water for horses and dogs, was given to the town by Antoinette Peet in 1895 in memory of her husband. The fountain was moved three times to different locations around the Nichols Green before its present installation next to the Starkweather House, where it serves as a welcoming monument to the village of Nichols.

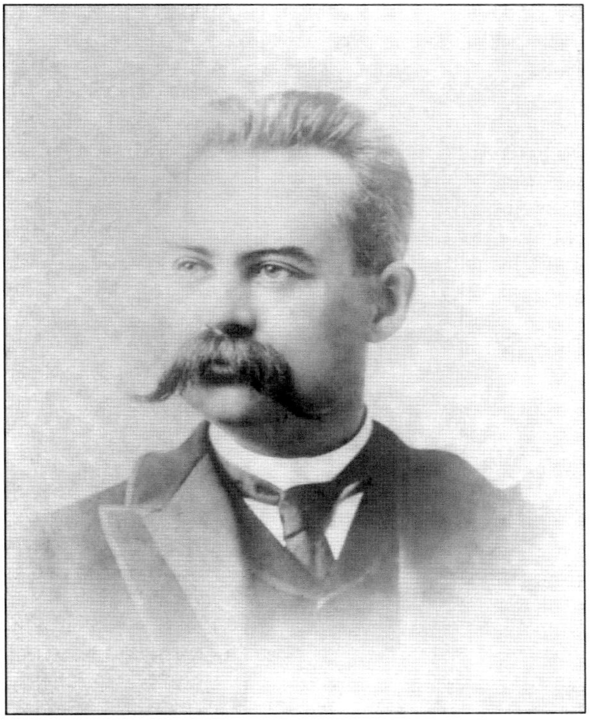

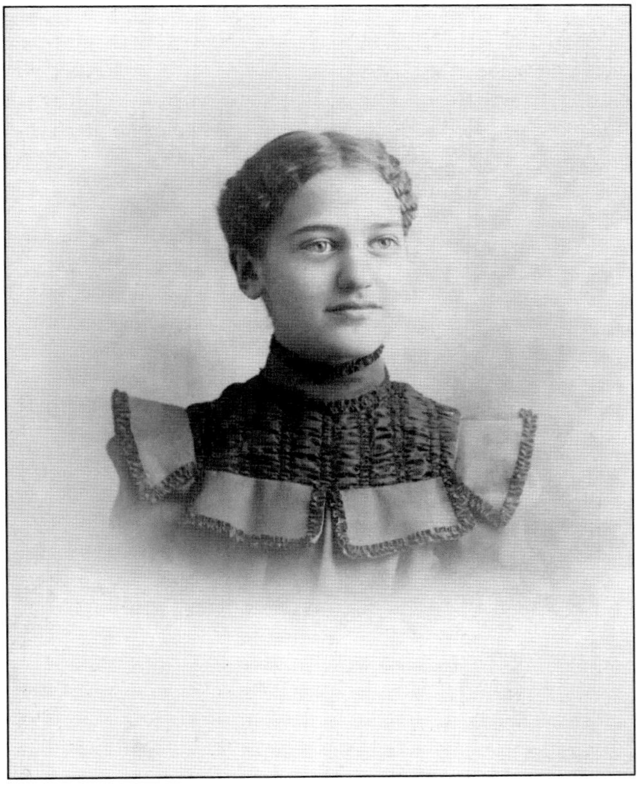

Alice Wellington served many years as librarian at the Fairchild Memorial Library, retiring in 1968 at the age of 82. She was known for her rapport with children and the beautiful gardens she tended at her home on Shelton Road.

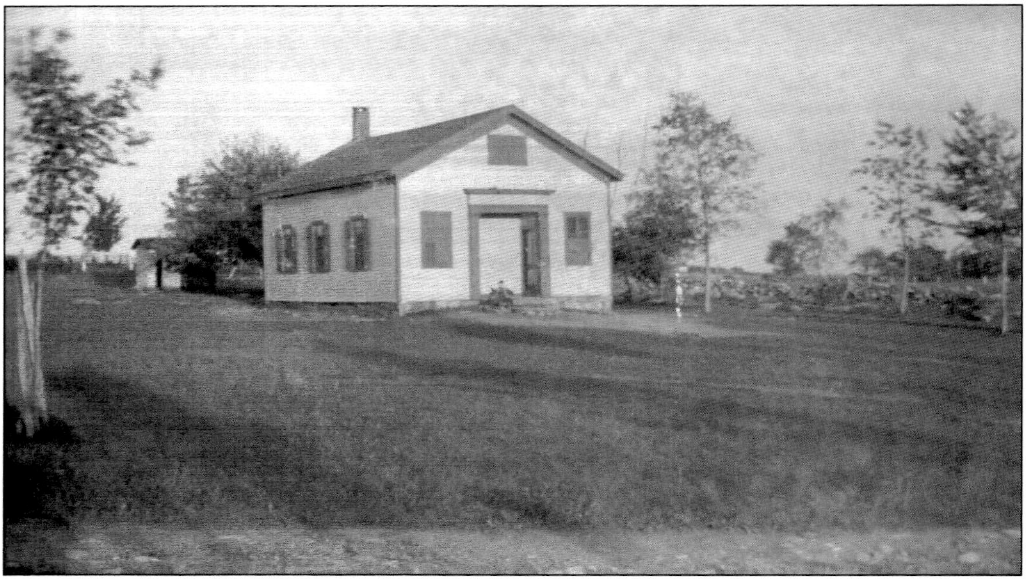

As the village of Nichols grew, so did the need for a schoolhouse. The first one-room schoolhouse was established on Huntington Turnpike in 1852. The school was later moved to Shelton Road, where this photograph was taken in 1866. Before Nichols had its own church, services and meetings were often held inside the school. Many of the boys could attend school only in the winter, as they had to help on family farms during the summer, spring, and fall.

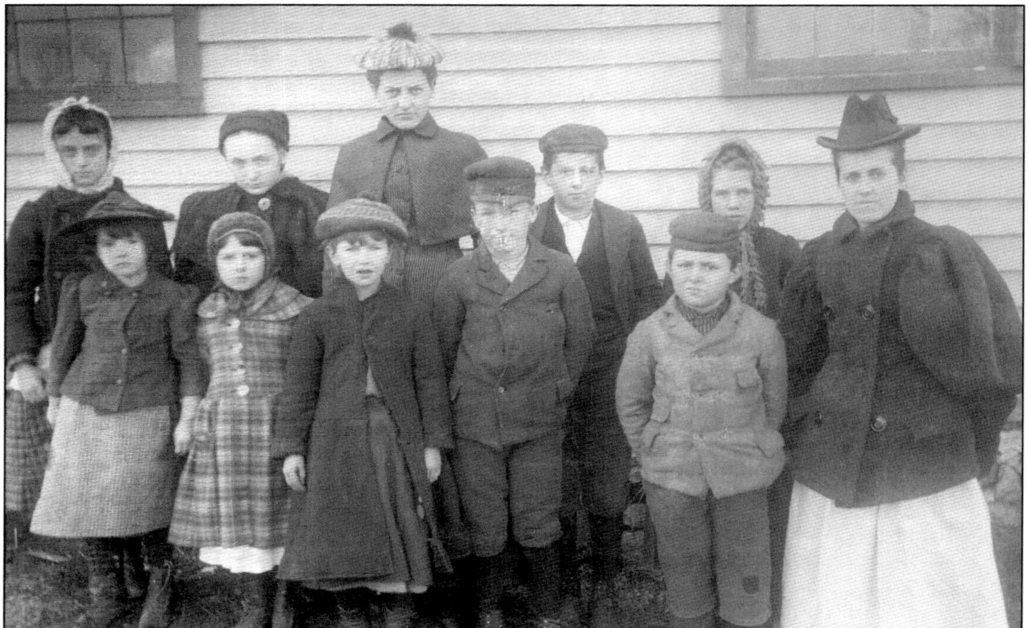

Above, Nichols students pose for a class photograph with their teacher Ida Williams, standing at right. From left to right are (first row) an unidentified Bassett, Nellie Wanzer, Hattie Bassett, an unidentified student, and Frank Honkey; (second row) Ina Nichols, Lily Hale, Alice Shellon, Will Weeks, and Sadie Bassett.

By 1912, when this photograph was taken, a second story had been added to the Nichols School to accommodate the growing number of students. Eventually, steam heat was also installed in the building. The school was used until 1920, when a new brick school was built at Priscilla Place. The old school eventually became the Nichols Fire Department and, later, a village library. It was torn down in the 1930s to make room for the present-day Nichols Fire Department Station House No. 1.

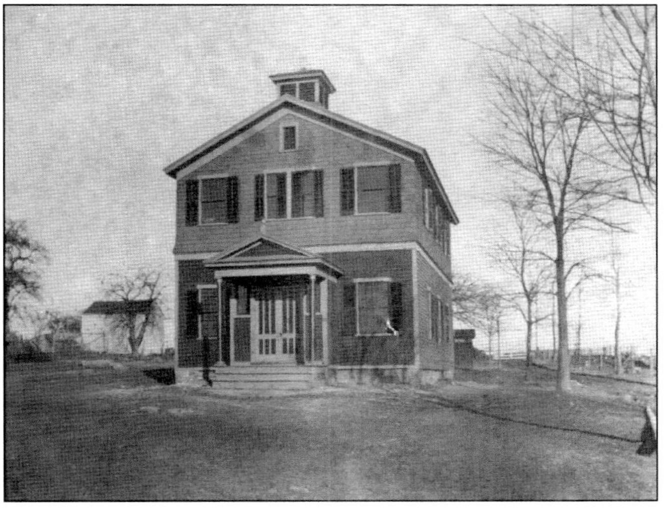

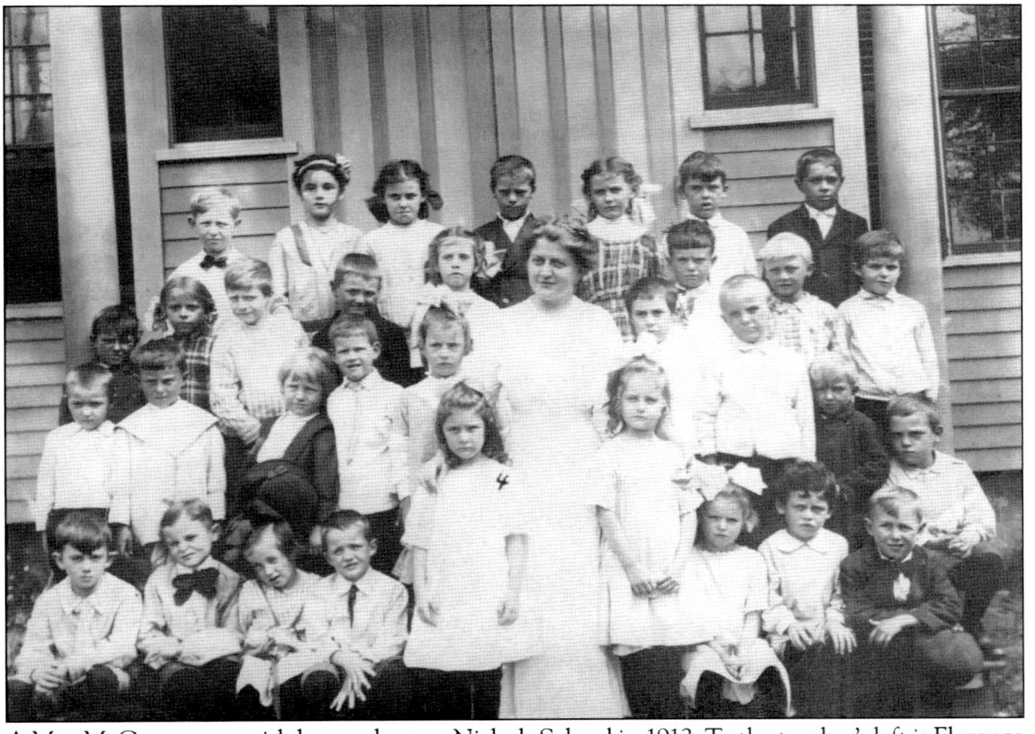

A Mrs. McCann poses with her students at Nichols School in 1912. To the teacher's left is Florence Hitt, who lived on Center Road in Nichols. Her father, Ernest Hitt, was a local blacksmith and also worked repairing carriages in the Nichols carriage factory. When Florence contracted tuberculosis at age 17, her mother refused to send her away to a sanitarium and instead nursed her at home. To keep Florence busy during her recovery, her mother collected prints and scraps for her to use in making a quilt. That quilt is now part of the permanent collection at the Trumbull Historical Society.

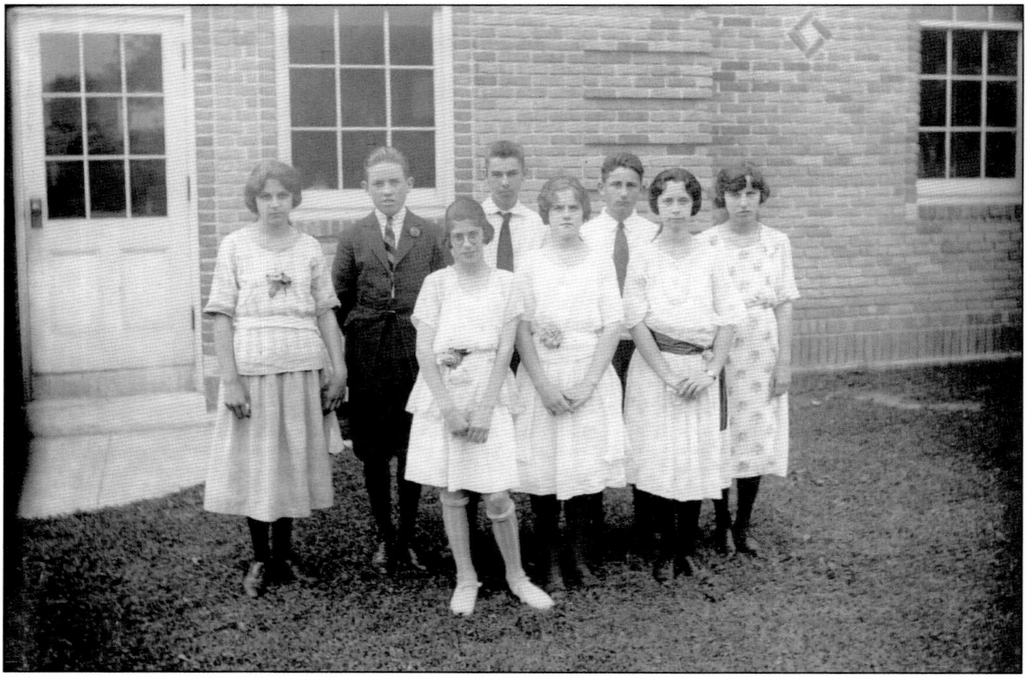

Above, members of the first eighth-grade graduating class pose in front of the new Nichols School in 1921. Built in 1920, the Priscilla Place school building had modern utilities and multiple classrooms. Graduates of this and other elementary schools would continue their education in Bridgeport until 1960, when a high school (now Madison Middle School) was built on Madison Avenue. After retiring as a school, the Priscilla Place building became Trumbull Senior Center. The original school-building flagpole is now in front of the Trumbull Historical Society. Below, a group of Nichols School students gather for a photograph.

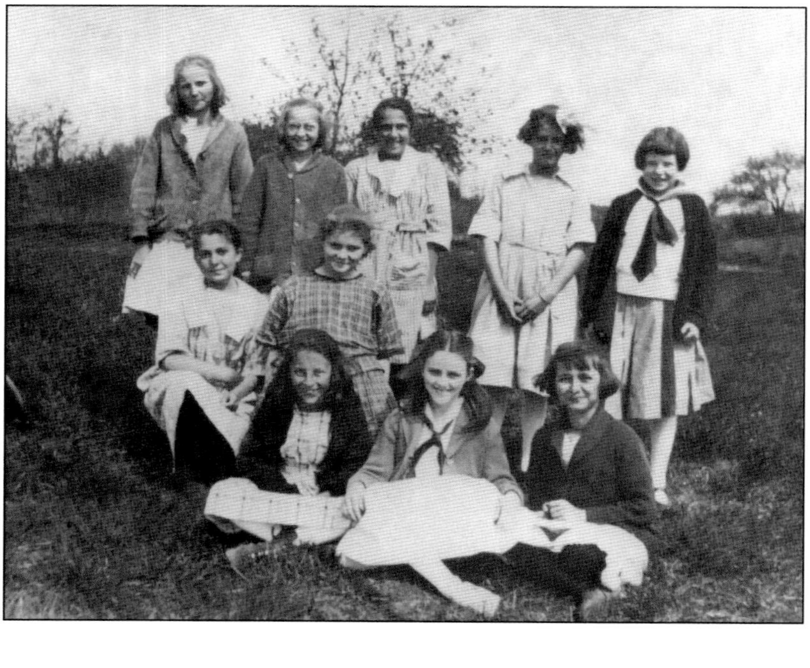

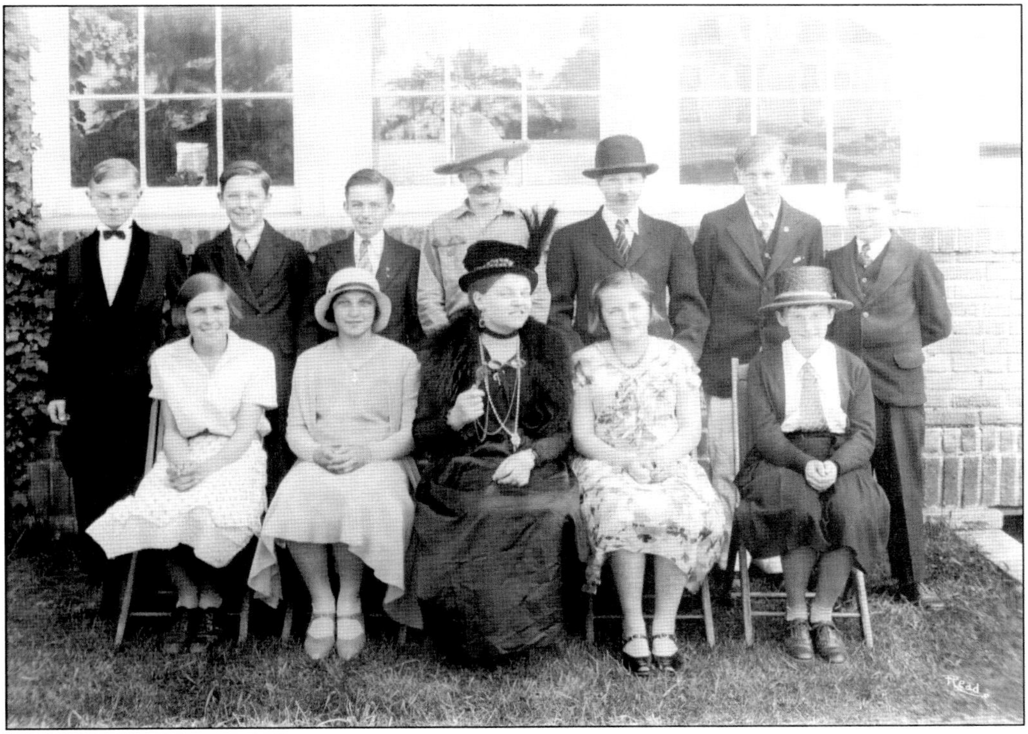

Above, students from Nichols School pose dressed in costumes for the play *Meet Uncle Sally* in May 1931. Eventually, Nichols children would start their education at an entirely new school on Booth Hill Road. Below, students take part in a dance festival at Booth Hill School in June 1965.

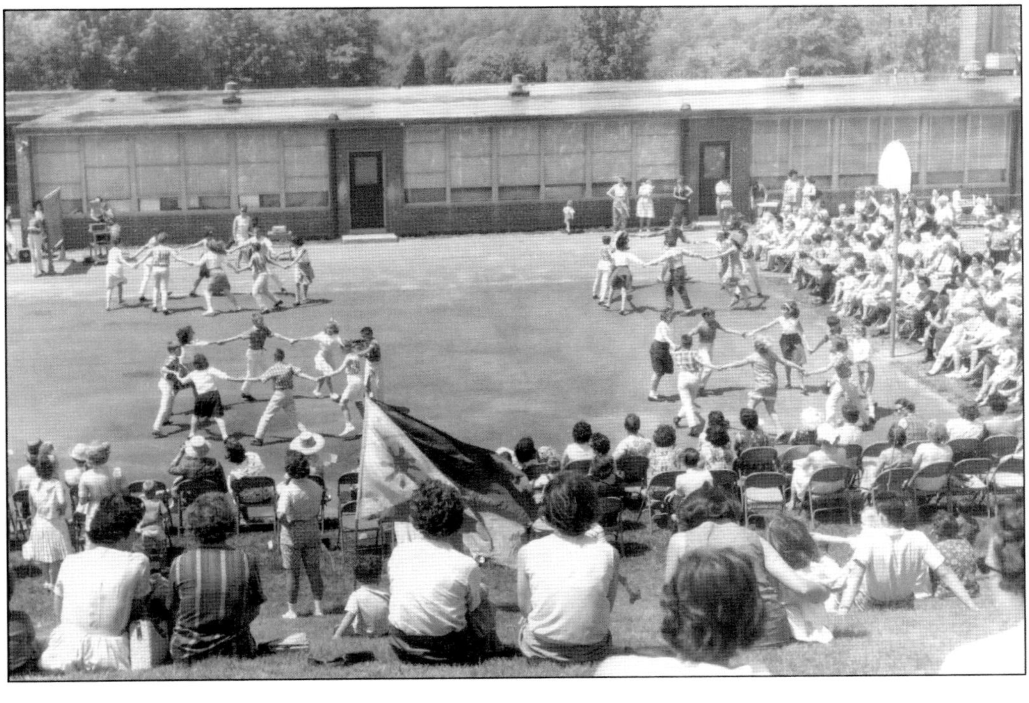

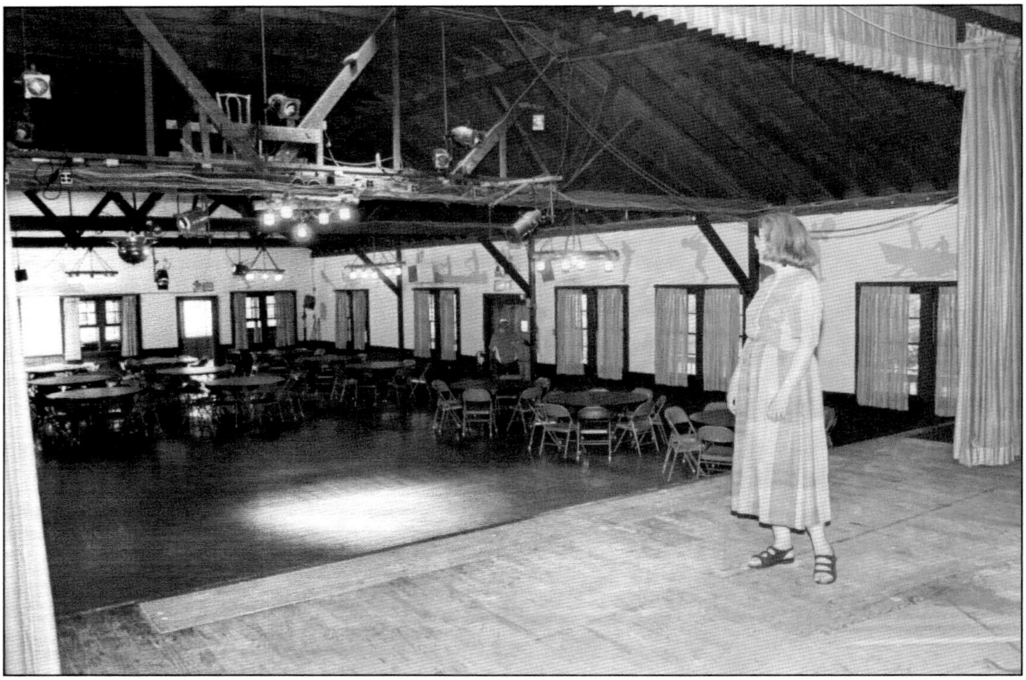

The unique revolving stage at Pine Brook Lodge drew notable actors and writers to Trumbull through the 1930s. The lodge was the centerpiece of a resort established by Benjamin Plotkin on the shores of what had been originally called Old Farm Pond, which was later renamed Upper Bunnell's Pond while under ownership of the Bridgeport Hydraulic Company. Plotkin renamed the site and built the lodge and a number of summer cabins. Following World War II, the resort fell on hard times and was divided into private building lots. The private Pinewood Lake Association now manages the lodge and facilities at the lake.

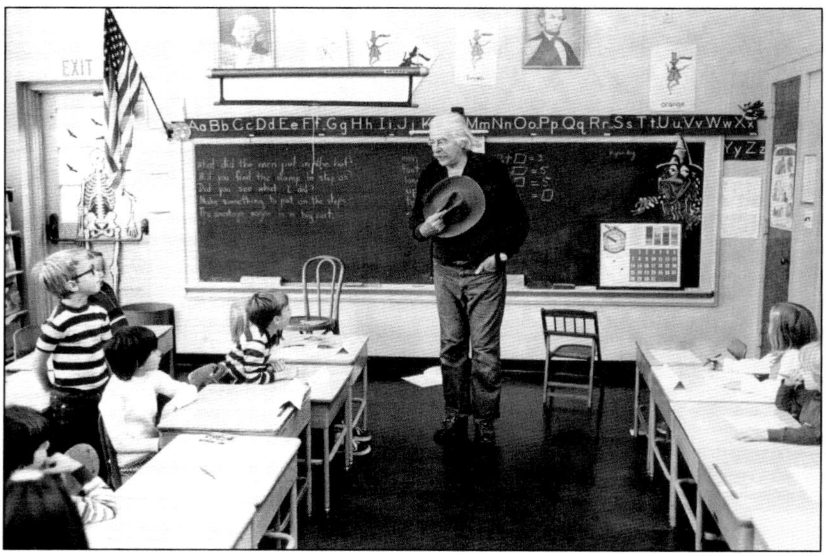

Actor Will Geer, known for his portrayal of "Grandpa Walton" on the television show *The Waltons*, was a Nichols resident in the 1970s, living in a secluded home off Nichols Avenue. Here, he visits a local school in 1975.

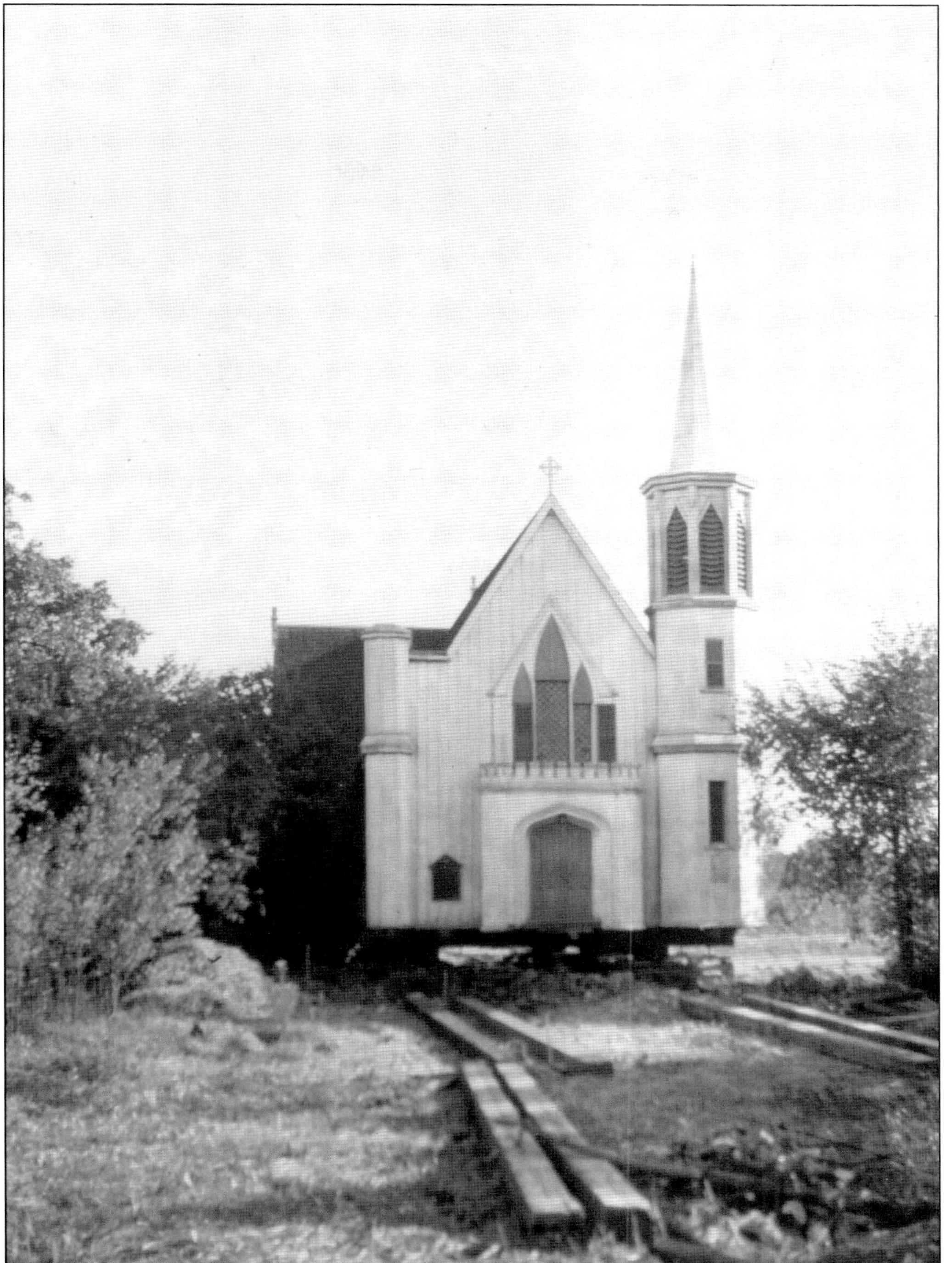

Finding itself within yards of the newly built Merritt Parkway in 1939, Trinity Church Nichols was moved from its original site at the corner of Huntington Turnpike and Jerusalem Hill Road to its present location farther north. This photograph shows the church, built in 1848, as it was being slid on huge timbers to its new location. (Courtesy Trinity Church.)

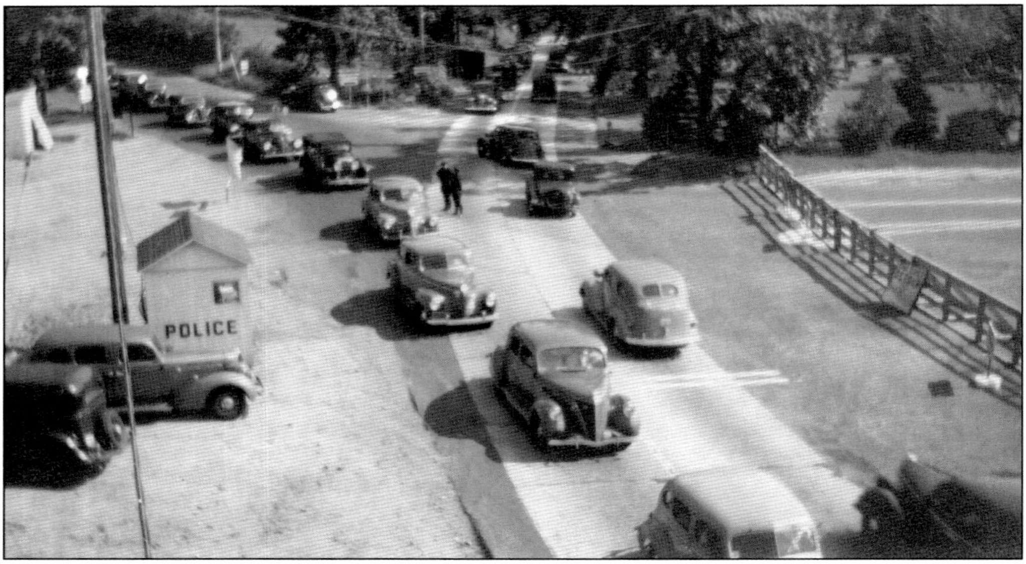

When the Merritt Parkway was first built, Nichol's Huntington Turnpike ran beneath the new highway. Above, a police officer directs traffic coming north from Nichols Avenue and Huntington Turnpike during construction in November 1939. Below is a view looking north at the framework of the original bridge. The intersection was reconfigured in 1979 to make the parkway pass under Huntington Turnpike. Ornamental panels from the original bridge were restored and affixed to the new one, where they can now be seen from the parkway. (Both, courtesy Trinity Church.)

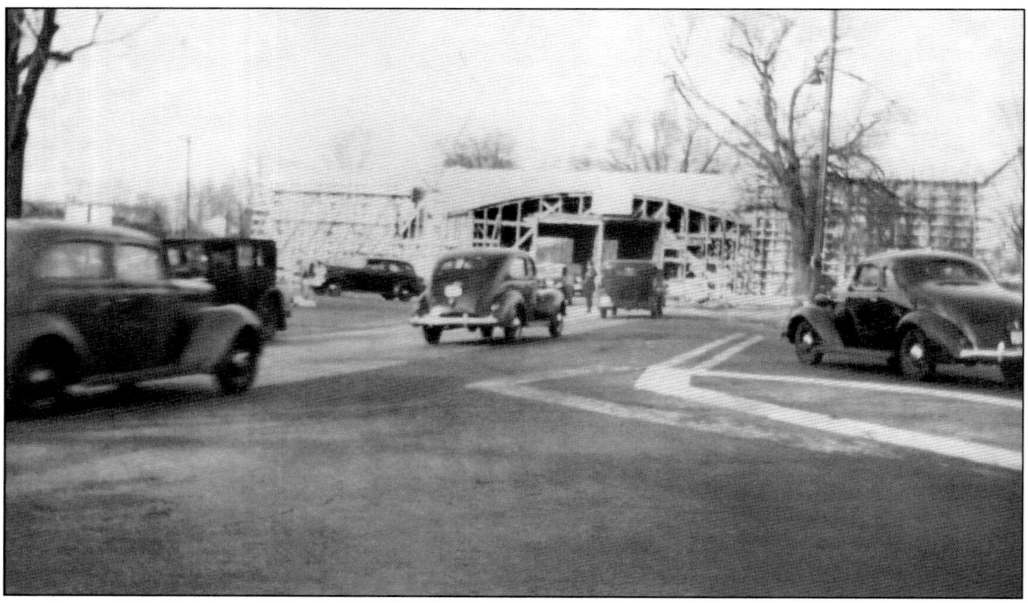

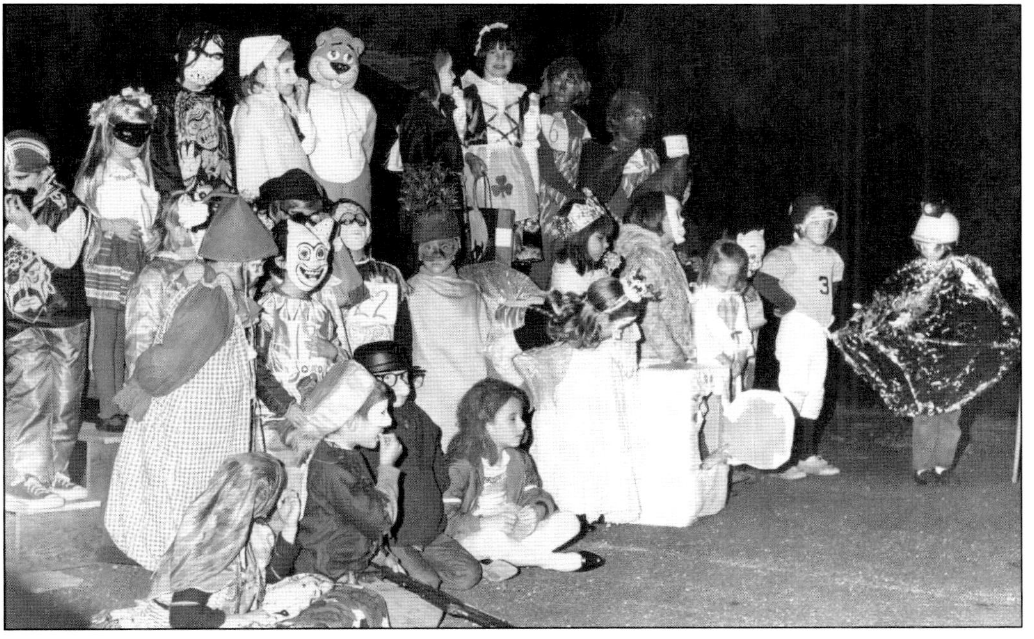

Established in 1889, the Nichols Improvement Association (NIA) is known for its stewardship of the iconic Bunny Fountain as well as its tradition of activities for Nichols families. Above, Nichols children dress up for the NIA's Halloween parade in 1967; below, families gather at the annual bonfire in 1975. Both events, and others, continue to evoke a solid sense of community.

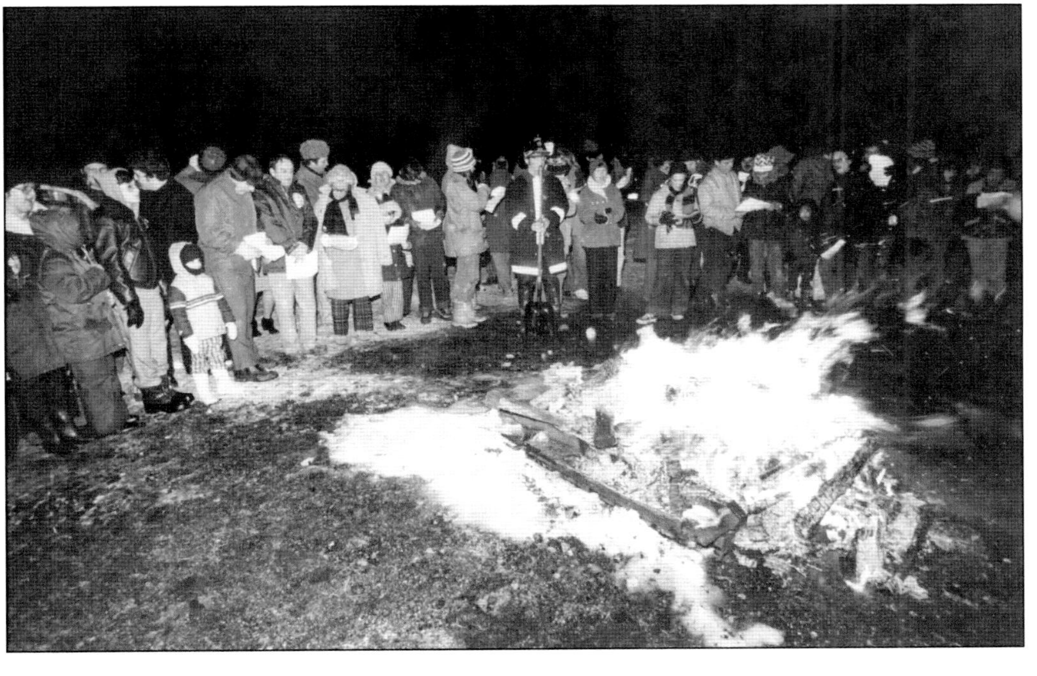

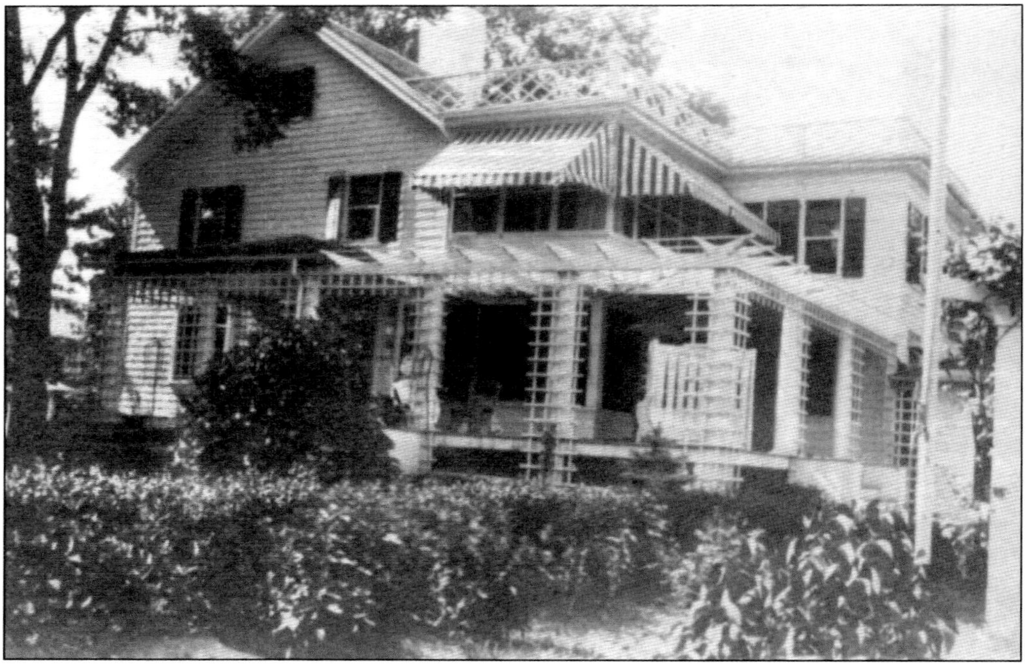

Above, the house on the estate of George and Florence Woods is now the home of the Trumbull Historical Society. This view from the southeast side shows an elaborate portico that was later removed. Below, George Woods shows off flowers in his garden.

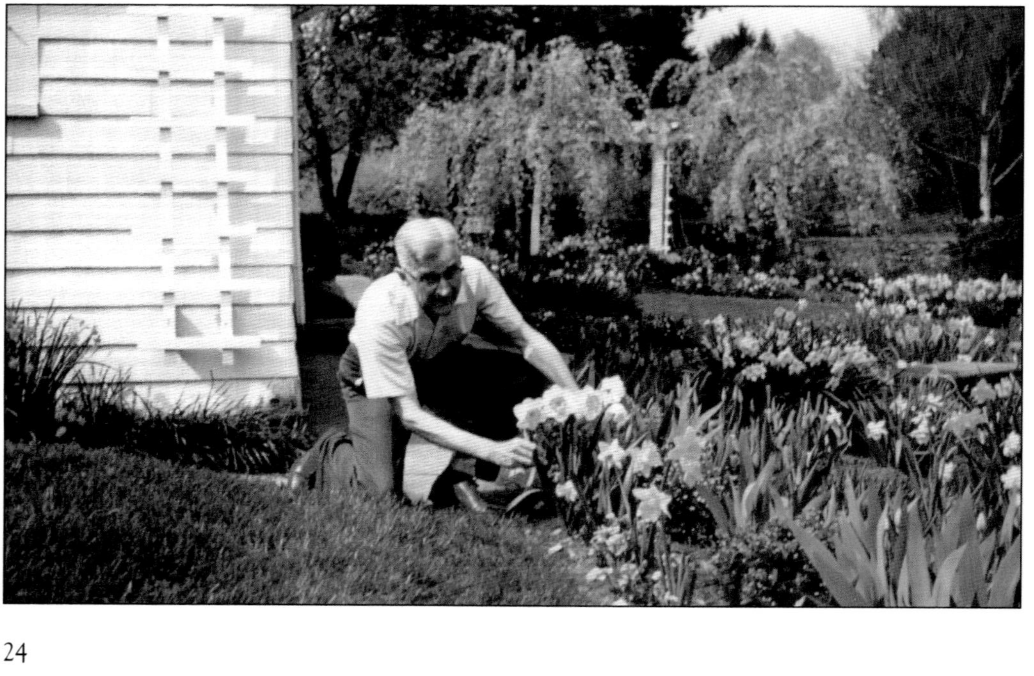

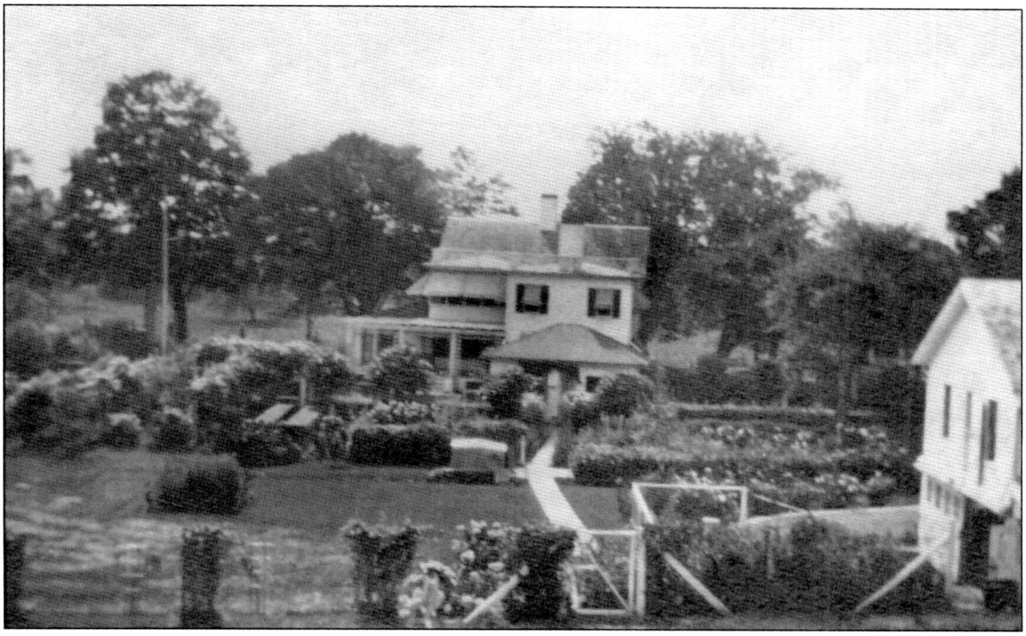

A distant view of the Woods home, above, takes in the estate's ample gardens. Both the grounds and the orchard in the rear of the former estate now make up Trumbull's Abraham Nichols Park. Below, a photograph taken during the Woods' ownership shows flowers filling the greenhouse that remains standing on the property today.

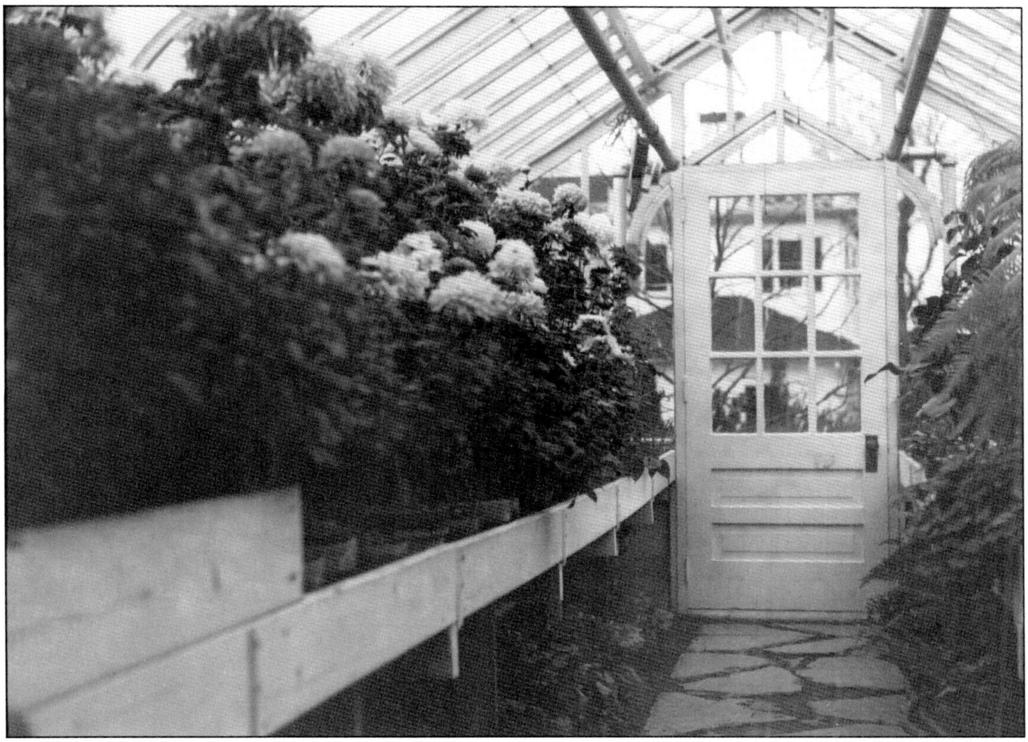

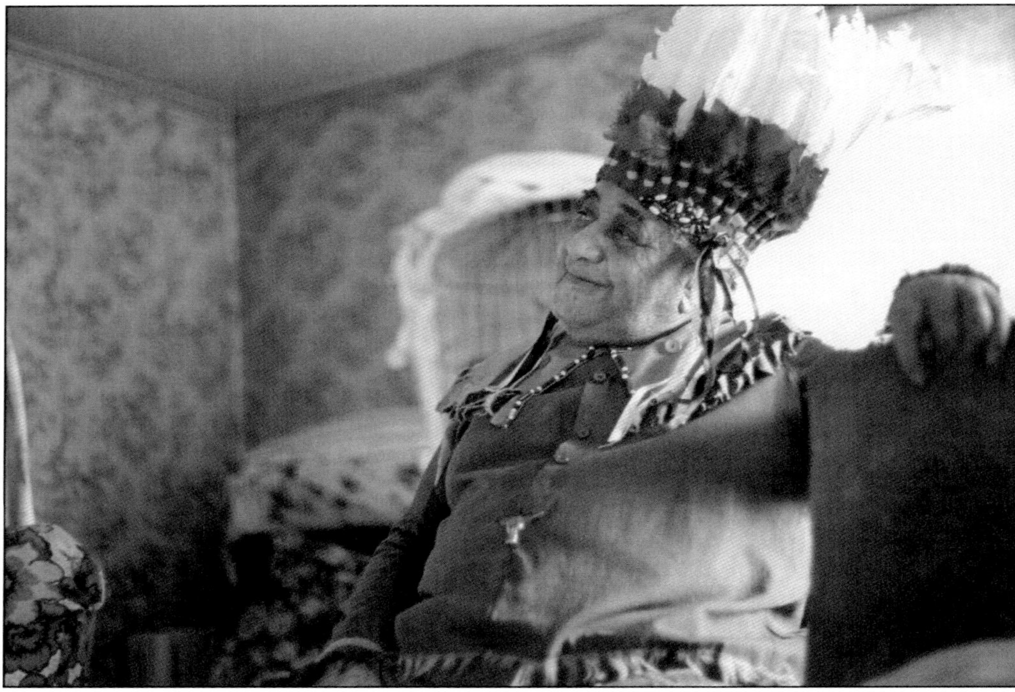

Edward Sherman, known as Chief Black Hawk, presided over the Golden Hill Paugussetts until his death in 1974. His nephew Aurelius Piper, or Chief Quiet Hawk, then assumed leadership of the tribe and, in a bid for federal recognition, filed lawsuits claiming that land throughout Fairfield and New Haven Counties had been stolen from the tribe centuries earlier. The tribe's petition for recognition was finally rejected by the Bureau of Indian Affairs in 2004. Sherman is buried in a family plot in Nichols Farms Cemetery.

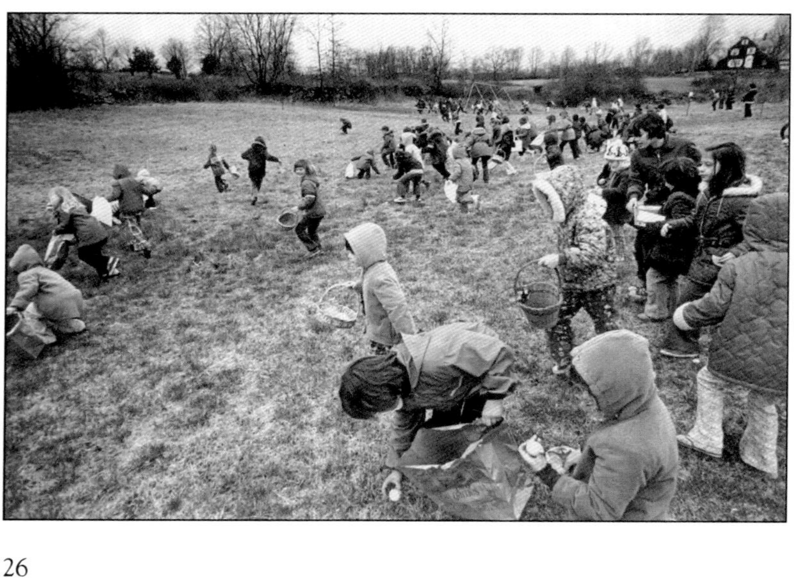

Children rush over the grounds of the Nichols Improvement Association during the annual Easter egg hunt in the fields behind the Starkweather House. Each participating family would dye a dozen eggs that would be hidden by volunteers for children to discover.

Two

TRUMBULL CENTER

The area known today as Trumbull Center was first settled in 1705. It lies adjacent to the southern part of Nichols and is connected via Unity Road. Early settlers found the land open and easy to farm. As more families came to this area, a road was laid out at what was then known as the White Plain. The first meeting of the Church of Christ in Unity was held at the area called Pulpit Rock on White Plains Road, next to the present-day Christian Heritage School. Leading the new church was the Reverend Richardson Miner, who also served as the community's physician.

By 1730, a meetinghouse had been built at the intersection of Unity and White Plains Roads. After the establishment of the church, the village of Unity developed quickly. With the Pequonnock River running through the village, it was a natural location for farmers to construct gristmills and sawmills. The first meeting of the Town of Trumbull in 1797 was held in Eliakim Beach's Tavern on Daniels Farm Road. Eventually, the intersection of White Plains and Daniels Farm Roads became a commercial hub known today as Trumbull Center.

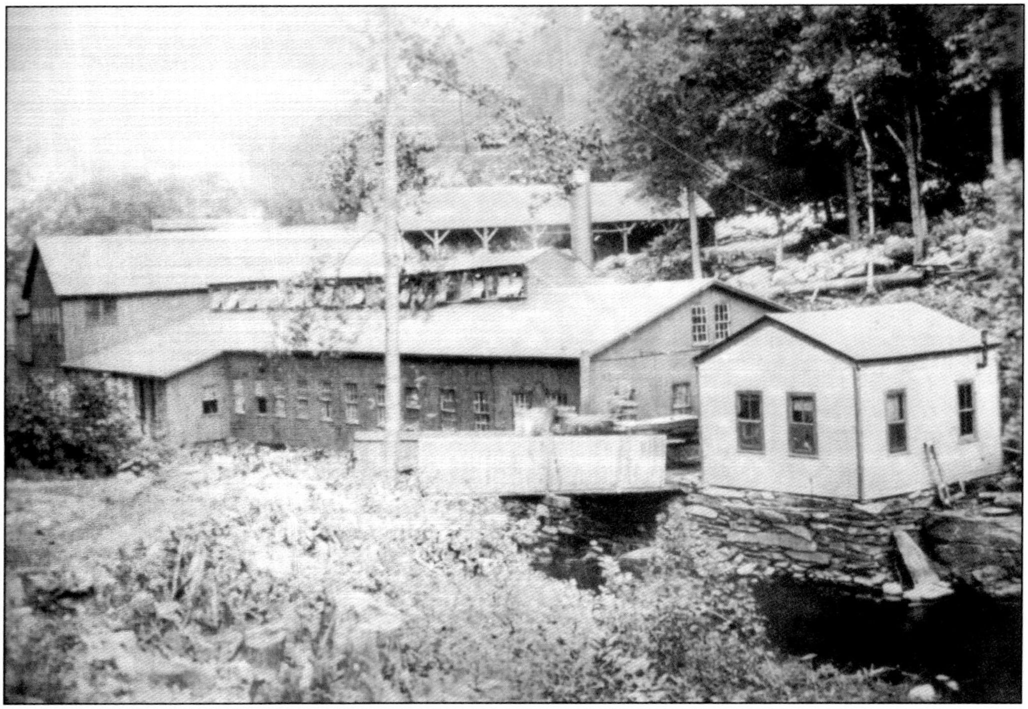

The Tait Paper Mill was located along the Pequonnock River, close to the present entrance of the Pequonnock River Valley's east trail. After working at the Fairchild Paper Mill located farther downriver, Andrew Tait started his own business. Established in 1836, the mill manufactured marbled paper until 1856, when Andrew's son William joined the family business. The A. Tait & Son Paper Mill began producing strawboard used in the packaging of corsets and other products. The mill was later sold to the Bridgeport Hydraulic Company.

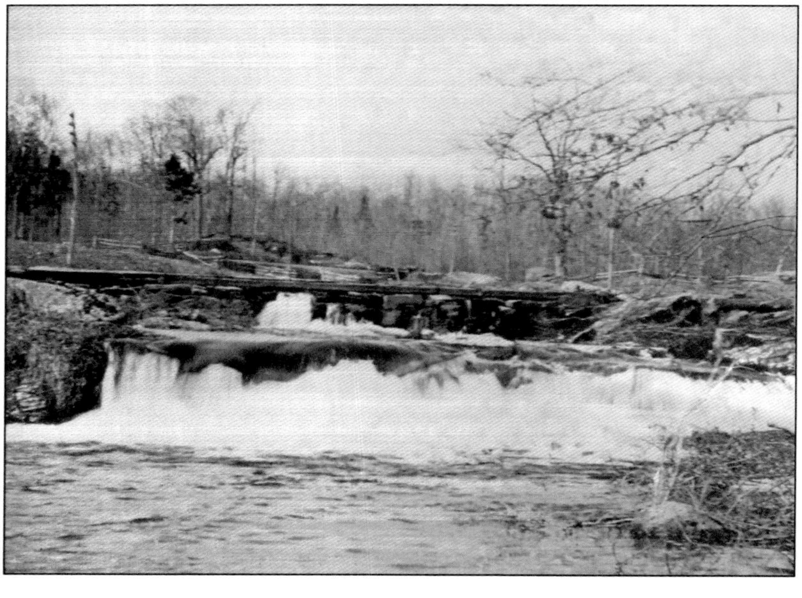

This 1894 photograph shows "The Falls" along the Pequonnock River on White Plains Road, where Col. Lewis Fairchild built Fairchild's Paper Mill in 1826. The mill, which stood near the entrance of the present-day Fairchild Memorial Park on Old Town Road, made high-quality white notepaper.

Andrew Tait was born in Scotland in 1799. He had spent his life working in the papermaking business and found work in Hartford, Connecticut, after immigrating to the United States. Successful in his adopted home, he sent for his fiancé, Isabella Ronaldson, in 1822. The two settled in Trumbull after Tait was offered a job as superintendent of the Fairchild Paper Mill in 1827. Tait worked there for several years before starting his own paper business on the Pequonnock River. The couple built their home next to the mill. Tait also served as town clerk for several years. He died in 1890, and both he and Isabella are buried side by side in Riverside Cemetery, not far from the site of the mill he founded.

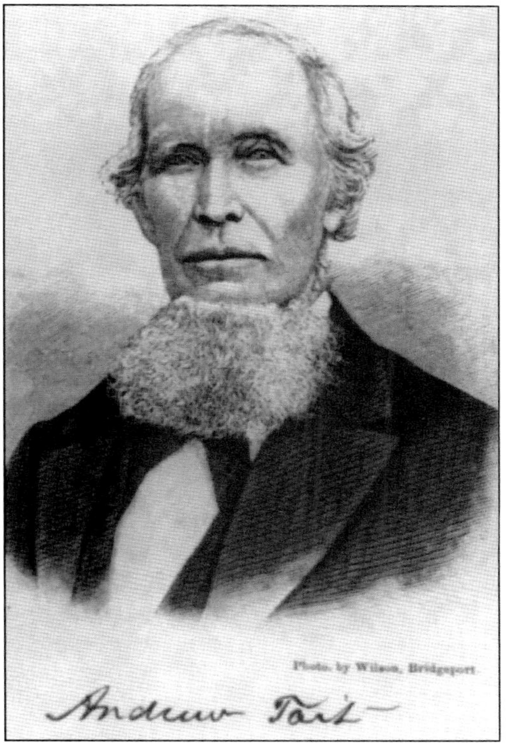

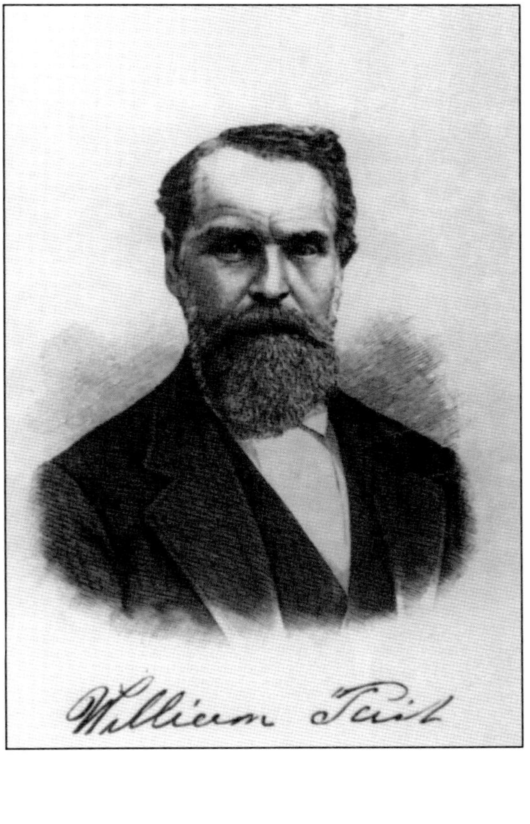

William Tait was born in 1824 in East Hartford, Connecticut, the second of six children born to Andrew and Isabella Tait. William eventually joined his father in the papermaking business, and the business was renamed the A. Tait & Son Paper Mill. Together, they ran the successful strawboard business for many years. William married Grace Camp in 1848 and served in the Union army during the Civil War in Company D of the 23rd Connecticut Regiment. After the war, he returned to Trumbull to work in the family business. He died in 1919 and is buried in Riverside Cemetery with his parents.

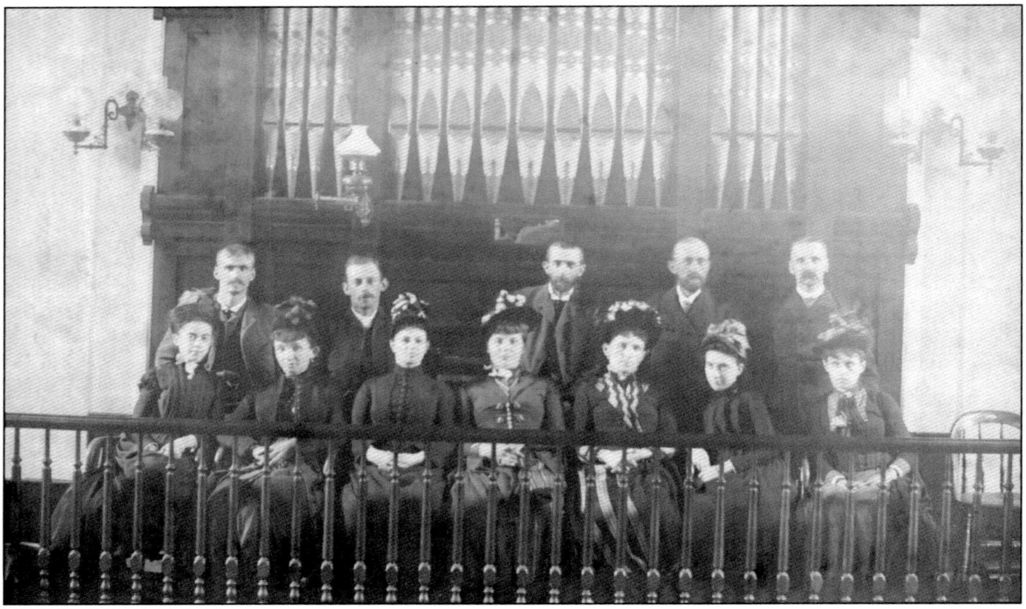

Members of the Trumbull Congregational Church choir appear dressed in their finest in 1887. They include Nathala Merwin Case, C. Frank Plumb, Mrs. William Tait, Wilbert French, Mrs. Willard S. Plumb, Mrs. C. Frank Plumb, Willard S. Plumb, Mrs. O.B. Burton, O.B. Burton, Florence Merwin, William Tait, and Mary Sterling.

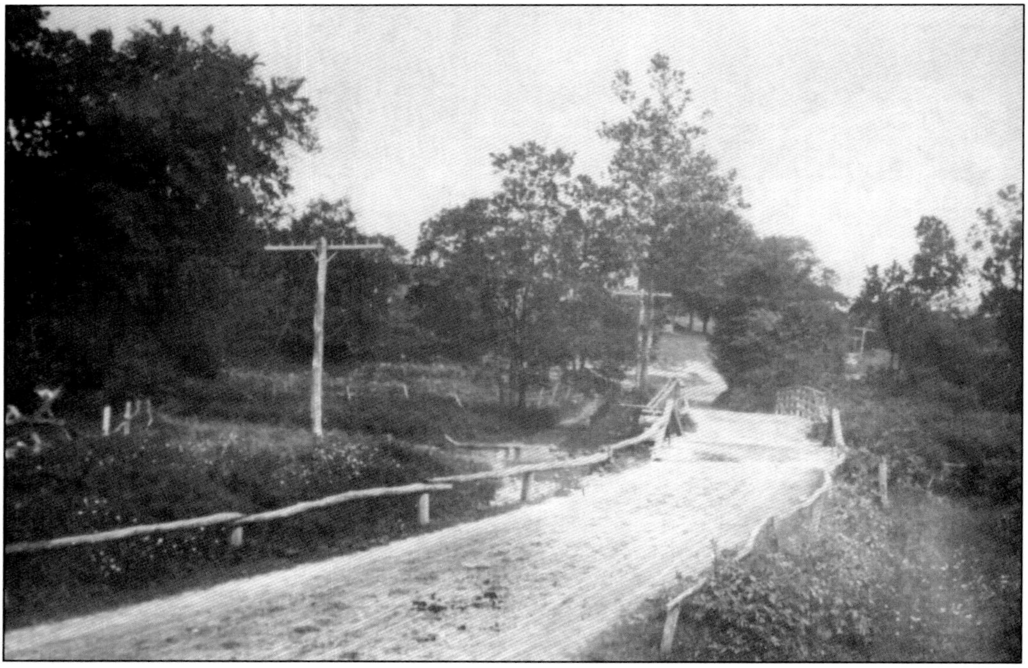

This early view of White Plains Road looking north shows the bridge crossing the Pequonnock River. Today, the view beyond the bridge is bisected by the Route 25 highway, and Veterans Memorial Park is located to the right.

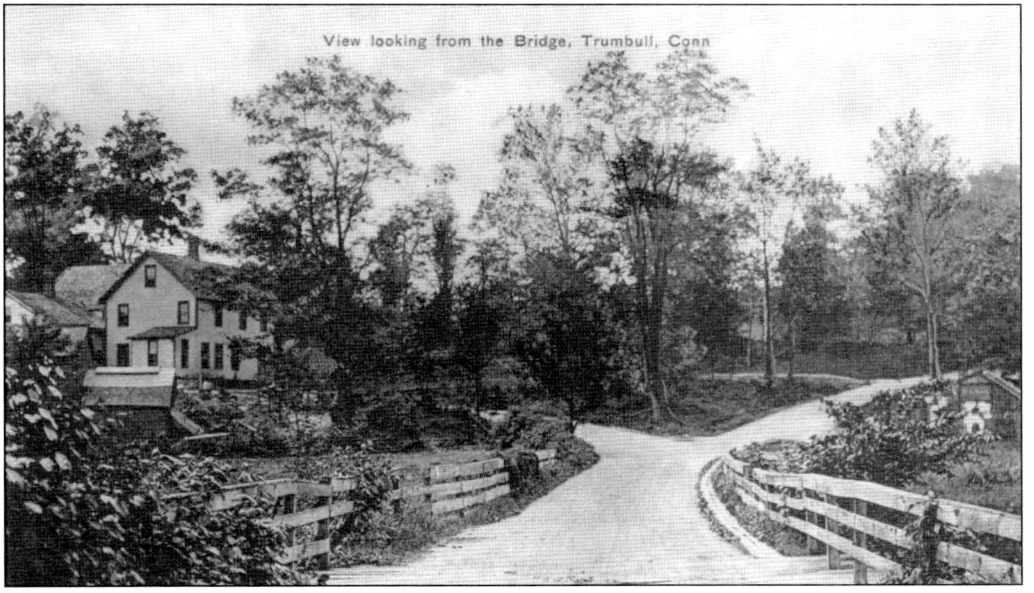

This view is taken from Daniels Farm Road where it leads into Trumbull Center. Parks' Store, later Kurtz's Store, can be seen to the left. A small portion of Church Hill Road can be seen on the upper right.

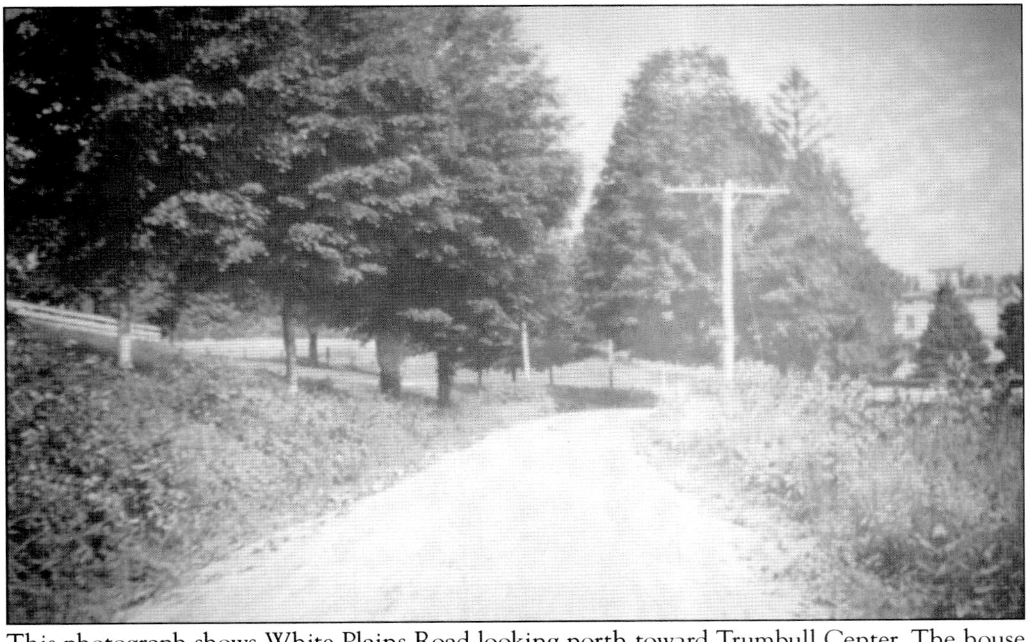

This photograph shows White Plains Road looking north toward Trumbull Center. The house on right is in the location of what would later become the Trumbull Center shopping area. The evergreens on the right mark Brinsmade Cemetery, later Trumbull Center Cemetery.

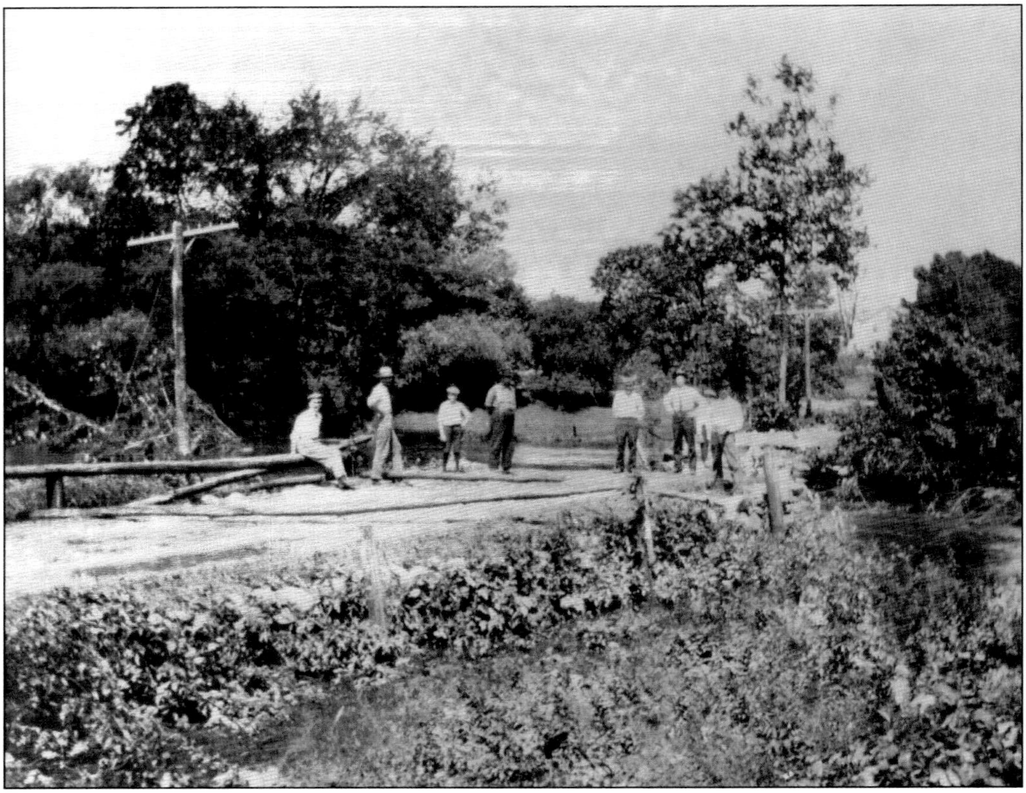

Men inspect the damage on White Plains Road following a massive flood in July 1905. Heavy rains resulted in the bursting of several dams, sending floodwaters cascading down the Pequonnock River. Houses were swept away, and 52 people were killed. The flood also disabled many of the mills that had drawn power from the river. Below, rubble from the floodwaters is strewn around Ward's Grist and Sawmill.

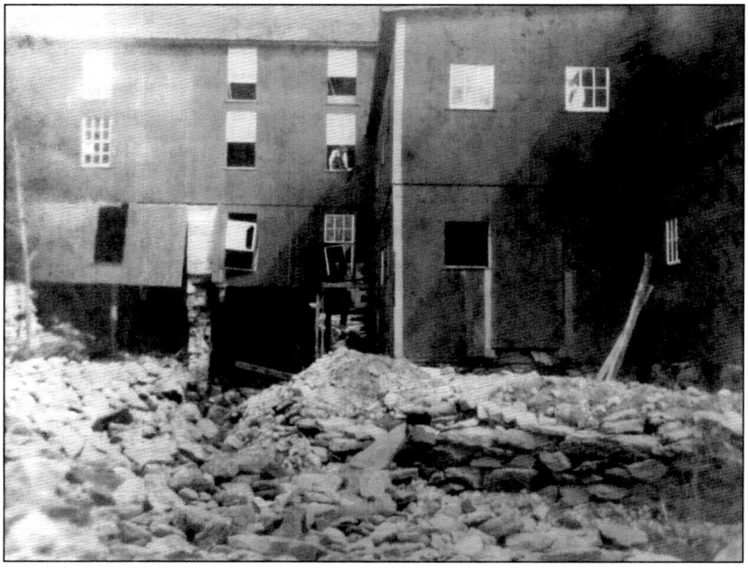

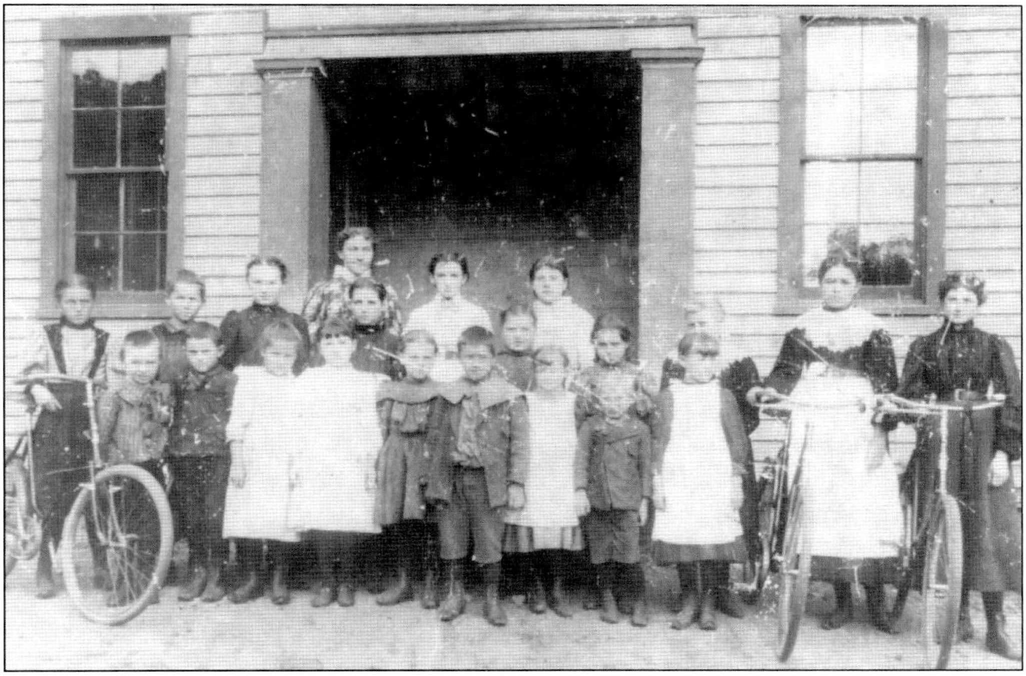

The bicycles in this photograph of students at White Plains School, taken on November 10, 1897, may be a clue as to how Trumbull students made their way to school. Only one person in the photograph is identified: the second girl on the right is Alice Nichols (later Mrs. William Fuller).

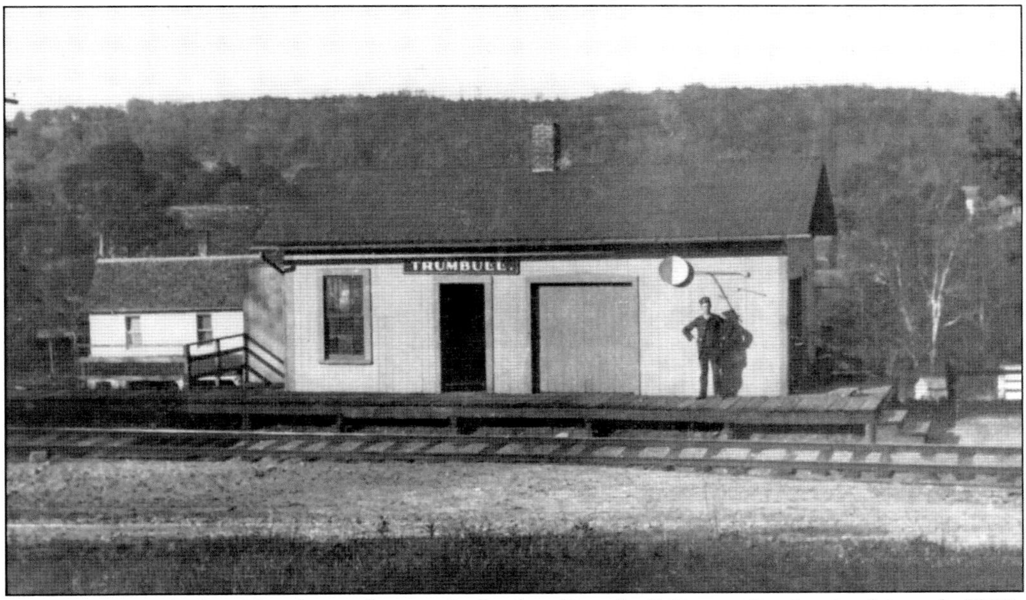

Stationmaster Arthur Plumb stands outside the first Trumbull Center Station in this early-1900s photograph. Plumb was the father of well-known town clerk Helen E. Plumb, for whom the old town hall, located just east of the station, was named. The stop was originally called Trumbull Church because it was located near the site of the second and third buildings of Trumbull Congregational Church.

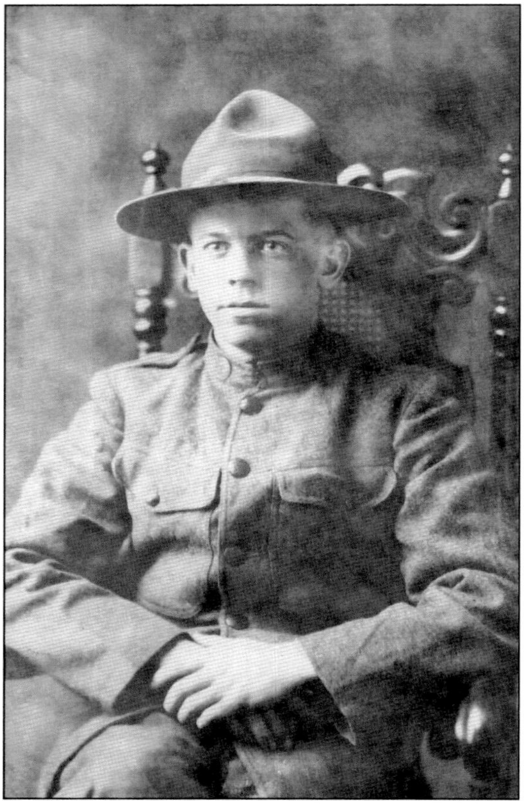

Dwight Brinsmade, photographed in uniform, was a descendant of one of the first families to permanently settle in Trumbull in the early 1700s. Born on August 27, 1900, Brinsmade grew up in a house on Brinsmade Crossing, near Trumbull Center. He died in 1982 and is buried in the Brinsmade Cemetery (now Trumbull Center Cemetery) on White Plains Road.

This photograph of students at White Plains Road School is dated June 15, 1921. Emma Linley was the teacher at the time. Schools in the early 20th century were crowded, the hours long, and the average wage for teachers about $8 a week. Several years after this photograph was taken, Trumbull school districts were consolidated and the building sold.

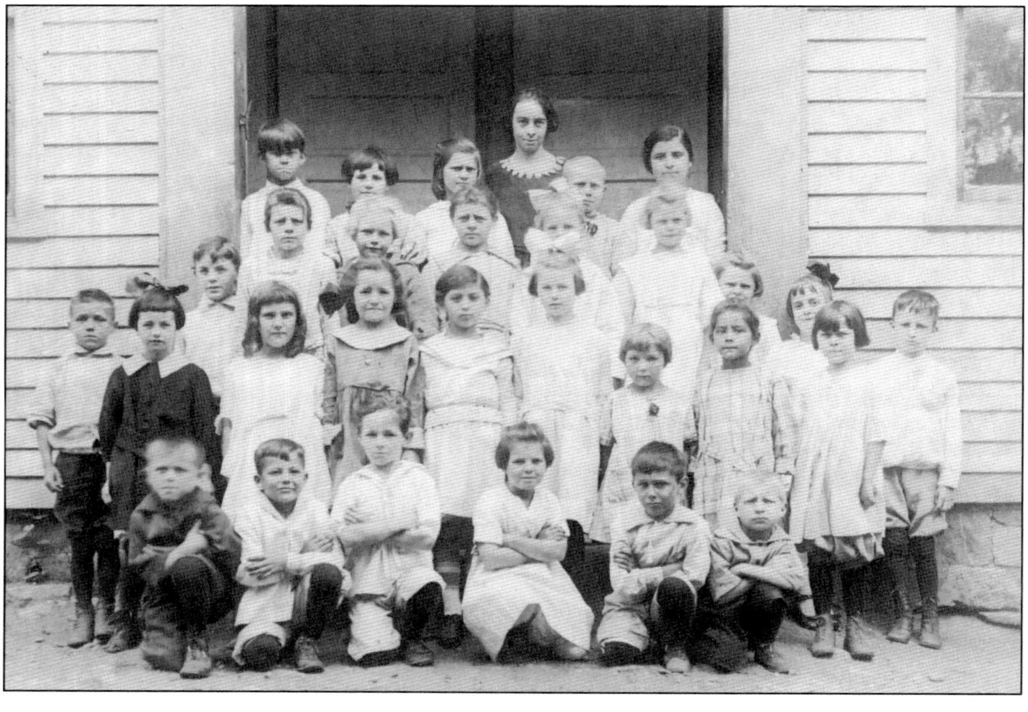

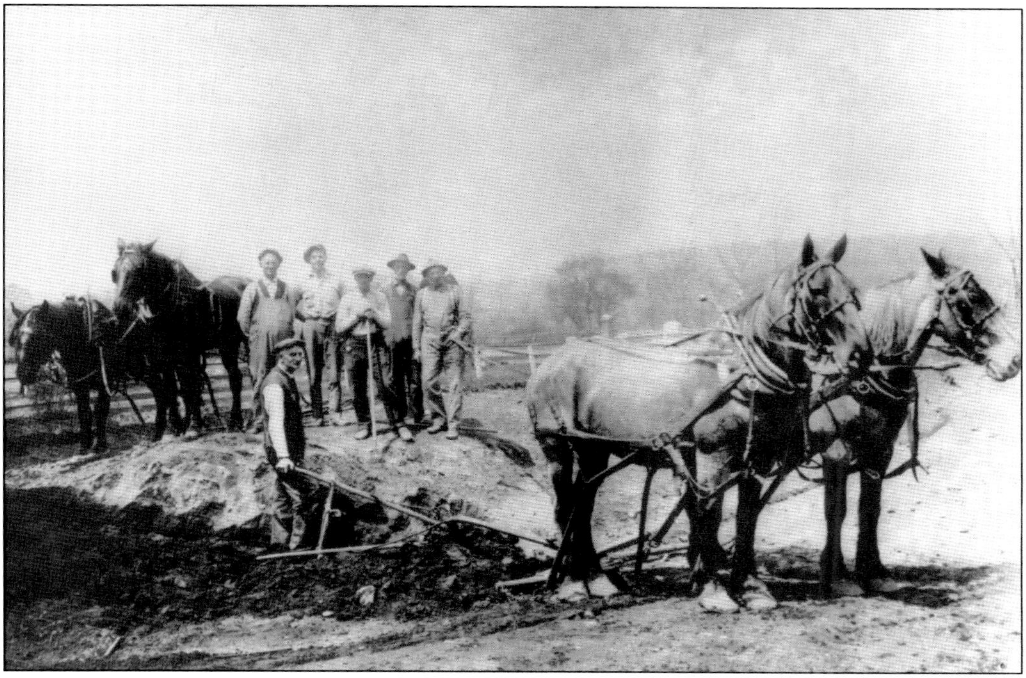

Above, local farmers use a plow to break ground for the new Center School on White Plains Road in 1925. Banford Beach stands with the plow. On the rise above him are, from left to right, Howard S. Beach, Herman Strobel, Joseph Kohler, Arthur Burr, and Arthur Jones. By the mid-1920s, the number of students in Trumbull made one-room schoolhouses impractical. In addition to Trumbull Center, new brick schools with multiple classrooms were built in Nichols, Long Hill, and on Edison Road. Below is a photograph of Center School as it appeared in 1945.

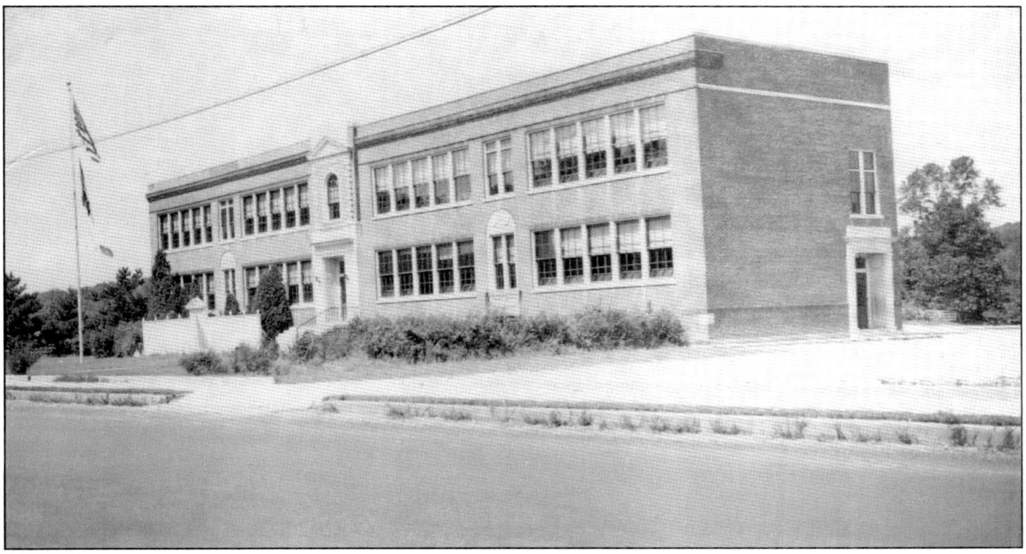

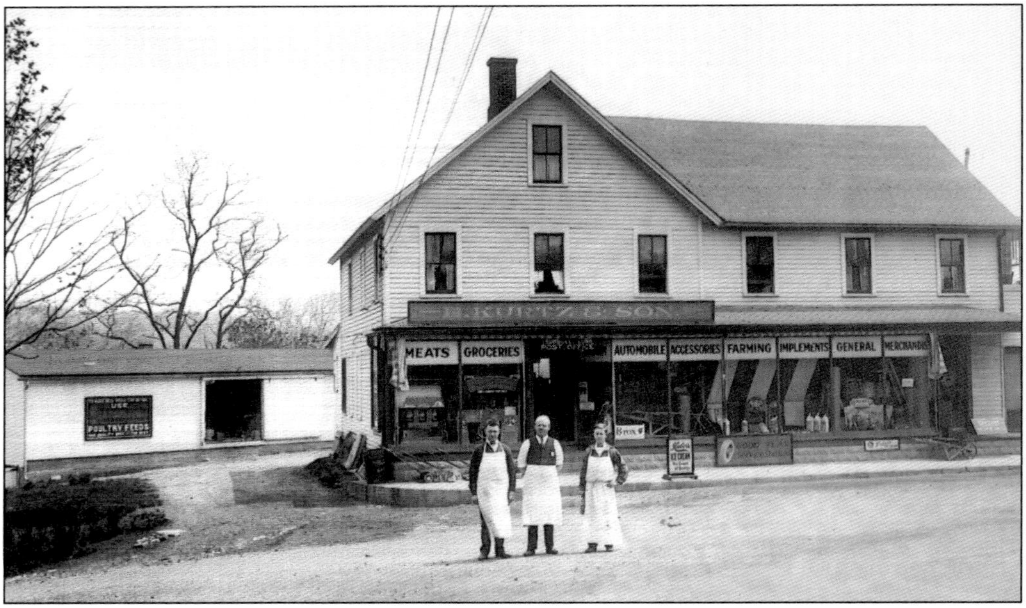

Emmanuel Kurtz, shown here with sons Charlie (left) and John (right) in 1925, purchased his general store from Stephen Parks in 1918. As the story goes, Kurtz, a local farmer, purchased a 50-gallon barrel of red barn paint from Parks for the bargain price of $10. Joking that he would set up a store to sell it off, Parks offered his. By the end of the conversation, Kurtz was the new owner.

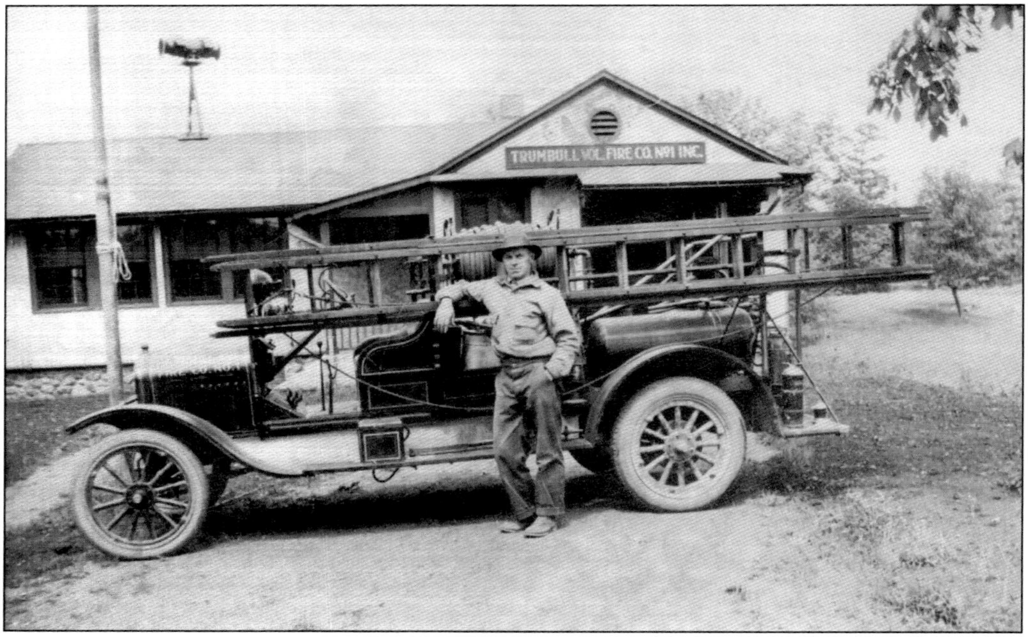

After a disastrous fire in 1922 on Daniels Farm Road, the people of Trumbull realized the need for an organized fire department. The Trumbull Fire Company was formed in 1923, followed by incorporation of the Trumbull Volunteer Fire Company No. 1 on August 25, 1925. Here, Fire Chief Carl Robert Peterson stands in front of the firehouse on White Plains Road. He served as chief from 1925 to 1927 and also from 1929 to 1944. (Courtesy Trumbull Fire Department.)

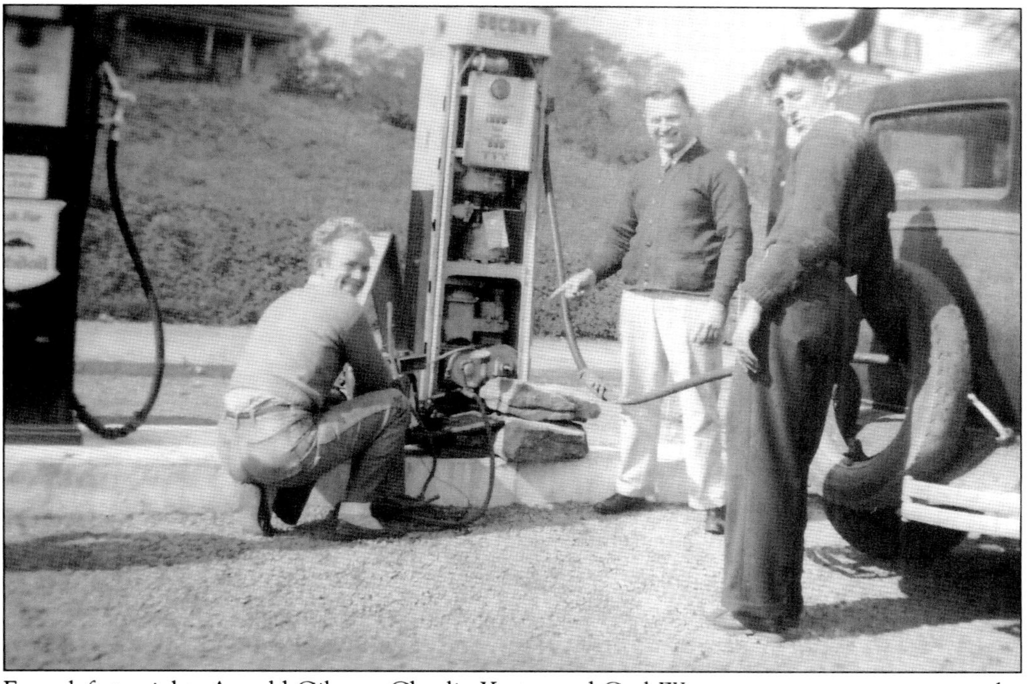

From left to right, Arnold Gibson, Charlie Kurtz, and Carl Wayne use a generator to get the gas pumps working at Dolan's gas station following the Great Hurricane of 1938. More than 250 New Englanders died in the storm, which swept through the region with 121-mile-per-hour winds. (Courtesy Cindy Hall Arendt.)

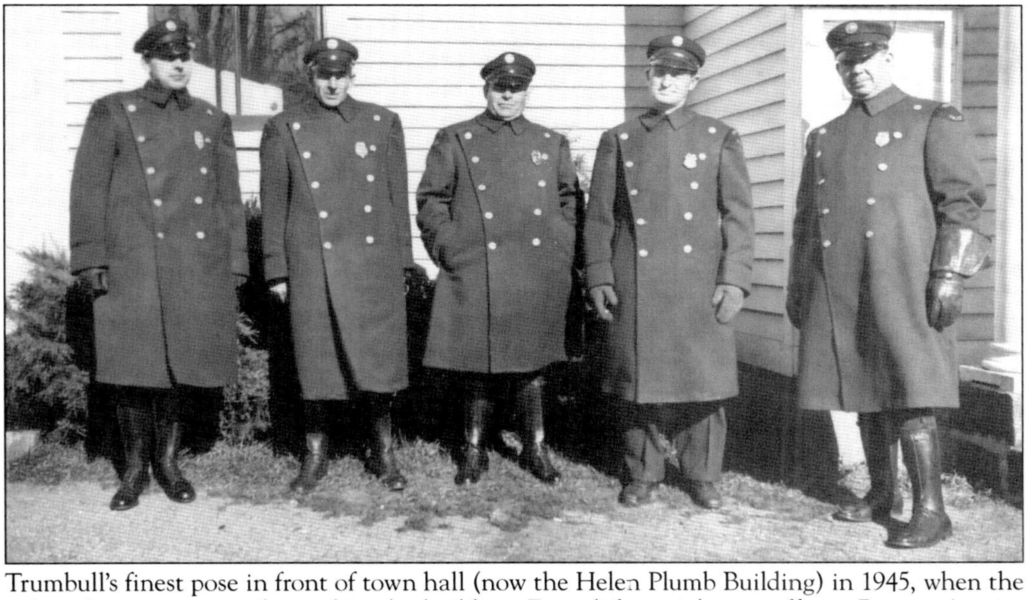

Trumbull's finest pose in front of town hall (now the Helen Plumb Building) in 1945, when the police department was housed in the building. From left to right are officers Berger, Austin, Jennings, and Haywood. Chief Raymond Beckwith stands on the far right.

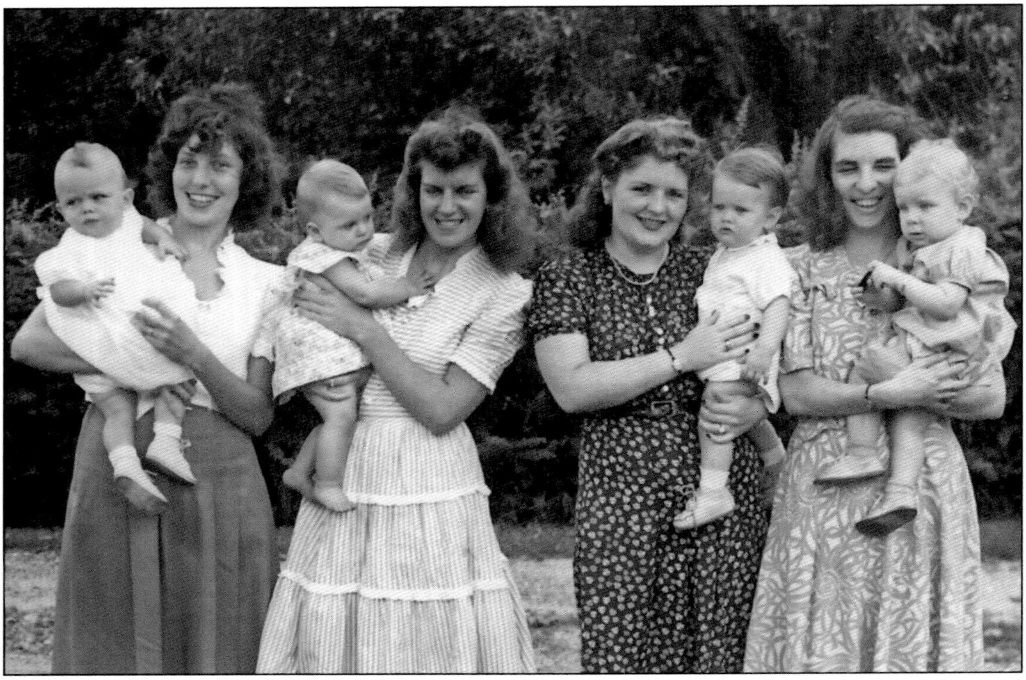

A newspaper photograph from 1945 captures four young women from Trumbull Center with their babies, awaiting their fathers' return from service in the war. From left to right are Jean Hughes Hayden, holding 11-month-old Nancy Lynn, whose father, Chester Hayden, was a military police officer; Jean Claud-Mantle Hall, holding Cynthia Jane, whose father, Charles Hall, was serving with the Navy in the Pacific; Edith Hickey Rogan, holding Charles Williams, whose father, Charles N. Rogan, was a paratrooper in Yokohama; and Jacqueline French Schwarz, holding 13-moth-old Marilyn Ann, whose father, John J. Schwarz, served in the Signal Corps in Manila. Below, a display at Center School remembers Trumbull troops. (Both, courtesy Cindy Hall Arendt.)

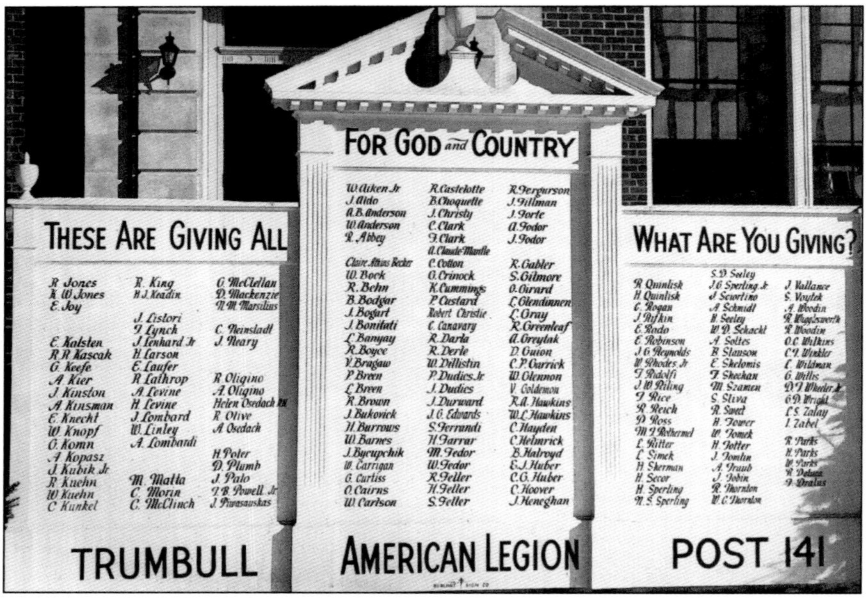

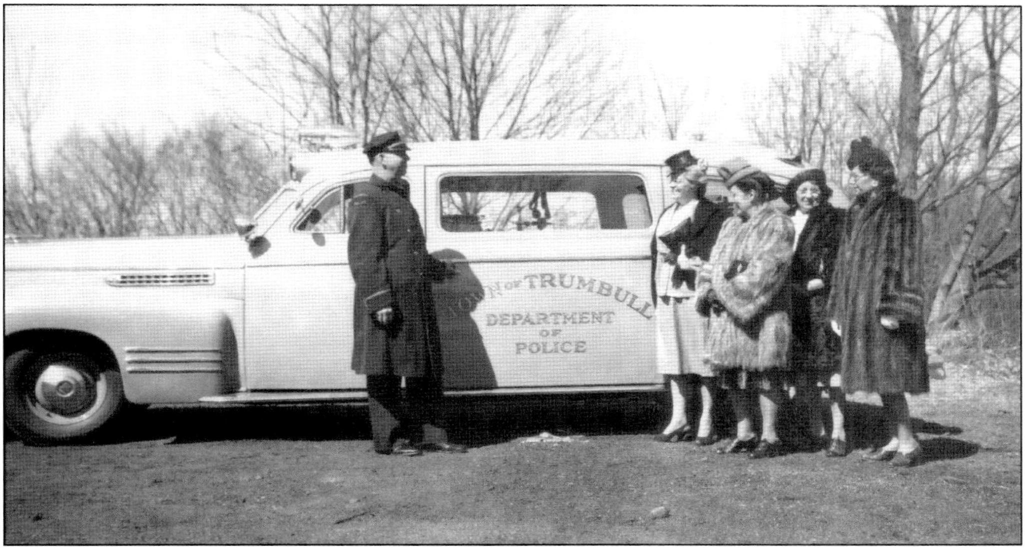

Trumbull police show off a new ambulance in February 1947. At the time, the town police also provided ambulance service. The ambulance was kept in a garage near the Helen Plumb Building, where the police were headquartered.

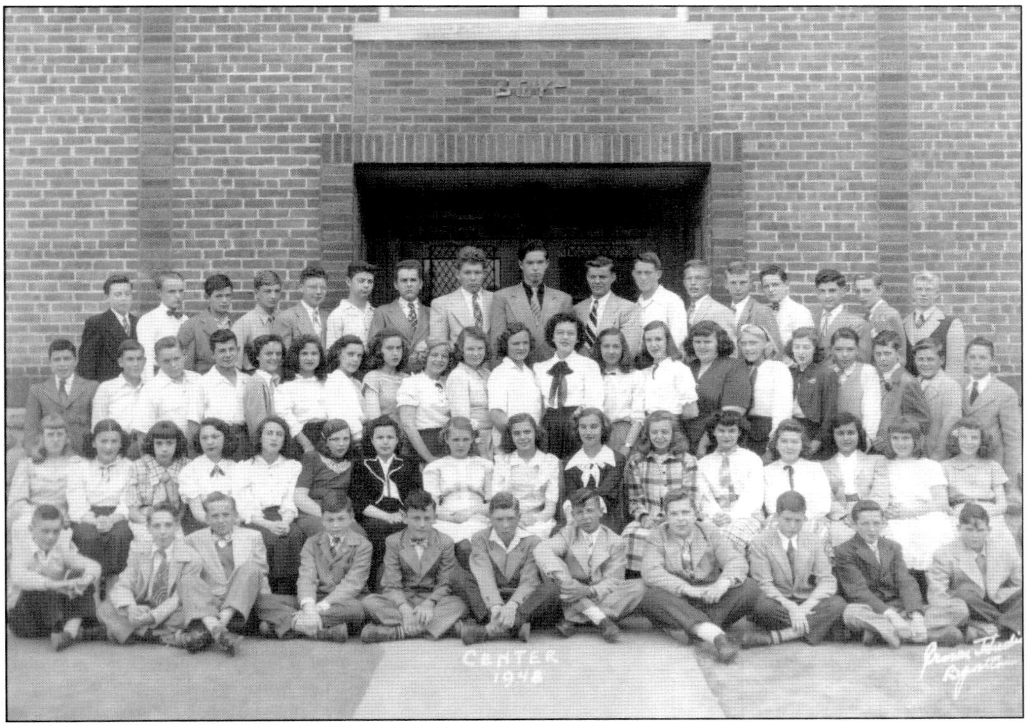

The graduating class of 1948 poses in front of Center School. With no public high school in Trumbull until 1961, students graduating from Trumbull's primary schools would continue their education at high schools in Bridgeport. The town's first high school, located on Madison Avenue, was converted to Madison Junior High (later Middle) School when a new high school was built on Strobel Road. (Courtesy Bill and Ruth Wakeley.)

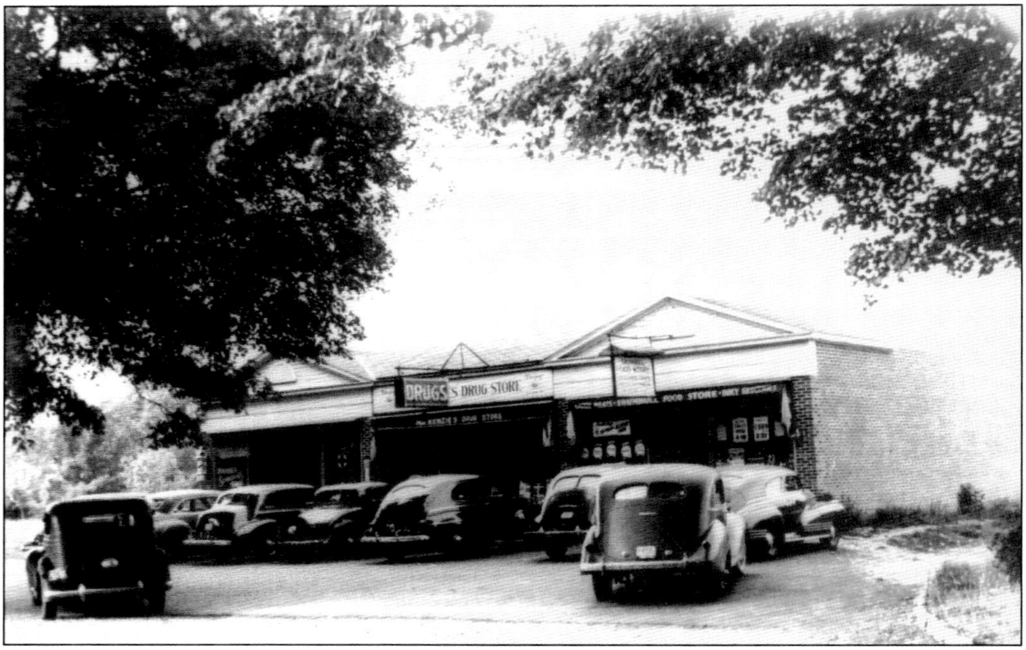

Above, Scortino's barbershop, MacKenzie's Pharmacy, and Herb Hay's Trumbull Food Store were among the businesses in Trumbull Center during the 1940s. The row of stores now holds a Starbucks and a CVS, which took the place of MacKenzie's in 2013. Below, in a later photograph, Trumbull druggist "Mac" MacKenzie (left) poses with Harry Brinkerhoff, a fellow pharmacist from Bridgeport, at Mac's Trumbull Center store.

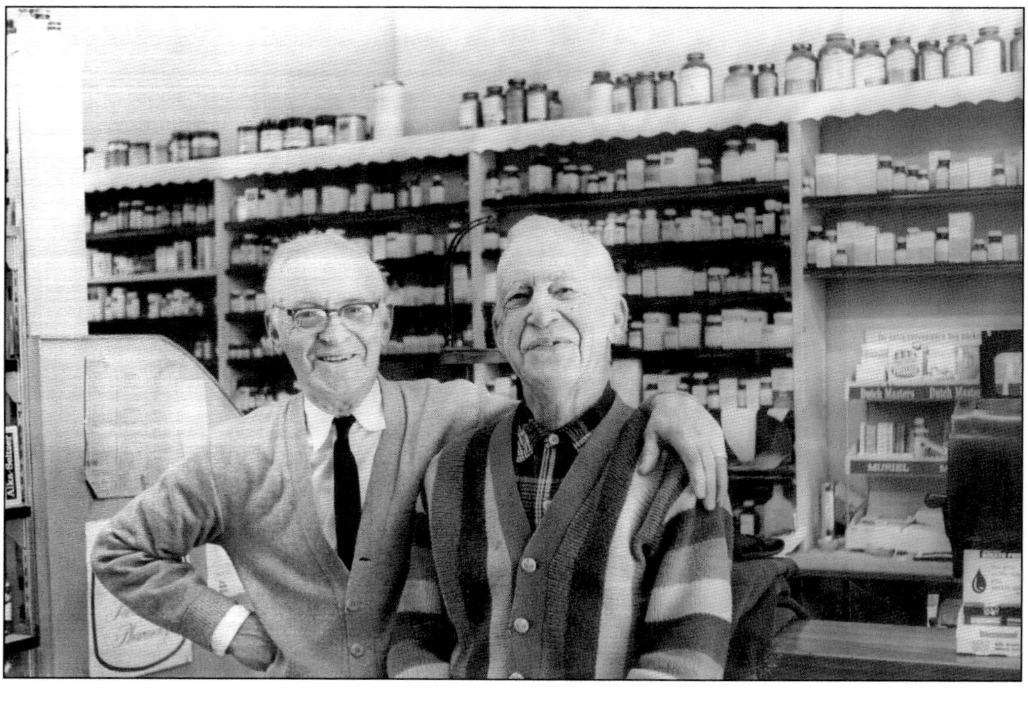

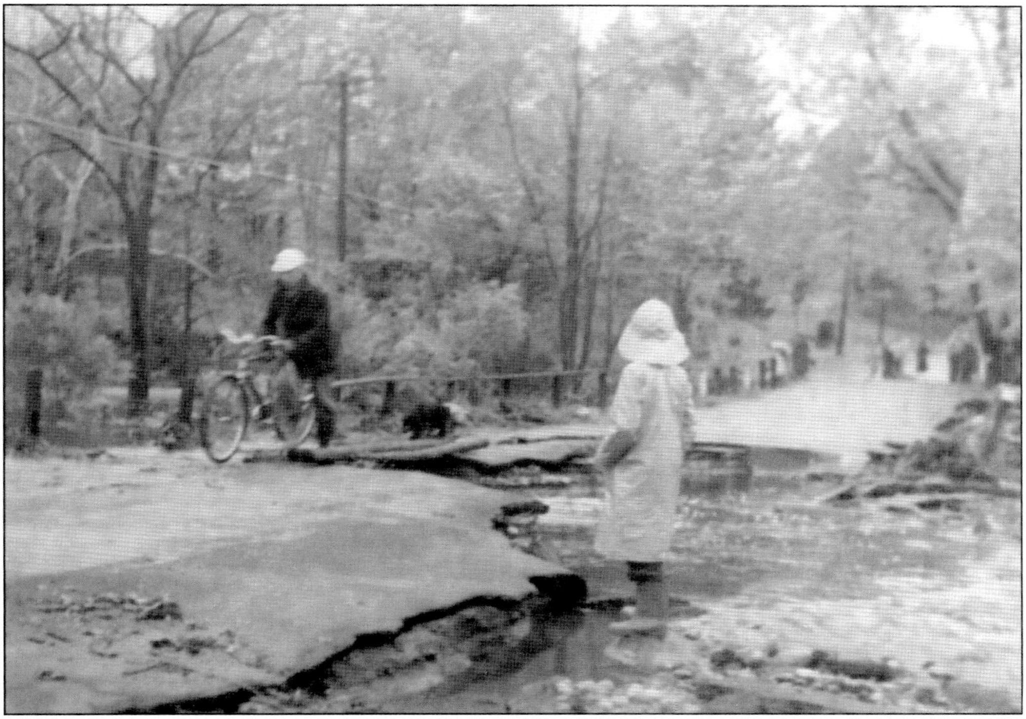

A section of roadway in Trumbull Center was washed out where the Pequonnock River surged in the flood of 1955. Floodwaters devastated much of the state when Hurricane Connie dropped 6 inches of rain, followed five days later by Hurricane Diane, which dropped an additional 14 inches in a 36-hour period.

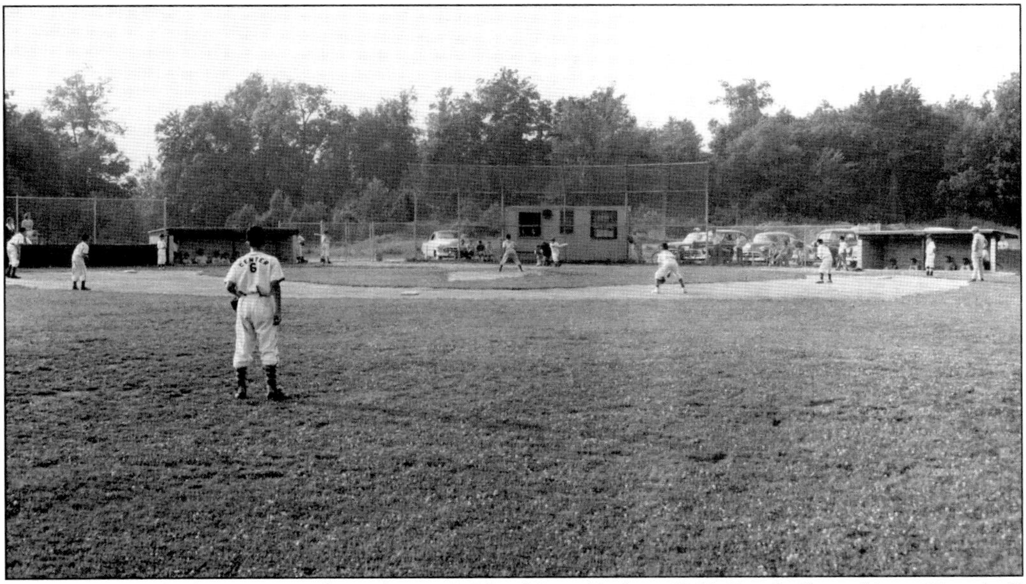

This photograph shows a view from the outfield at Unity Park in 1955. Baseball would put Trumbull on the map in 1989, when the Trumbull National All-Stars would defeat a team from Taiwan to win the 43rd Little League World Series Championship.

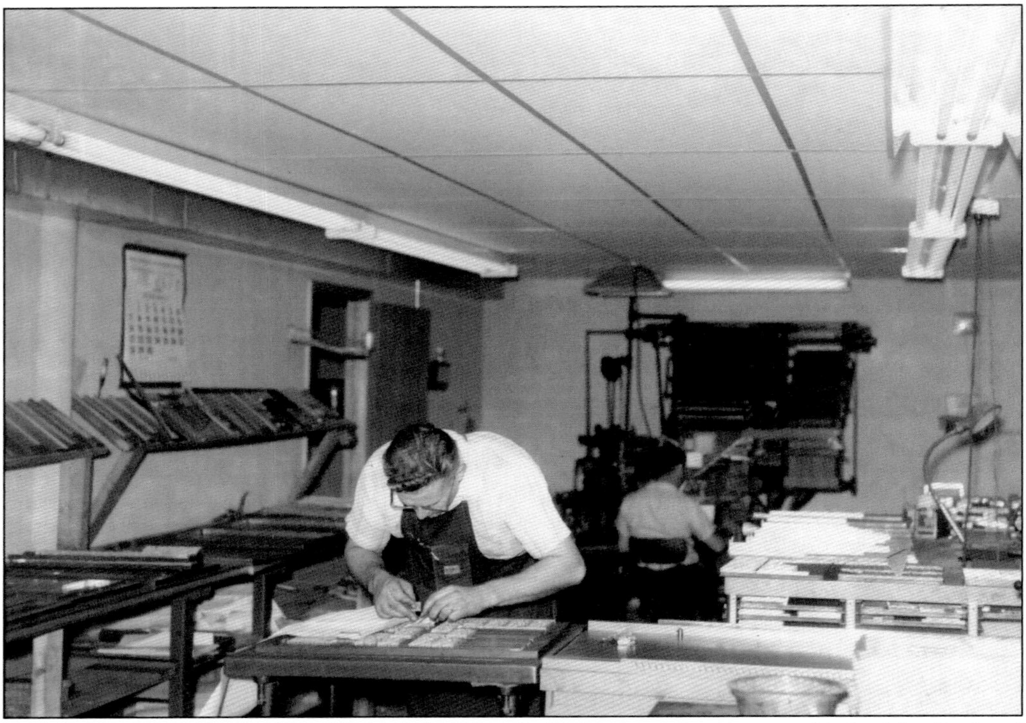

A compositor works in the office of the *Trumbull Times* newspaper, established by Richard Diamond in 1959. At that time, the newspaper had its offices in the Trumbull Center shopping area. Its offices are now located in Shelton.

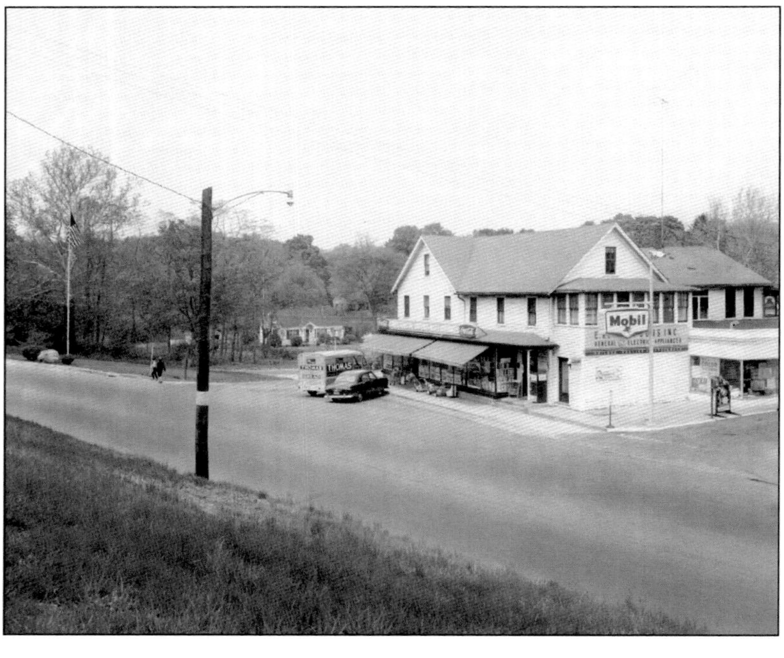

In the 1950s, Trumbull Center was still a relatively quiet suburban hub, with Kurtz's store and Dolan's Trumbull Center Mobil station anchoring the corner of Daniels Farm and White Plains Roads. This photograph is taken from a hill near the former location of Brinsmade Crossing.

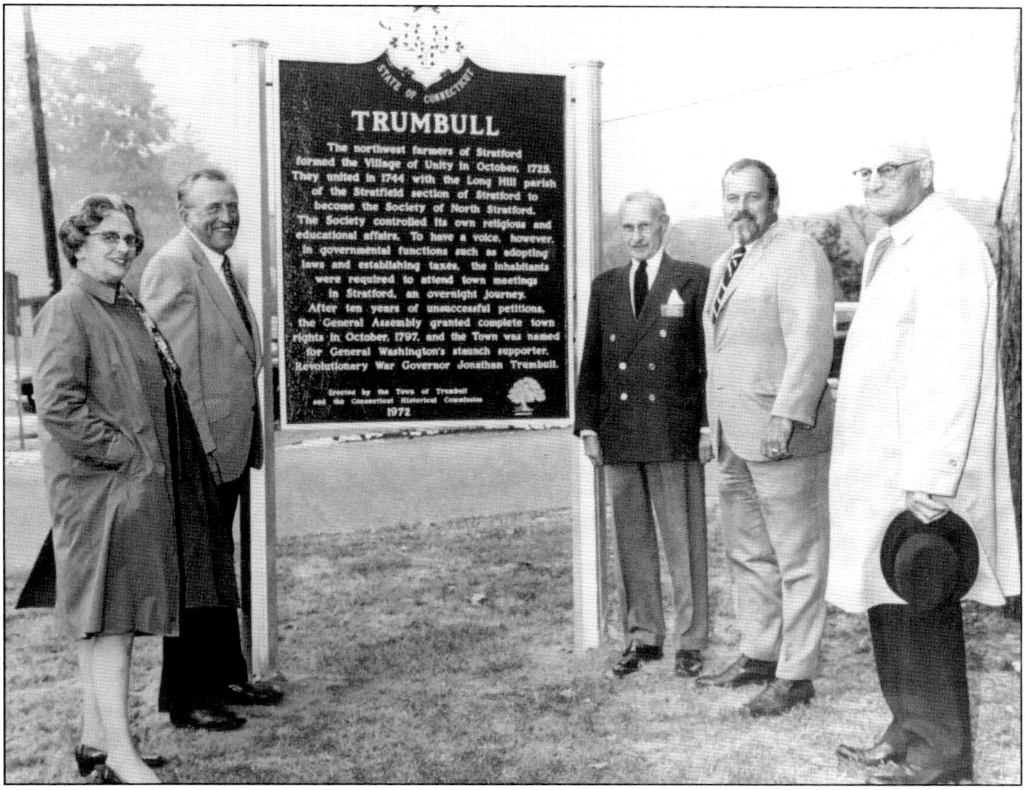

Officials pose beside a Connecticut Historical Commission marker—the first of its kind in the state—at the corner of Unity and White Plains Roads. The unveiling took place on October 12, 1972, to mark the town's 175th anniversary. Pictured from left to right are Helen Plumb (town clerk and chair of the town's 175th anniversary committee), Clarence Heimann (first selectman), Eric Hatch (chairman of the Connecticut Historical Commission), Elwood C. Stanley (president of the Trumbull Historical Society), and E. Merrill Beach (town historian and founder of the Trumbull Historical Society).

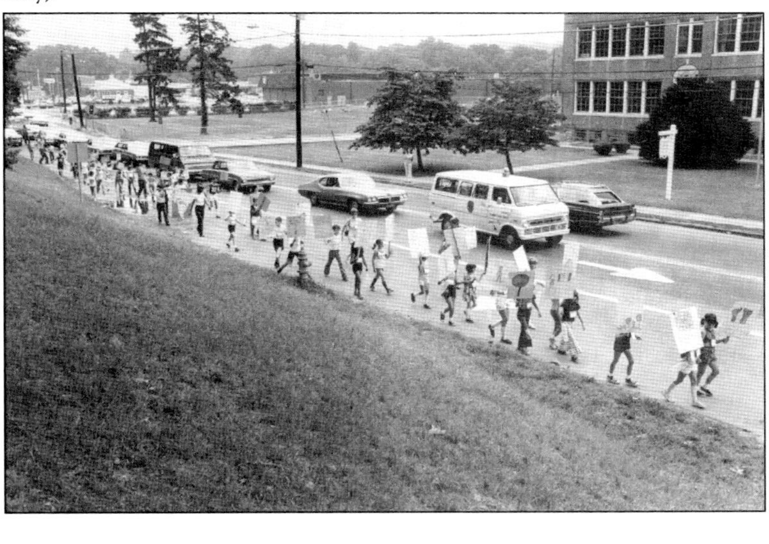

Trumbull fourth graders hold a march for hunger along White Plains Road in 1975.

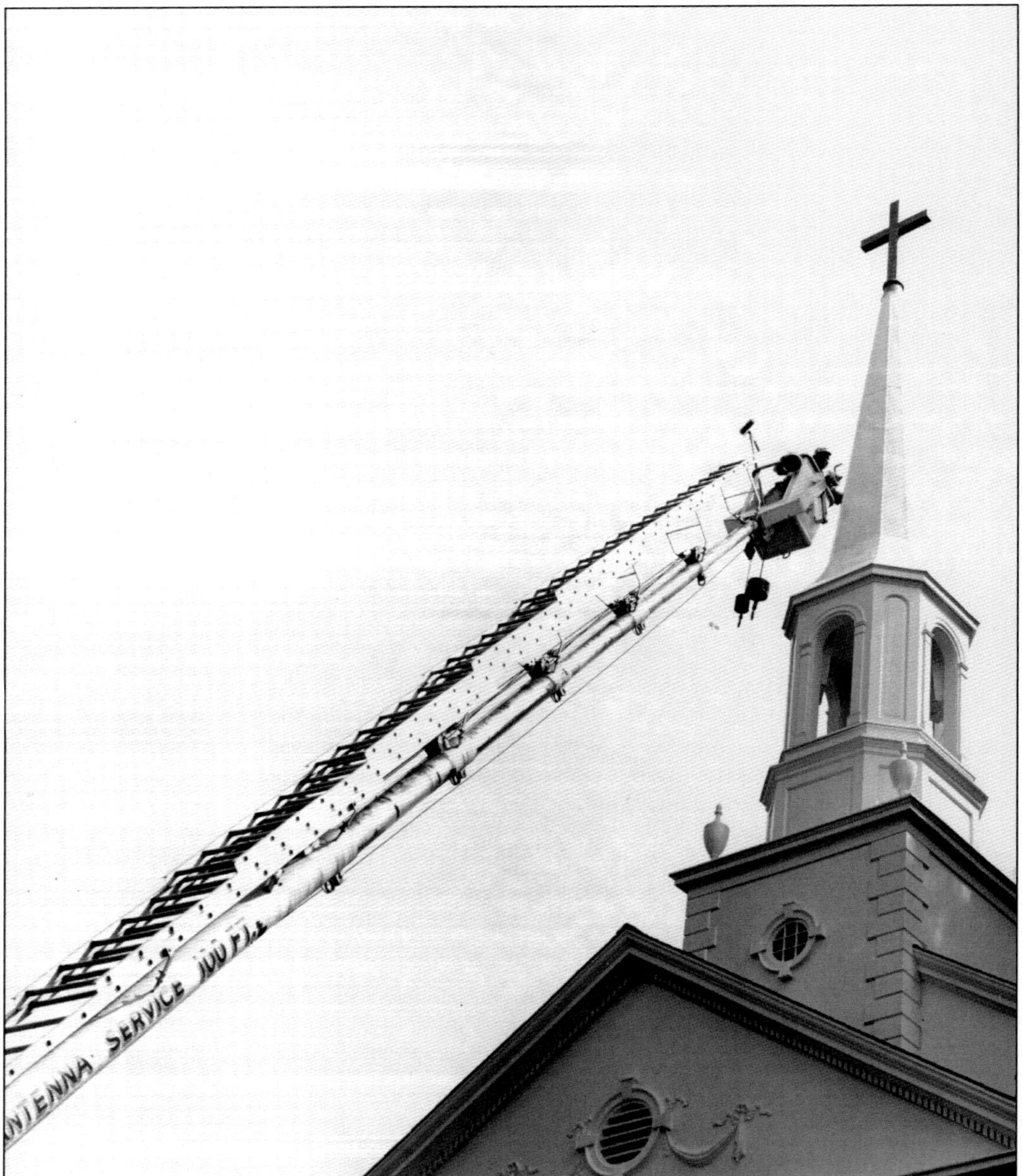

A worker paints the steeple at the Calvary Evangelical Church on White Plains Road on June 8, 1968. The white steeple still serves as a Trumbull landmark for those passing on the nearby Merritt Parkway.

Three

Long Hill

Long Hill—located north of Chestnut Hill, west of the Pequonnock River, and east of Tashua—was first settled in 1728, when the Turney, Walker, and Middlebrook families built homes there. Soon, more families settled this area, and the Long Hill parish was established in 1740.

In 1744, the villages of Long Hill and Unity petitioned the Connecticut General Assembly to combine and become the Society of North Stratford. Long Hill remained a village controlled by the town of Stratford until 1797, when the town of Trumbull was established.

As the population increased, mills and factories were built along the Pequonnock River. The Long Hill Green, created when the Newtown Turnpike (now Main Street) was rerouted and straightened, became a center for commerce. During the 19th century, Long Hill's industries flourished with the manufacture of shirts, underwear, glove linings, cigars, and carriages, all within close proximity of the green. Other nearby industry included a gristmill, sawmill, icehouse, tungsten mine, and an amusement park, with local businesses that included shopkeepers and the village blacksmith.

Over the years, Long Hill has been home to several inventors, including Long Hill native Harvey Hubbell II, who invented the electrical plug and socket and pull-chain light switch; helicopter maker Igor Sikorsky; and submarine pioneer Simon Lake, whose farm was located near the top of Lake Avenue.

Complementing its industry, the primary occupation of Long Hill's residents was dairy farming. Soon after World War II, however, Long Hill's bucolic farms were rapidly transformed into new housing for the wave of young families moving from the cities to the suburbs. Long Hill has kept pace with progress throughout its history, providing its residents an ideal place to raise a family.

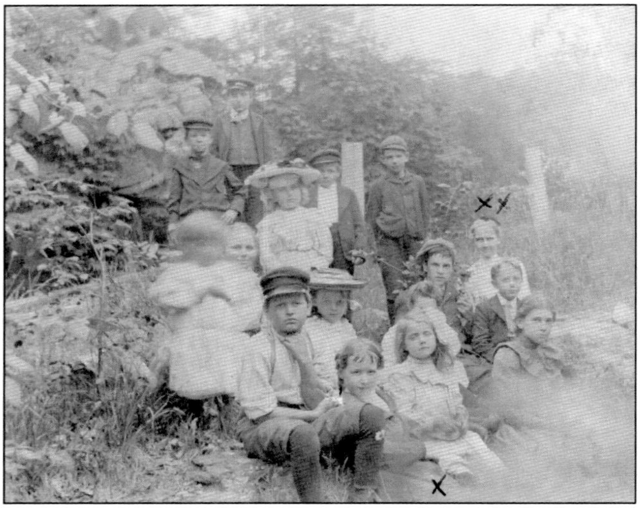

With no buses to transport students, class trips in the days of the one-room schoolhouse were confined to places within walking distance. But that did not prevent classes from taking nature hikes and exploring the nearby woods with picnic lunches that the children would bring from home. This 1890s photograph shows children from the Lower Long Hill School on a field trip. Teacher Lena Beers is identified with a double "X." The girl indicated with the other mark is Francis Cole, and the other children are unidentified.

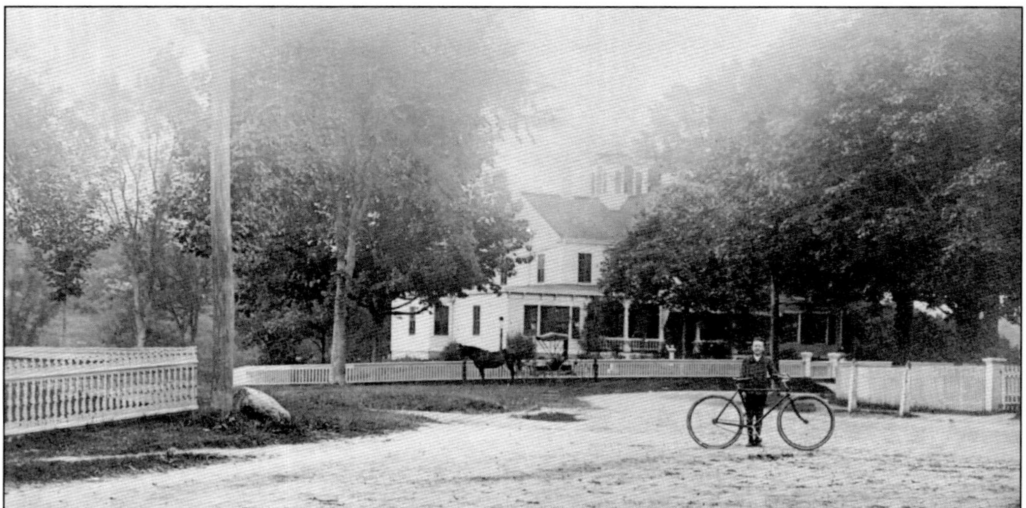

This postcard, dated 1923, is taken from the Long Hill Green and shows the Toucey house, which stills stands on Whitney Avenue. While some sources date the green to the 1700s, evidence exists that the green was created as late as 1842, when the path of the Newtown Turnpike was straightened out and moved to the west. On August 19, 1904, the Long Hill Village Green was purchased by 23 Long Hill residents from the estate of Emiline A. Hall, wife of Austin Hall, for $25. The deed specified that the land would "forever remain as a lawn or park" and that "no building of any description shall ever be erected, moved onto, or be allowed to remain on said tract of land."

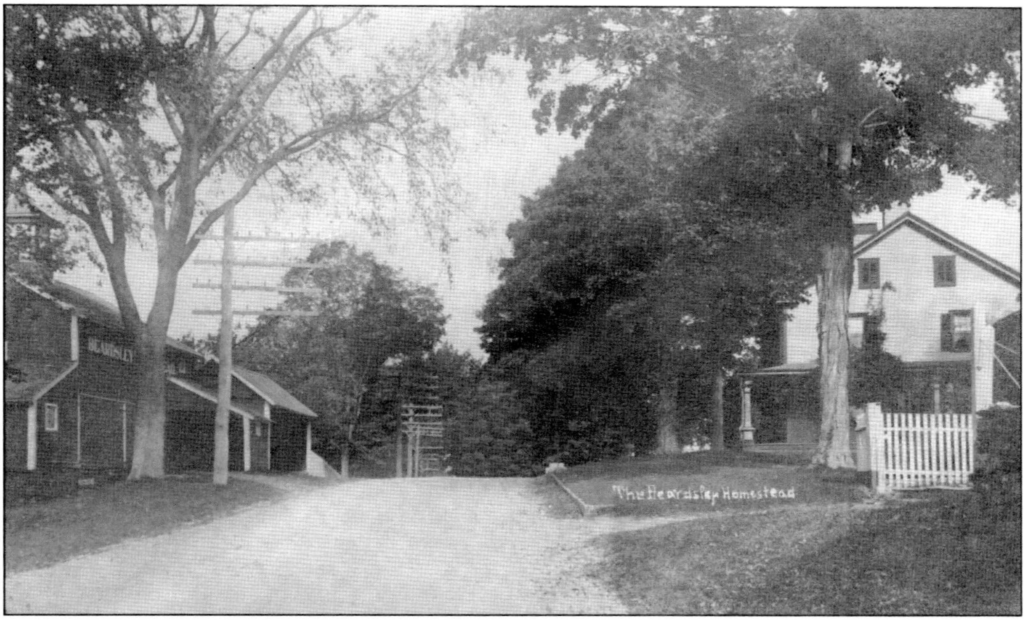

The Beardsley Homestead can be seen in this postcard view of Main Street, standing just south of today's Trumbull School administration building. The Beardsley family had long established roots in Trumbull, with a 110-acre farm that extended from Main Street east to the Pequonnock River. When the railroad came through, cow tunnels were built so the Beardsley cows could graze on pastureland between the rail bed and the river. Across the street was the family's large red barn with "Beardsley Homestead" painted on it in large white letters. The barn stood as a Long Hill landmark for many years, with its large clock mounted on top of the barn.

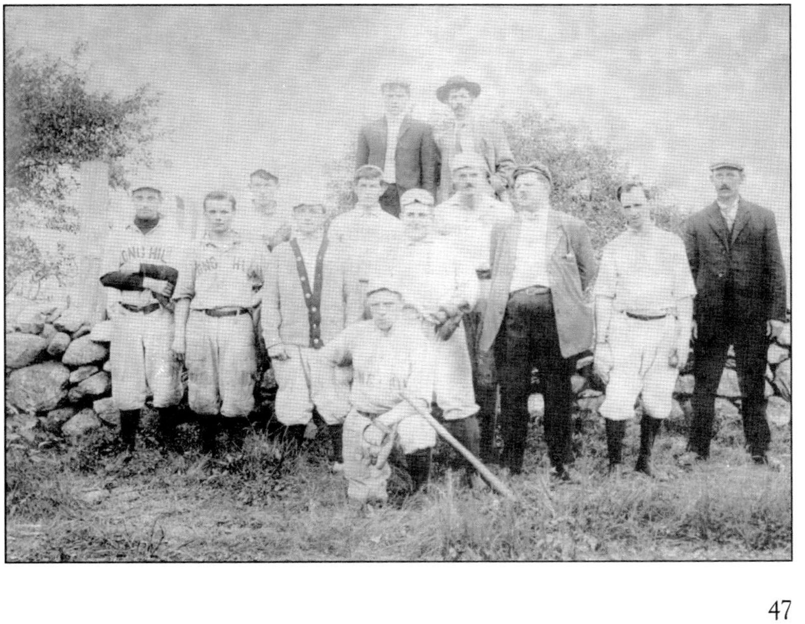

Even after Parlor Rock Amusement Park closed, the baseball field adjacent to the park continued to be used for a number of years. Pictured here is Long Hill's 1912 Parlor Rock baseball team, which included Leo Gabler, Roy Eastman, and Charles Randall.

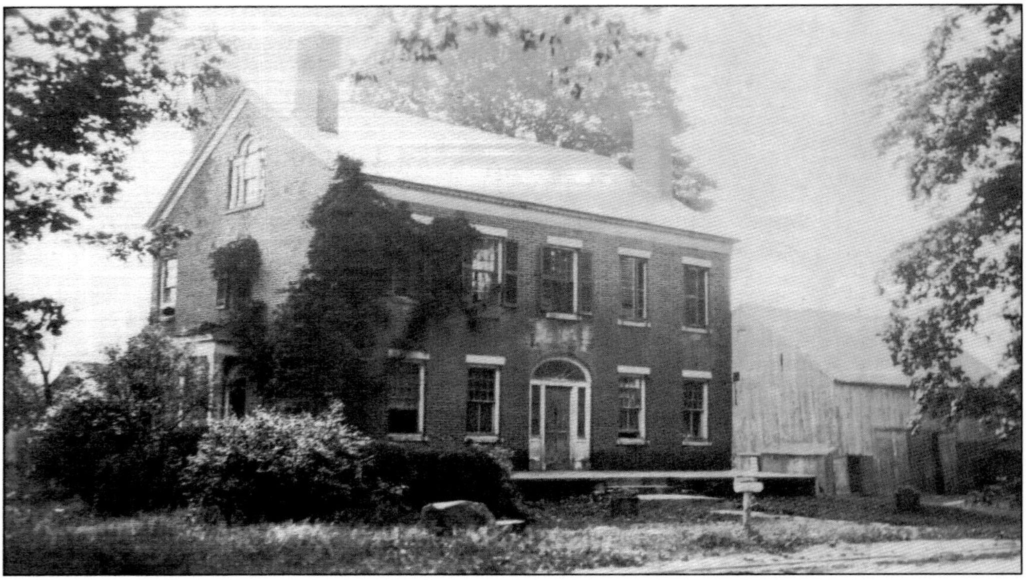

Called Stepping Stones, this beautiful house located at 6071 Main Street was built in 1824 by Dr. Elijah Middlebrook and his wife, Comfort. Dr. Middlebrook practiced medicine and also authored *Middlebrook's New England Almanac*, a popular journal that was first published in 1806. Local stories allege that the house's bricks were made from clay collected from the banks of a small brook that runs behind the house.

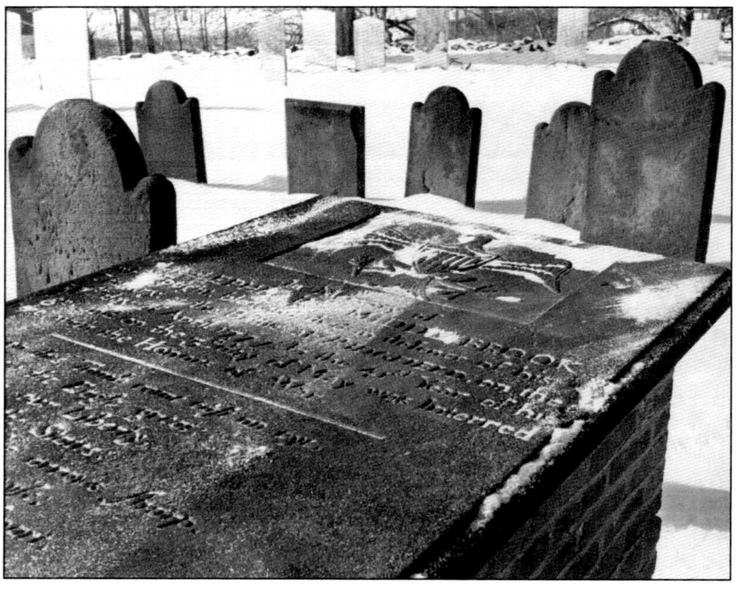

A solemn memorial marks the grave of Lt. Ephraim Middlebrook, who was killed at the Battle of Ridgefield on April 27, 1777, at the age of 41. Middlebrook was laid to rest in the Long Hill burial ground after his body was transported home from Ridgefield by oxcart, a trip requiring two days' travel. Middlebrooks Avenue, adjacent to the cemetery, is named after the Revolutionary War hero.

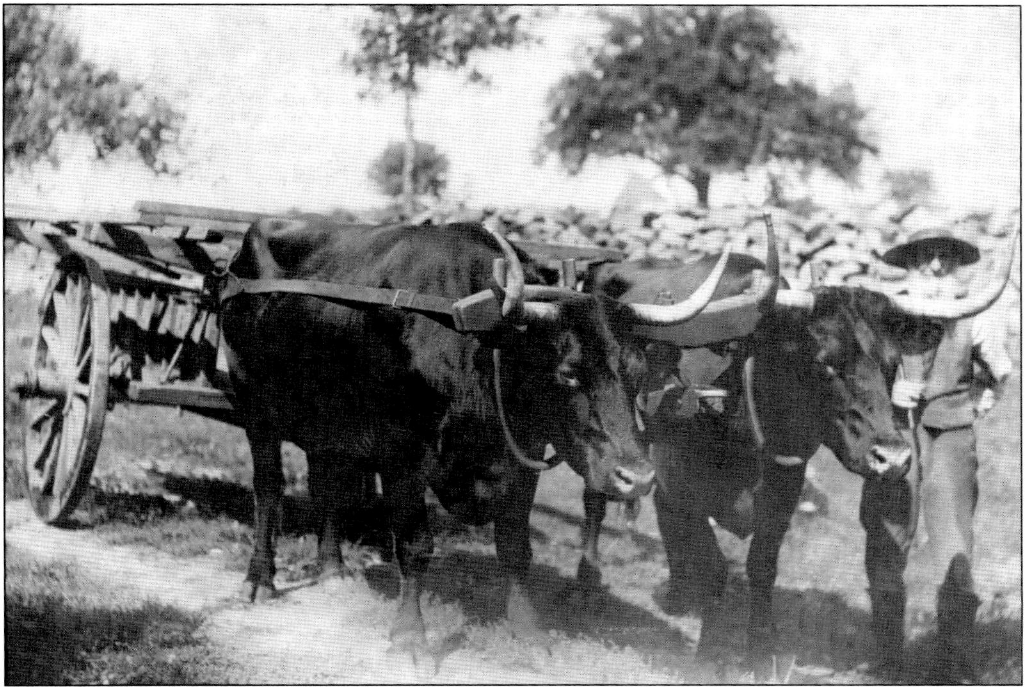

Joseph Spagele, who lived at 125 Teller Road, died a most unfortunate death when he fell asleep, fell off his wagon, and was run over. He is buried in Long Hill Cemetery.

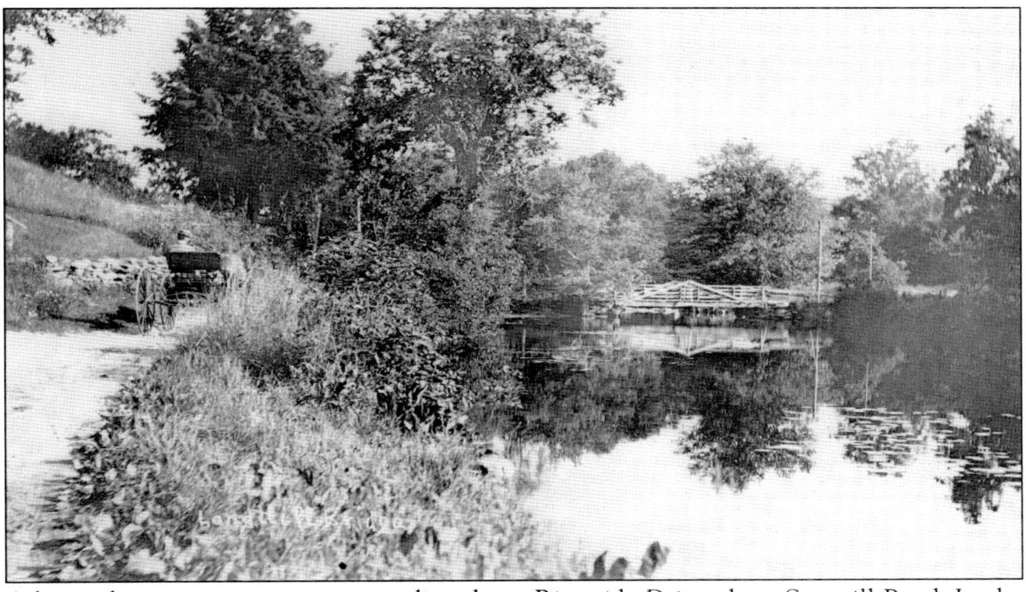

A horse-drawn carriage is seen traveling down Riverside Drive along Sawmill Pond. In the background is the Radcliffe Bridge, where the Pequonnock River flows under Whitney Avenue. At the time of this photograph, Whitney Avenue was known as Sawmill Road. South of this bridge on the west side of the river was the Long Hill sawmill. Radcliffe's knit mill was slightly farther downstream on the east side. The dammed water from the pond was used to provide power for the sawmill's operation.

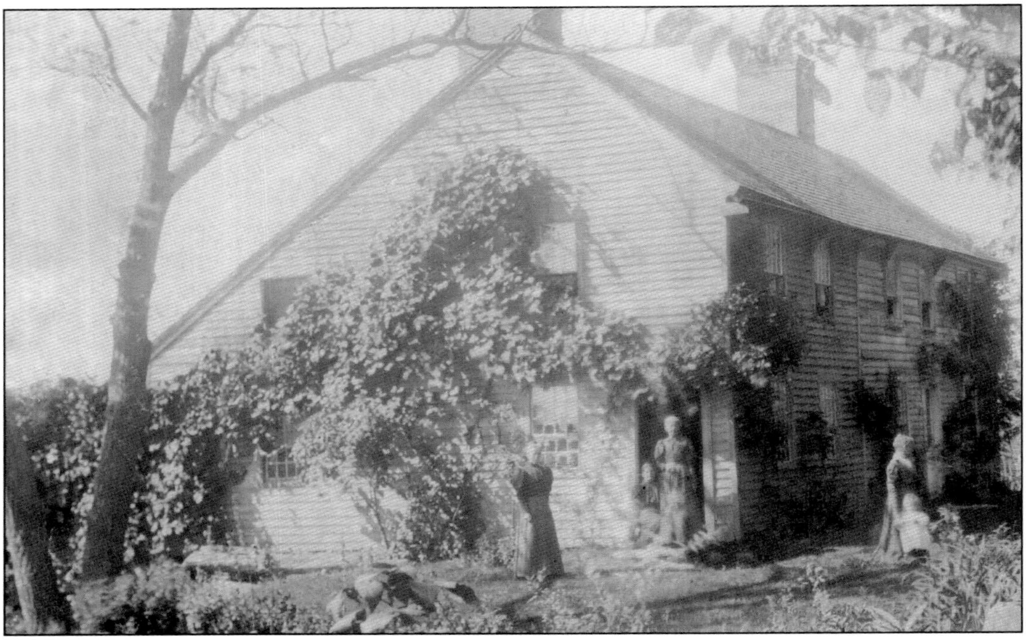

Frances Jennie Walker Coe stands with her young daughter in the front yard of their home at 5937 Main Street. One of the oldest houses in Trumbull, the saltbox was built in 1745 by John Wildman. It was the home of the Walker family for many years.

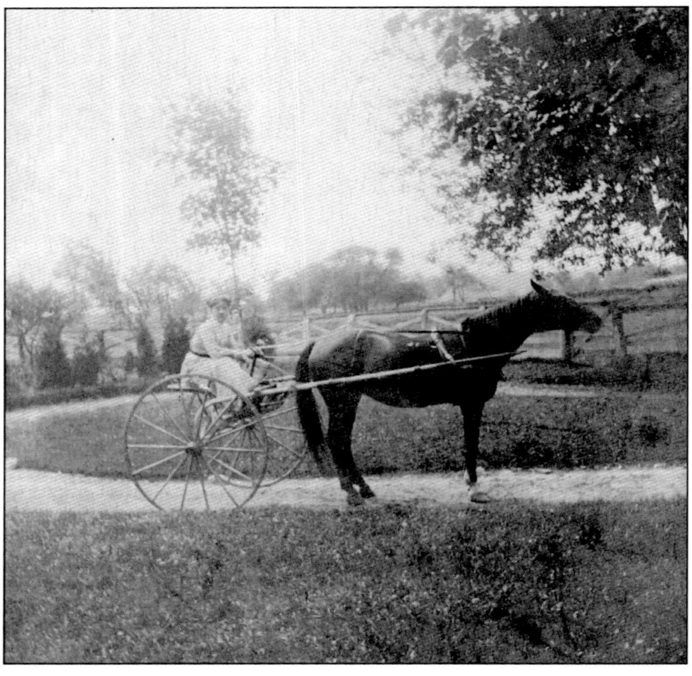

Ethel Davis drives a cart down Main Street in this undated photograph. Ethel's family moved to Trumbull in 1891, when her father bought a house at the corner of Middlebrooks Avenue and Main Street. Ethel attended the Lower Long Hill School in the 1890s and graduated from Bridgeport High School at a time when it was uncommon for girls to continue past eighth grade. After passing a certification test administered by the Trumbull Town School Committee in 1906, she started teaching at the one-room Chestnut Hill School. The job paid $12 a week.

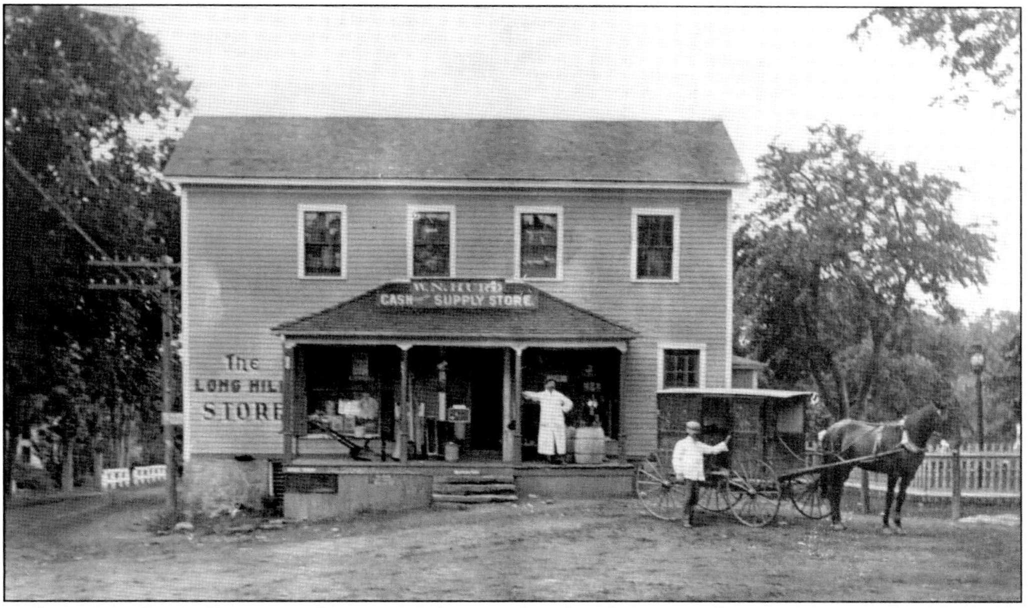

Wilson Hurd ran this general store on the north side of Long Hill Green from the late 1800s until 1921, when it was purchased by George Smith. For many years, the store also served as the village post office until that service was moved to the Downs residence on the east side of the green. The store was later purchased by Charlie Tomer, owner of the nearby Kimberly Inn. It was demolished on May 22, 1974, by the state Department of Transportation to make way for a planned Route 25 exit ramp that was never built.

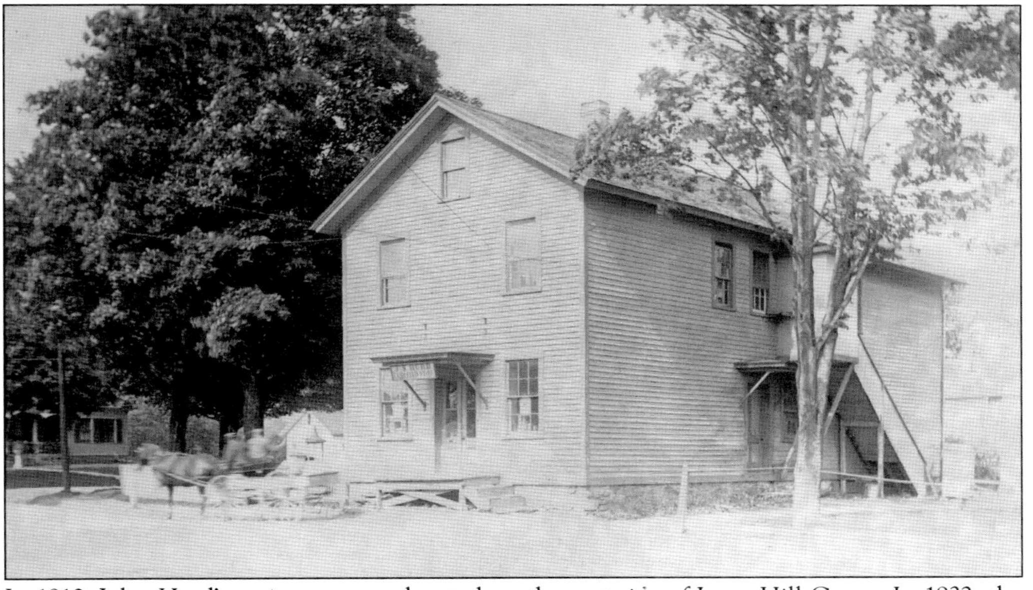

In 1910, John Hurd's grain store was located on the east side of Long Hill Green. In 1932, the building was moved to the opposite side and, in the process, was left sitting for one night in the middle of the green in apparent violation of the deed that prohibited any building from occupying the space. Once in its new location, the building served as Lackman's Feed Store, a hardware store and a carpet store. It was torn down in 1973.

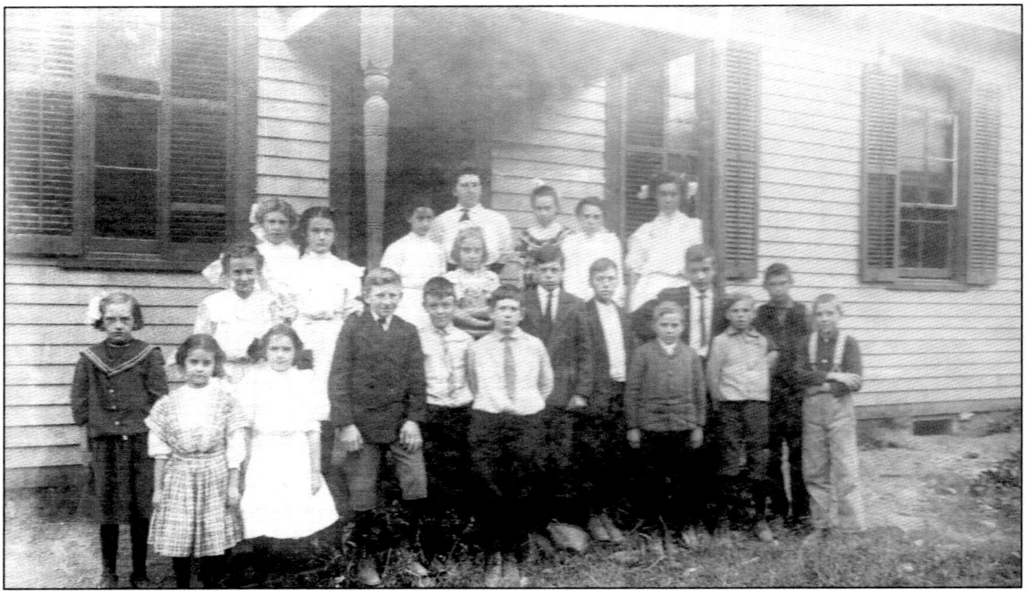

The Upper and Lower Long Hill school districts were formed when the Long Hill School was divided in half in 1895. Children living north of Long Hill Green attended Upper Long Hill School, pictured here. Originally named North Long Hill School, the school was located at 1910 Main Street, on the east side of the street roughly across from Gisella Road. The wood stove that once heated the school is on permanent display at the Trumbull Historical Society.

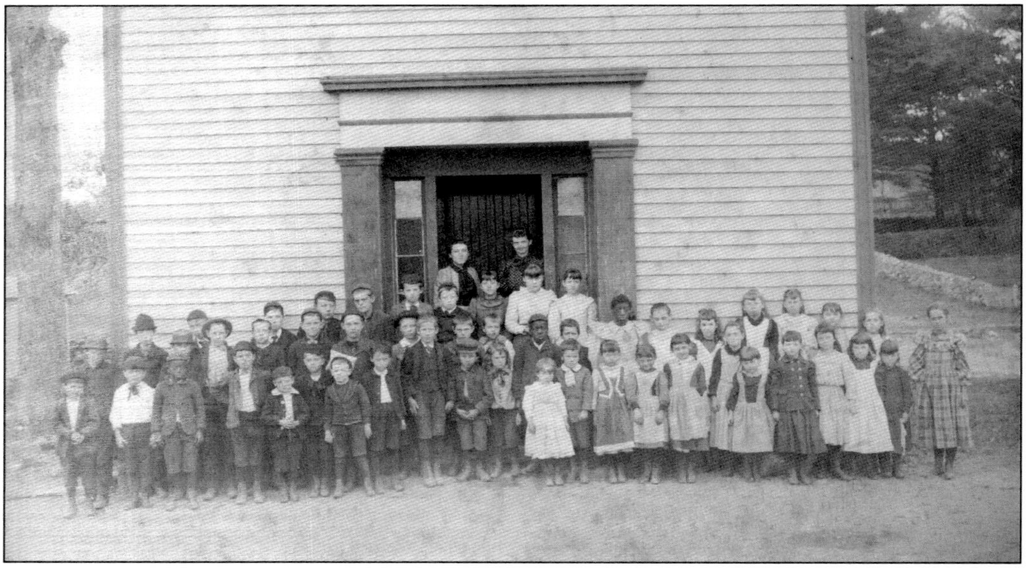

Lower Long Hill School teachers Lena Beers and Frances Walker gather their students for a group photograph in 1891. The two-room schoolhouse was located on a triangular plot of land at the corner of Main Street and Lake Avenue. Established in 1856, the school taught students from grades one through eight. One teacher taught in the first-floor classroom, while the other taught in the upstairs classroom. The school was closed in 1920 with the opening of the new Long Hill School on Main Street (now the Trumbull Board of Education offices). The old schoolhouse was later moved a short distance and converted to a residence on Lake Avenue.

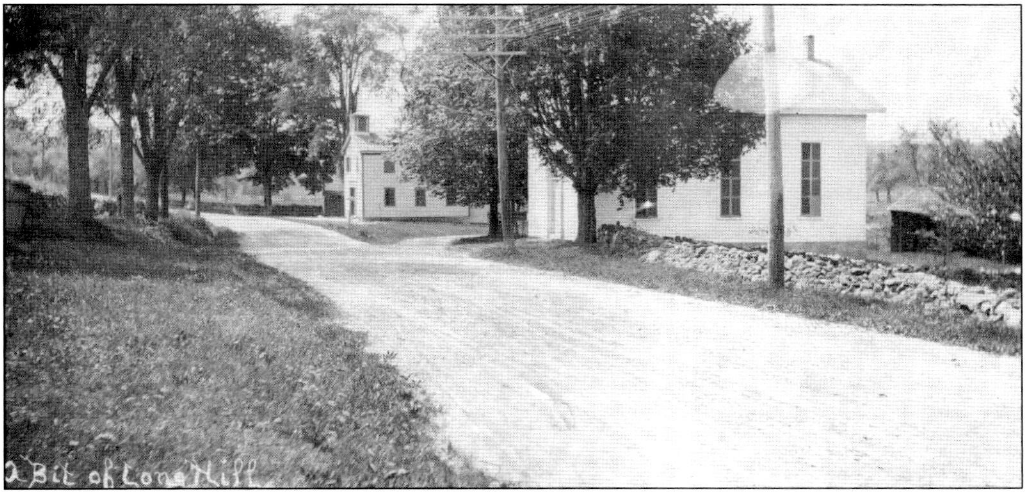

These buildings stood on the corner of Main Street and Modesty Avenue (now known as Lake Avenue). In the background is the Lower Long Hill School. In the foreground is Morgan Chapel, an early Methodist church built in 1857. The chapel was sold in 1911 to a bus company and later served as an auto garage and grocery store. By 1969, when the photograph below was taken, it operated as the Long Hill Food Mart. The store was popular with local children, who would go there for ice cream and penny candy. It was owned and operated by Nathaniel Caminiti before it was torn down in 1969 to make way for a new gas station.

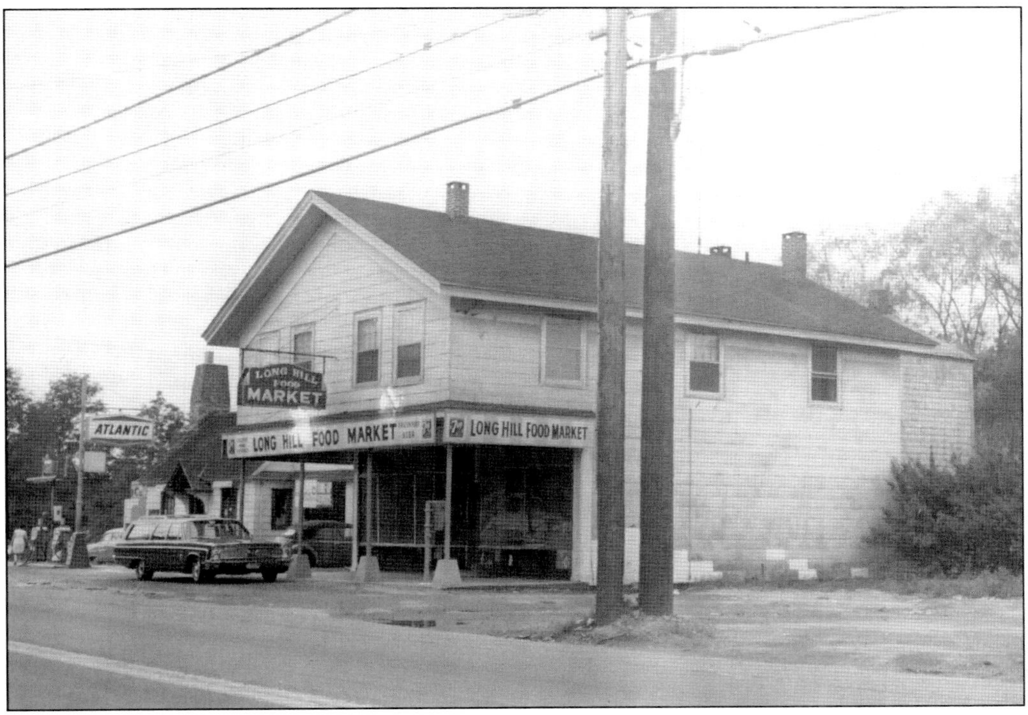

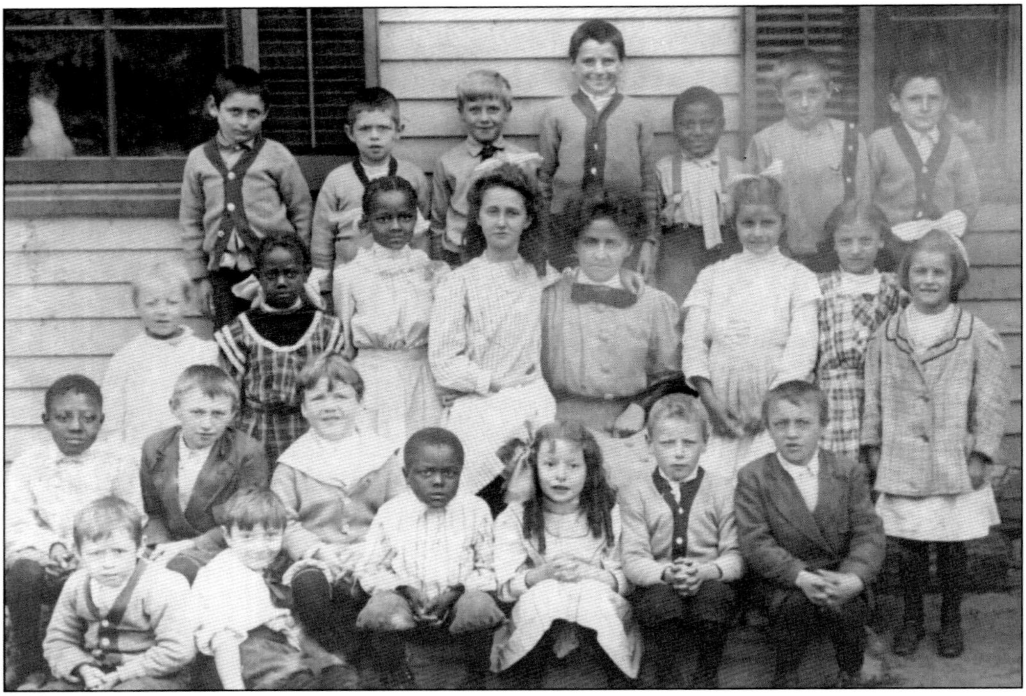

Pictured are children who attended the Upper Long Hill School before it was merged with Lower Long Hill School in 1920. Prior to the mass development of the town after World War II, Long Hill was a place where the greatest amount of ethnic diversity existed in Trumbull. Black families, some with long-standing roots in the area, were joined by Italian and Irish immigrants in the late 1800s in making Long Hill their home.

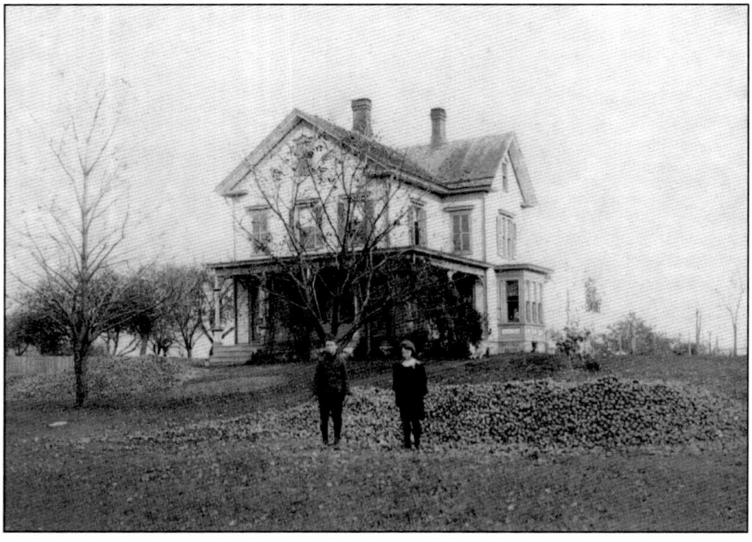

The Burroughs children stand in front of their house on Main Street. Two huge piles of apples are gathered on the front lawn, waiting to be made into cider in the mill across the street. The house, constructed in 1891, was purchased by the town in 2002 and moved slightly farther south to serve as a town hall annex, the Judge Aram Tellalian Building.

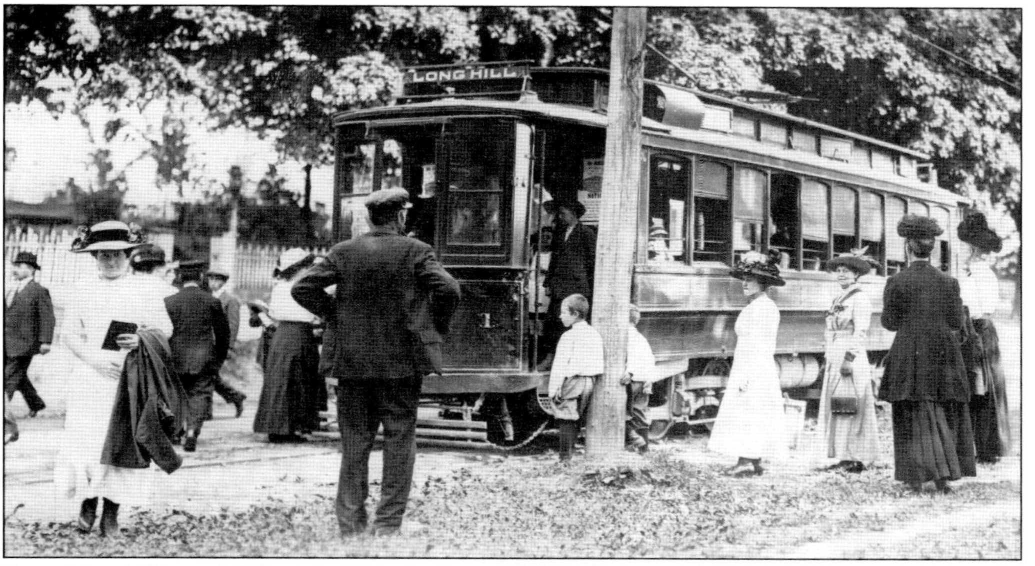

From May 1913 until February 1919, the Long Hill Trolley provided transportation along Main Street from Stonehouse Road to Bridgeport. Nicknamed the "Grasshopper" because of its green color and tendency to jump the tracks, the trolley soon gave way to buses and automobiles.

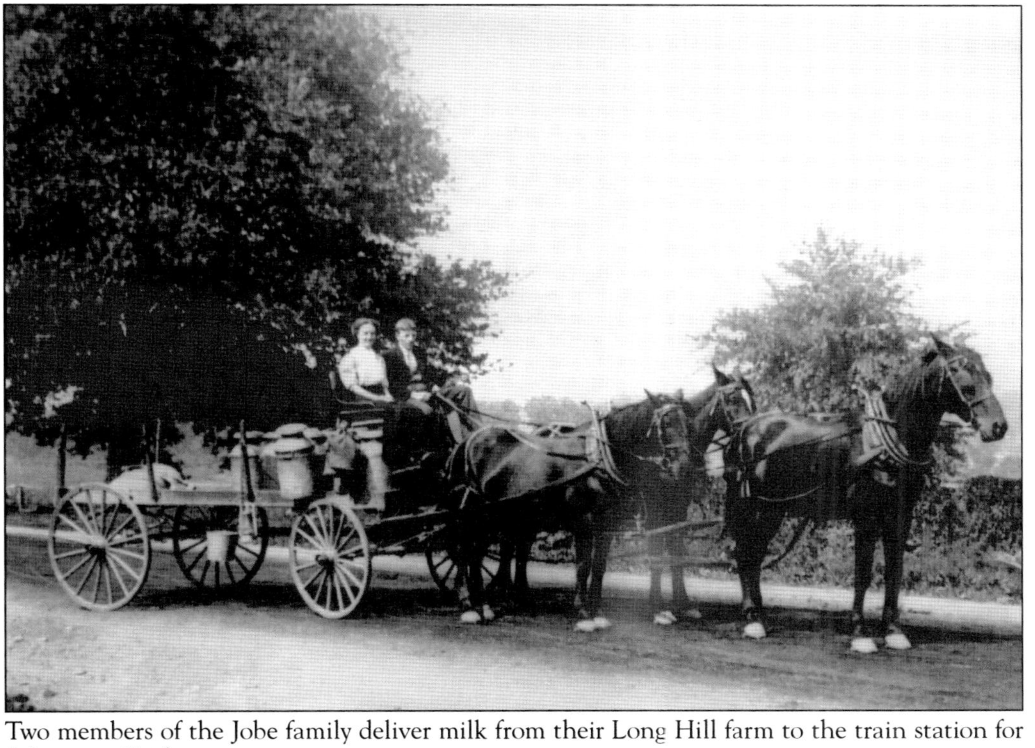

Two members of the Jobe family deliver milk from their Long Hill farm to the train station for delivery to Bridgeport.

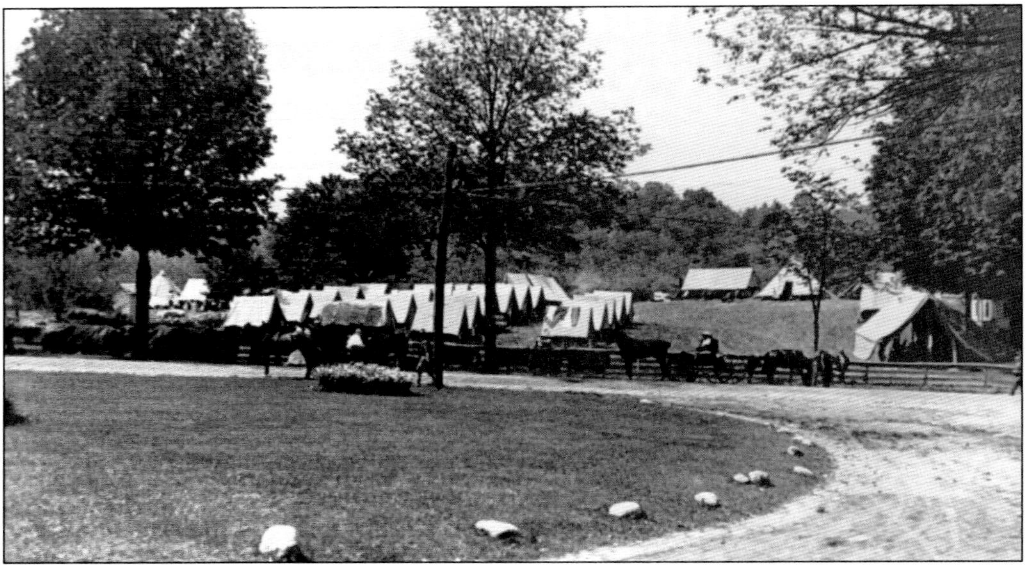

With political tension rising in Europe, US soldiers gathered at Camp Miles on the west side of Long Hill Green for war games in August 1912. The games, a mock attack on New York, involved 20,000 men divided into two "armies." Military dignitaries from Great Britain, Russia, and Mexico came to witness the "battle," along with more than 50,000 local spectators. The exercise marked the first time planes were used in war games, with planes taking off and landing in Stratford and Danbury. The games also pitted the performance of the truck against the standard army mule for the first time. By the end of the maneuvers, the trucks proved themselves superior to the mules, and the airplane proved itself a very useful new weapon for war.

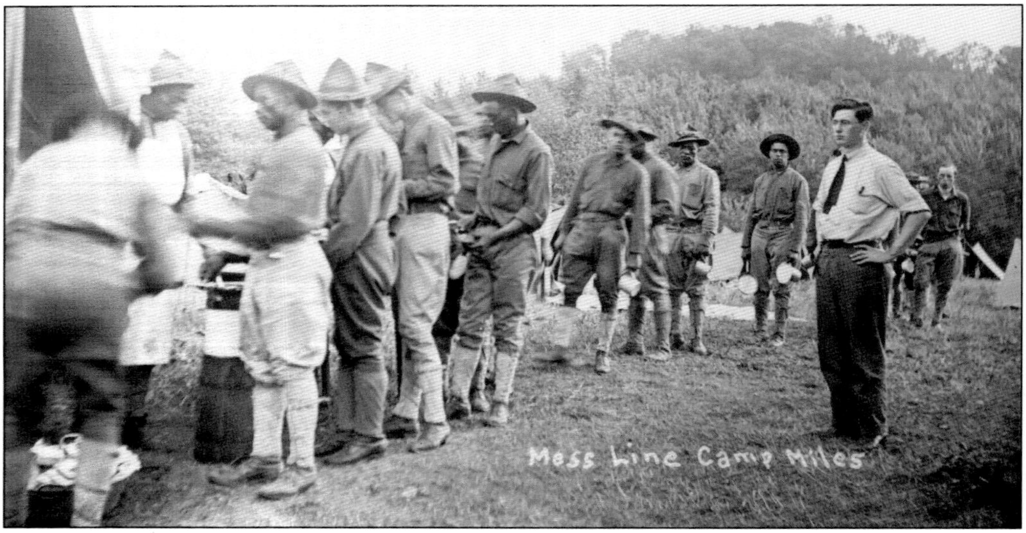

A description on this photograph identifies it as the mess line at Camp Miles. Howard Dillistin of Long Hill, who would serve in the approaching war, told a story of selling ham sandwiches to the soldiers for 10¢ apiece; however, when they realized how hungry the soldiers were, they raised the price to 25¢. Town folk provided lemonade and other cold drinks for the troops. In many local families, stories have been passed down that tell of young children handing out fresh-baked cookies to the men encamped nearby.

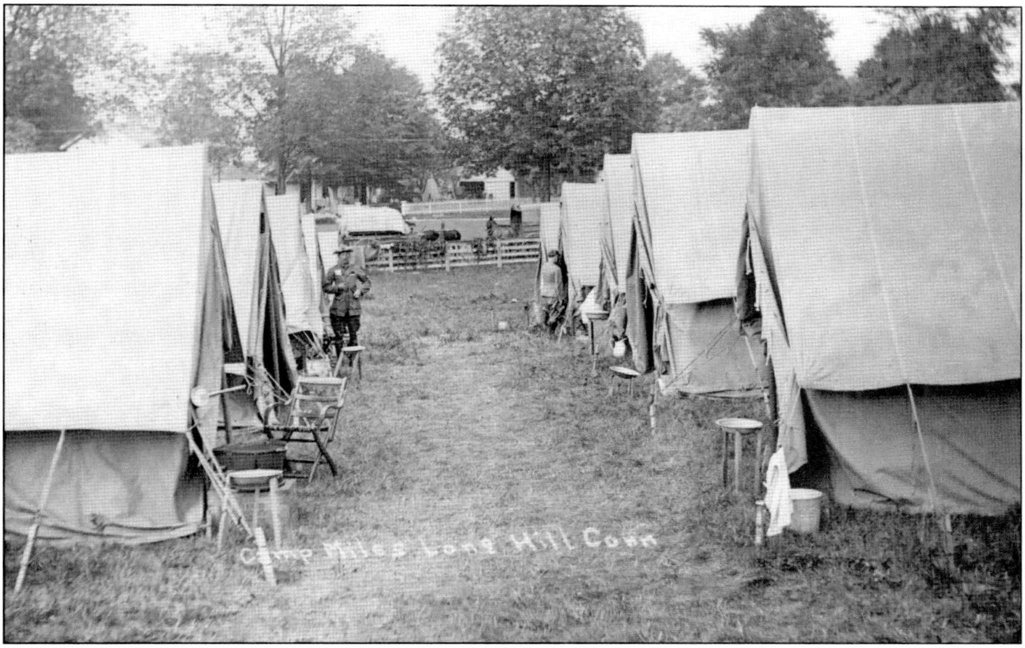

The soldiers that camped in Long Hill were members of the 71st Regiment of New York and made up the enemy "Red" army who were to engage with a "Blue" army representing the United States. The goal of these exercises was to defend a major New York City water supply at Croton Dam, located about 22 miles north of New York City.

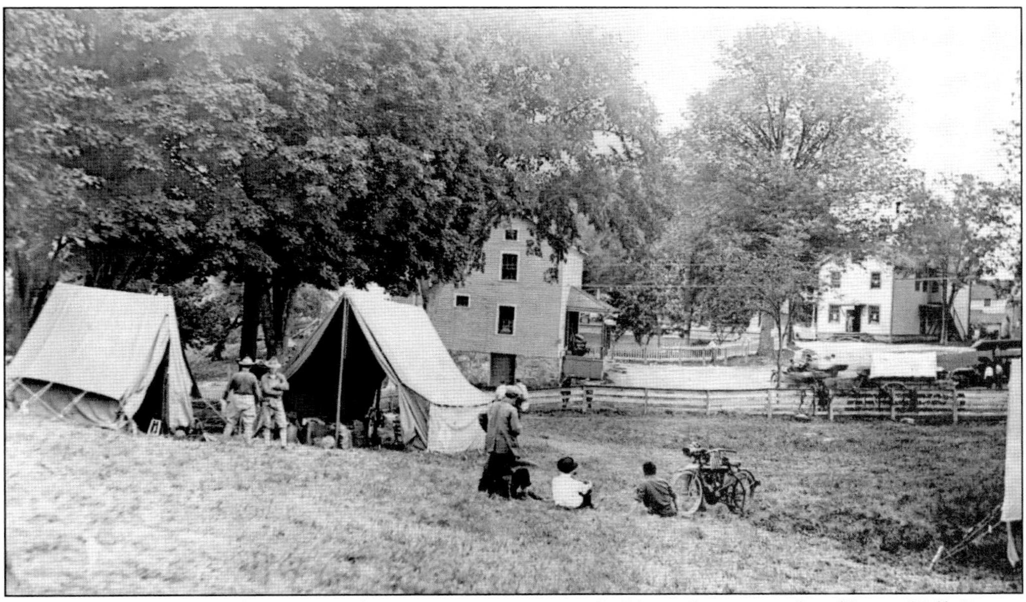

This was the scene looking east of US Army maneuvers held on the west side of Long Hill Green in 1912. Soldiers arrived by train and lined up on Whitney Avenue hill, where they staged a mock battle. John Hurd's feed store can be seen on the east side of the green, along with the general store of Wilson Hurd. Main Street runs between the general store and the fence around the field where the soldiers are encamped.

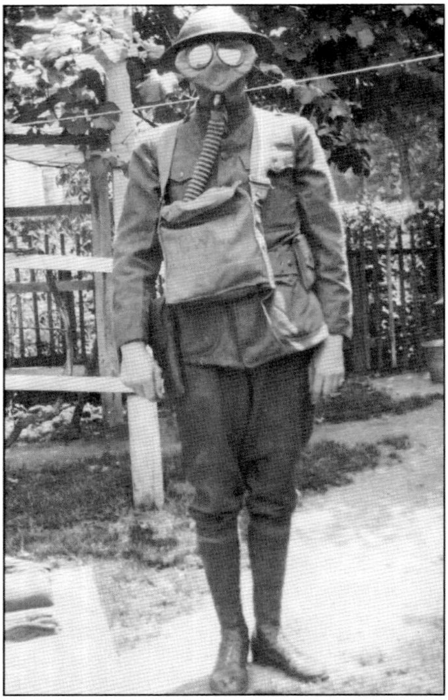

Edward Platt Downs was a Long Hill resident who was wounded in action in World War I and declared dead. He did not actually die, however, until 1948 at the age of 59.

Rallies to promote the sale of Liberty Bonds were a common event in 1918, when this gathering was held at Long Hill Green. First issued in 1917 to support the war effort, the bonds were promoted by politicians and celebrities at rallies like this one throughout the nation.

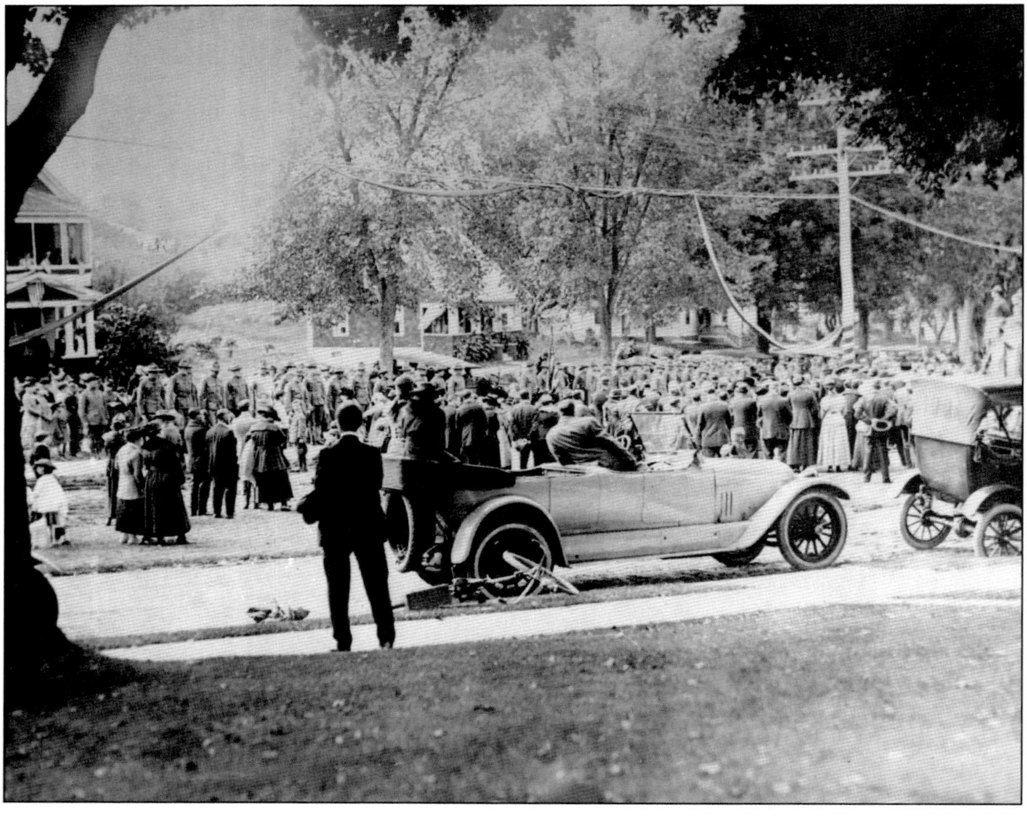

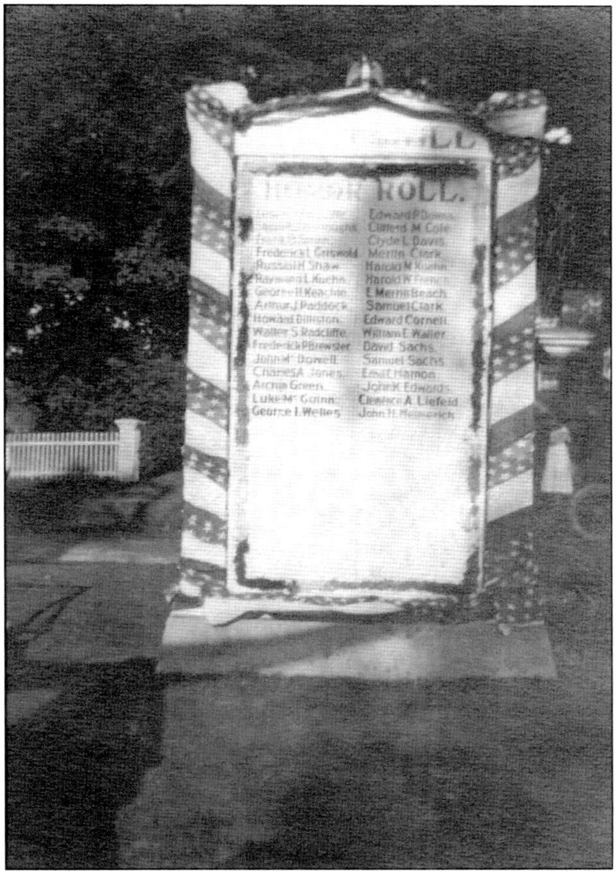

In 1919, the people of Long Hill erected a wooden monument on the green bearing the names of 33 men who had served in World War I. Unveiled with great celebration, it was nonetheless replaced in 1926 by a more durable monument, pictured below. The new memorial consisted of a boulder in which was set a bronze plaque bearing the names of Trumbull's 36 war vets, all of whom returned home safely. The boulder was transported to the site from the Chestnut Hill Road property of Francis E. Beach. Long Hill residents raised about $300 to pay for the tablet cast by the Monumental Bronze Co. of Bridgeport.

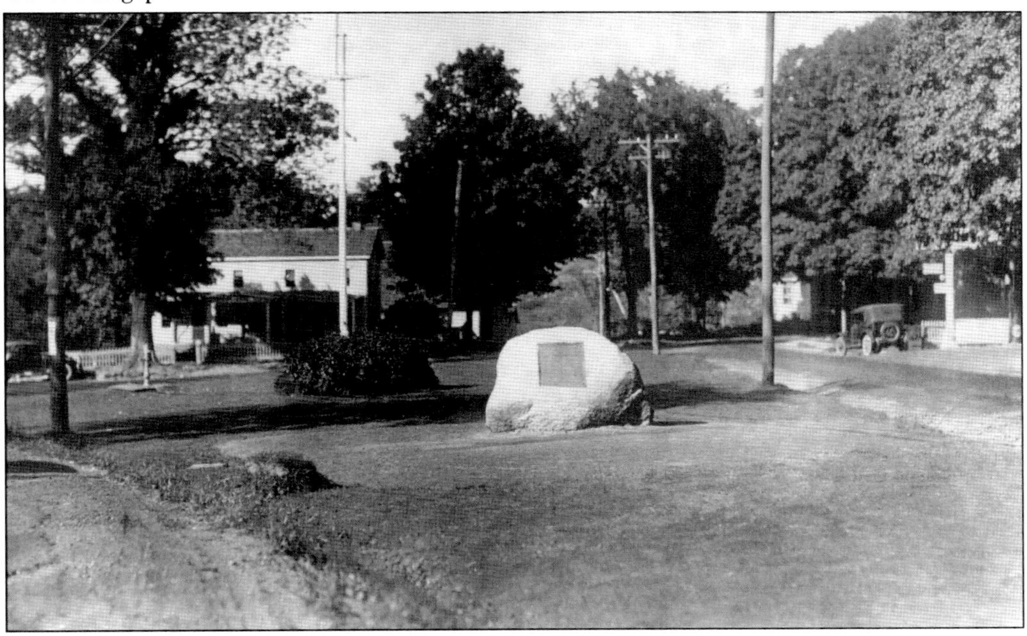

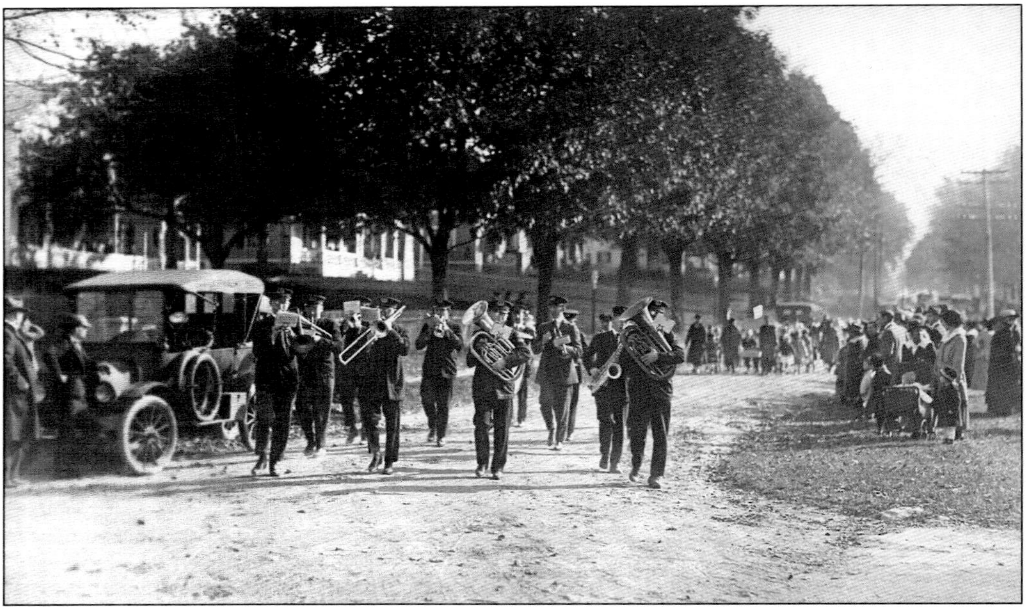

In the early 20th century, the Long Hill Green was the site of many political and patriotic events. In 1918, a large rally was held to promote industrial development in Long Hill. That same year, a bond rally was held to encourage the sale of Liberty Bonds. Just after World War I, in 1919, local residents gathered to dedicate a wooden honor roll bearing the names of veterans of that war. In 1926, they gathered on the green once more, this time to dedicate a second, more durable, stone monument. The patriotic tradition continues today, with Trumbull's Memorial Day parade starting off near the green.

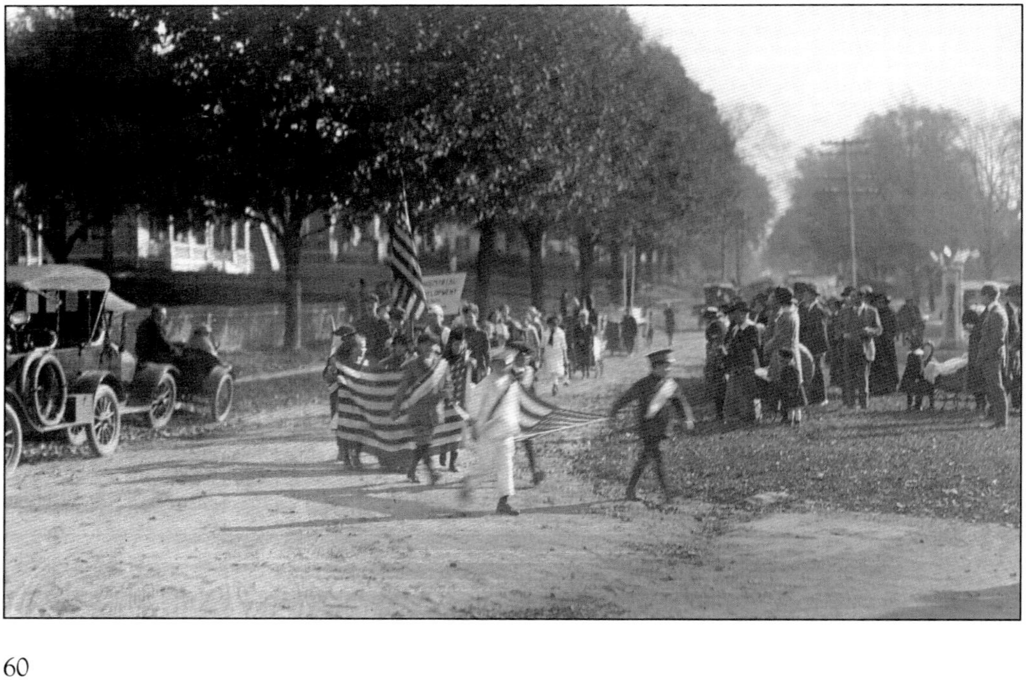

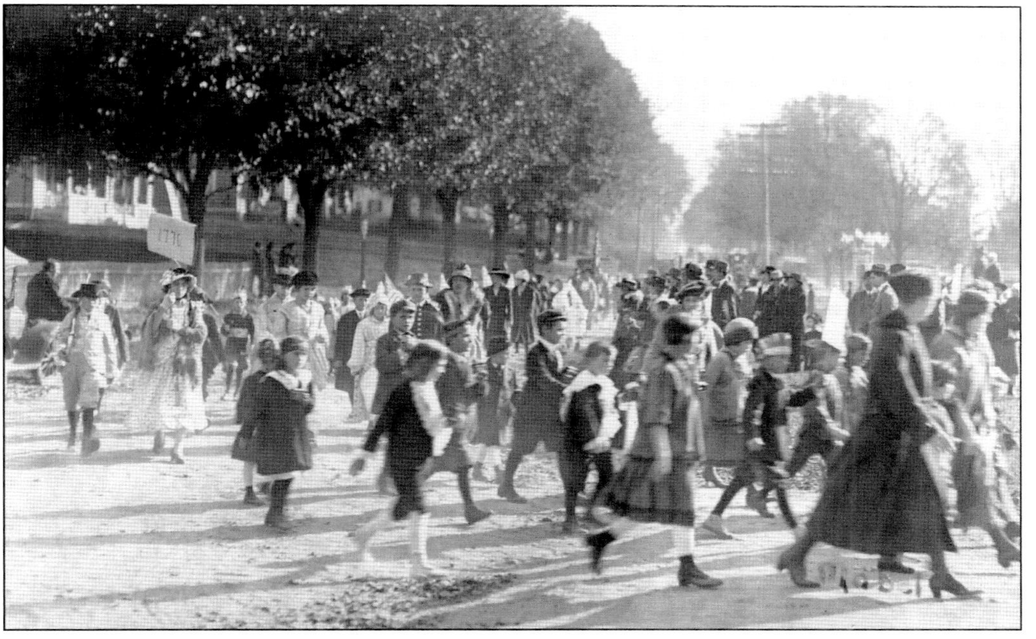

The signs carried by participants in these photographs indicate that this was the rally for industrial development held on the green in 1918. As the 20th century progressed, the village green hosted other events, including whistle-stop tours, political debates, Easter-egg hunts, and a tree-lighting ceremony. Tragedy struck on the green in 1957, when Chester Main, Long Hill's assistant fire chief, was electrocuted while decorating the large evergreen tree. A plaque was placed on the green in his memory.

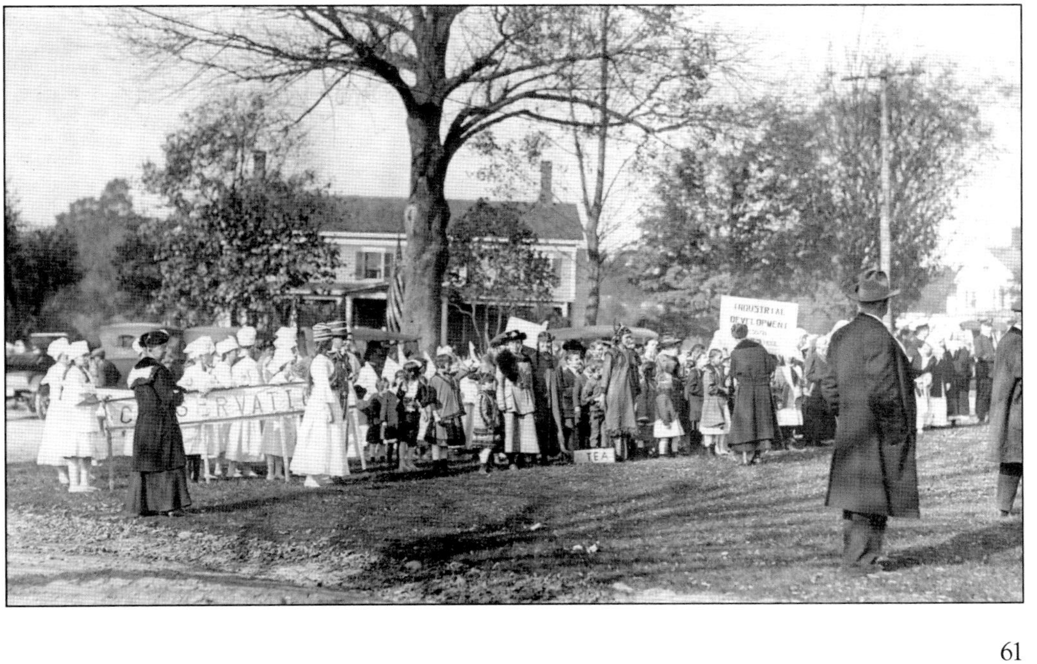

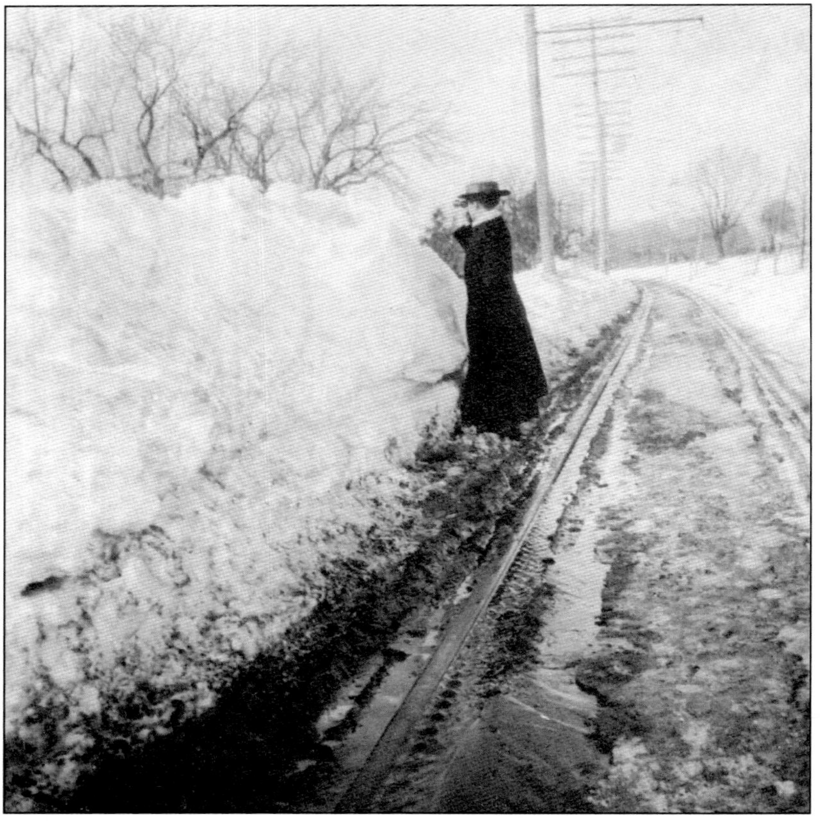

Louise Coe looks over the snow banks alongside Main Street in Long Hill on March 23, 1915. Notice the trolley tracks in the street. Born in 1879, Louise was the daughter of Francis and Fredrick Coe.

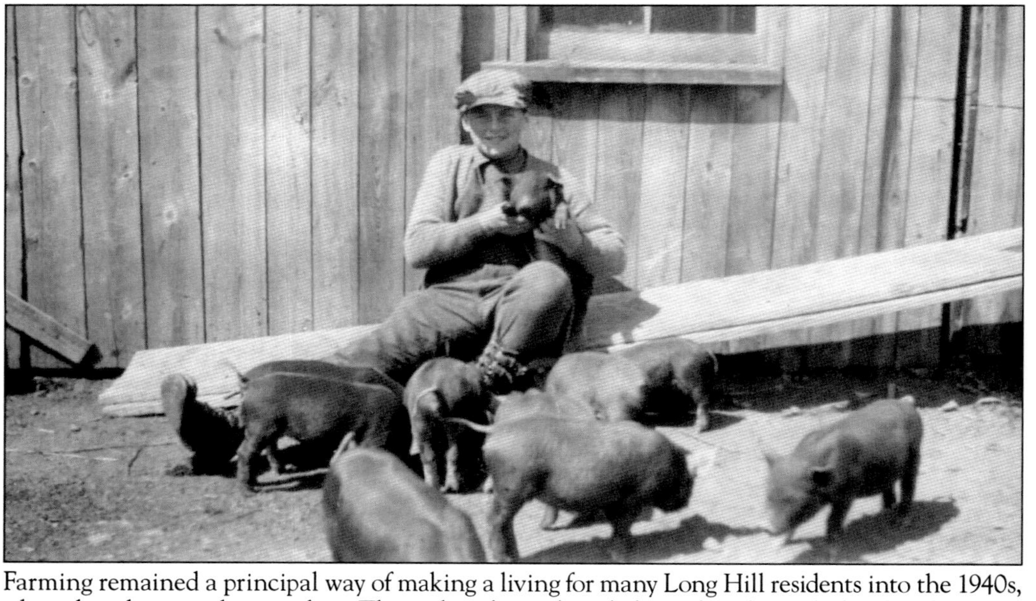

Farming remained a principal way of making a living for many Long Hill residents into the 1940s, when this photograph was taken. The piglets shown here belonged to the Cole family, who had a farm on Main Street. As Long Hill changed from an agricultural to a suburban community, some of the street names also changed, including Park Lane, which was originally named Pork Lane.

The Radcliffe knit mill, which began operation in 1862, was located just south of Whitney Avenue on the east side of the Pequonnock River. Under the mill, a large waterwheel with an attached shaft powered the looms and machinery inside. The shaft still remains at the site of the mill along with the ruins of the building's stone foundation and sluiceway. The mill made wool wristlets for gloves until 1938.

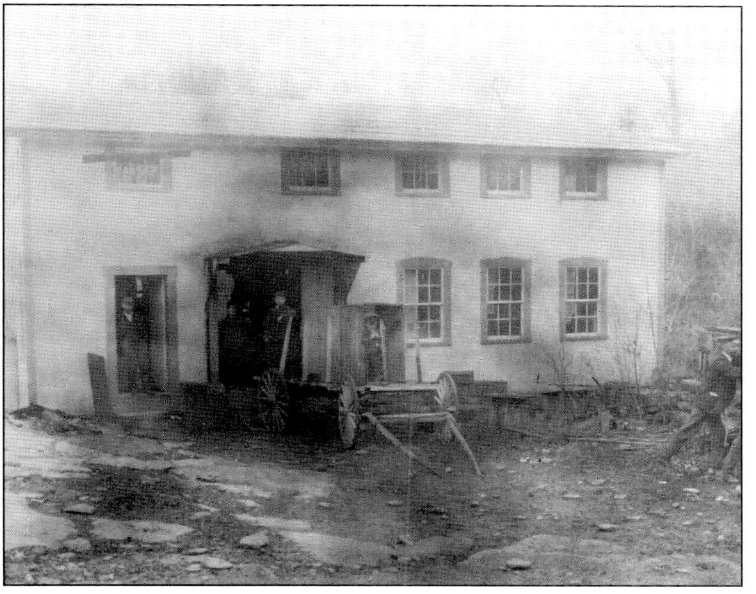

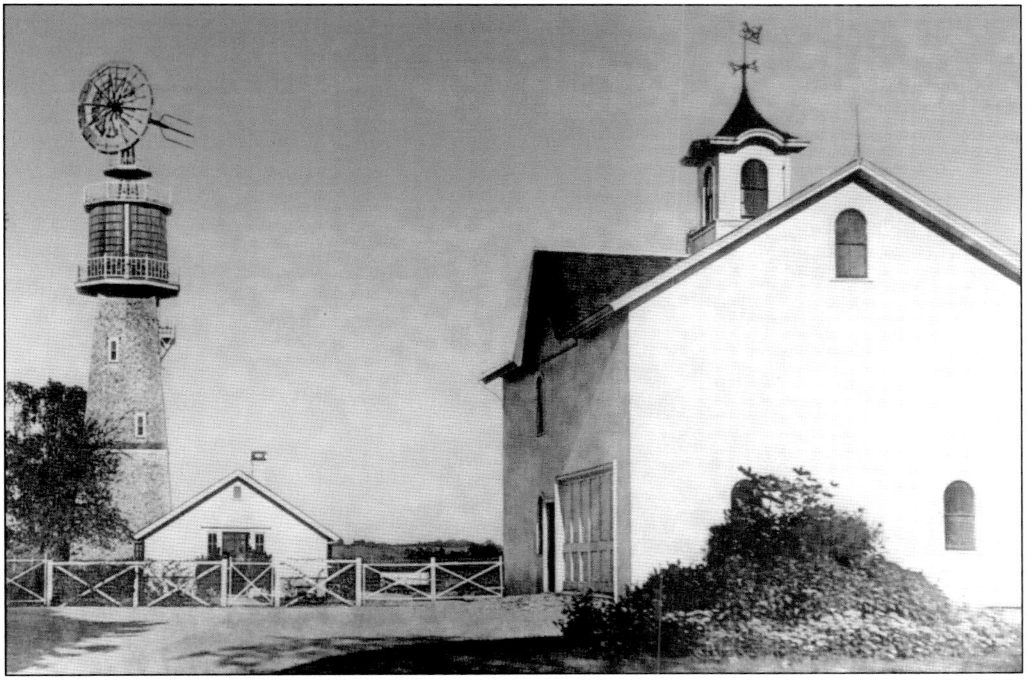

This 100-foot-tall windmill was part of a shirt factory on Main Street owned by Harvey Hubbell. His son Harvey Hubbell II, founder of Harvey Hubbell Electric Inc. in Bridgeport, invented the electrical plug and the pull-chain socket. A newspaper report in 1878 described "Hubbell's Factory of Long Hill" as "a very thriving business" with "labor given to hundreds of people; the sewing machines are run by steam power, and fifty hands are employed to attend them (mostly women)." By that time, the business was run by Hubbell's stepson G.F. Hadley. The property is now owned by St. Joseph's Manor. The windmill was torn down in 1976.

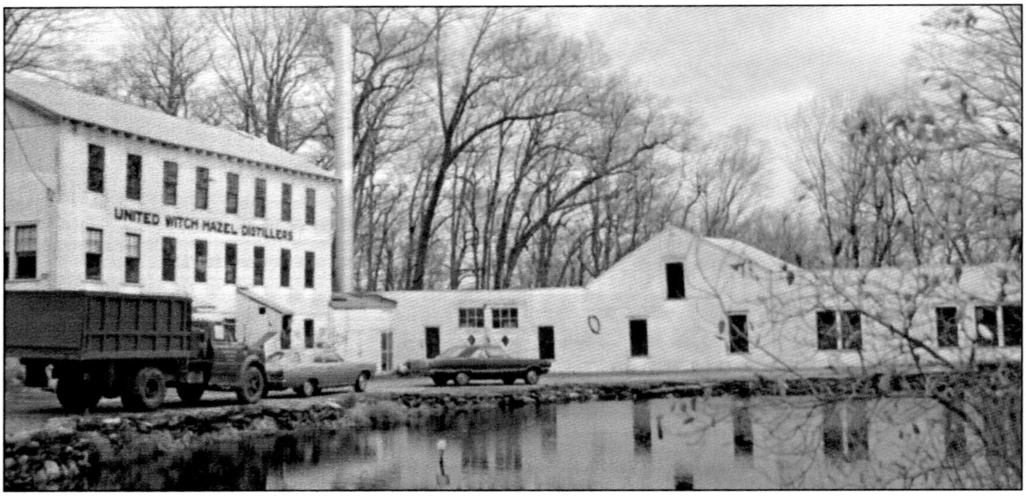

This 1970s postcard captures the United Witch Hazel Factory on Broadway Road not long before it was destroyed by fire in 1974. The complex was originally the Toucey factory, established during the Civil War period for the manufacture of fine muslin underwear for men. In 1923, the factory began making witch hazel as the Stepney Witch Hazel Company. Witch hazel, an alcohol-based astringent commonly used to sooths sprains and bruises, is made by steaming and boiling parts of the witch hazel bush. Only three witch-hazel factories existed in the United States during this century, all of them in Connecticut. Ownership and name of the factory changed several times. The factory was owned by the United Witch Hazel Distillers when a fire destroyed the building. The fire that destroyed it was the result of a distilling accident the day after Halloween in 1974. Interestingly enough, it occurred one week after a large silhouette of a witch flying on her broom was stenciled on the east addition.

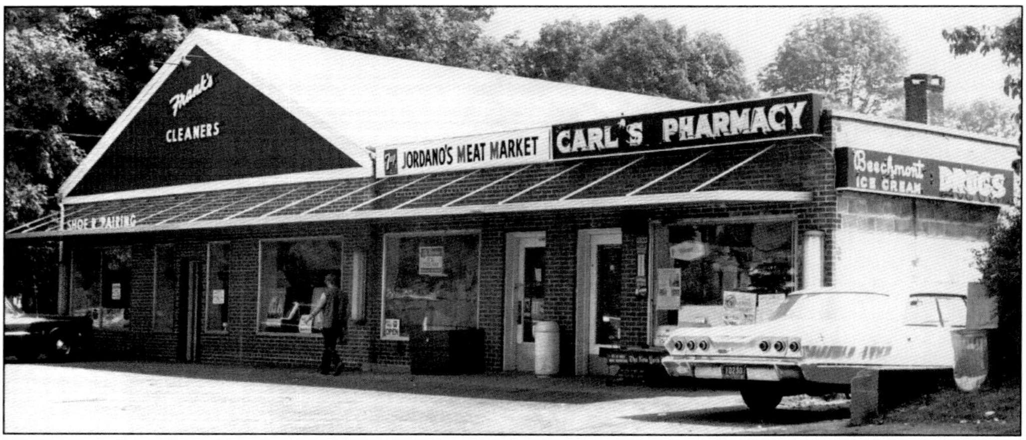

Shops on the east side of Long Hill Green—including Frank's Cleaners, Jordano's Meat Market, and Carl's Pharmacy—are pictured on July 27, 1970. The original portion of the building, where the cleaners was located, was a Studebaker dealership and auto garage. During World War II, the building was used as a machine shop to make submarine parts. Later, the property also housed a shoe-repair shop whose cobbler plied his trade in the front window where passersby could watch him at work. Carl Pember operated the pharmacy with a soda fountain next door. When Pember retired, The Original Bike Shop took over the space. When Luigi's Pastry of Bridgeport was looking to expand, they bought out the property and opened a shop formerly occupied by the dry cleaner. Franco Gianni's Restaurant was established where the market and pharmacy had been.

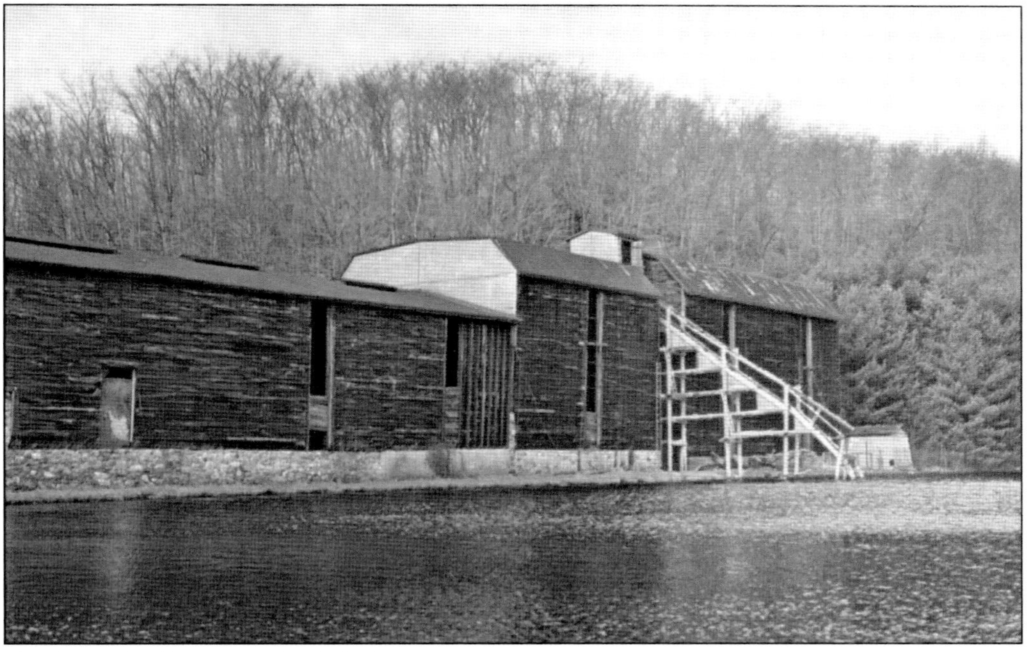

The Kaatz family operated this icehouse, located beside a pond on Whitney Avenue, from 1904 to 1955. Large blocks of ice were cut in the winter, lifted by an elevator, and then stacked in the icehouse, where they were covered with sawdust to prevent melting in the warmer months. Before refrigerators were available, people would place their perishables in an icebox. The iceman delivered the blocks of ice to homes with his horse-drawn carriage, from which he usually would also sell coal and, sometimes, rags. A placard was placed in the windows of homes requiring ice with a number indicating the block size to be delivered. In 1969, the town acquired the property. Although accepted into the National Register of Historic Places and believed to be the only structure of its kind standing in Connecticut, the building was razed in 1978 because town officials felt the structure's dilapidated condition made it unsafe. Today, the Trumbull Veterans Organization, comprised of American Legion Post 141 and VFW Post 10059, have a meeting hall located at Kaatz's pond. At right, Erich Kaatz stands in front of the icehouse conveyor in January 1967.

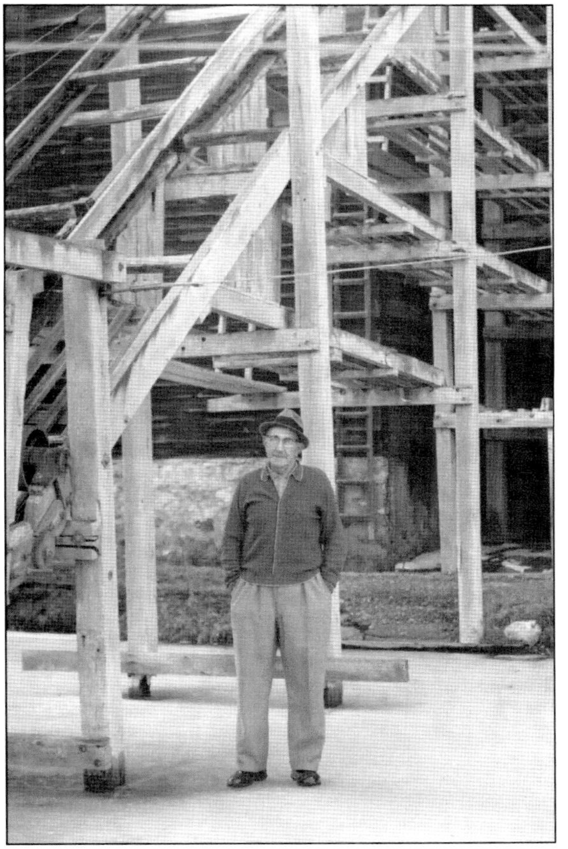

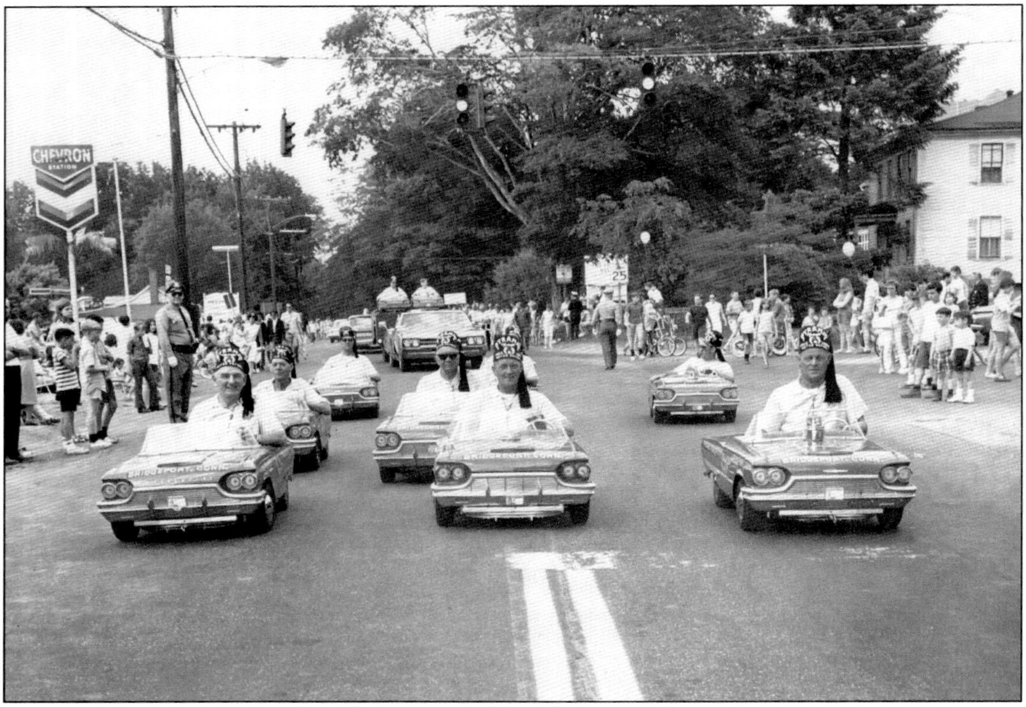

Since shortly after World War II, Trumbull has celebrated Memorial Day with a street parade down Main Street.

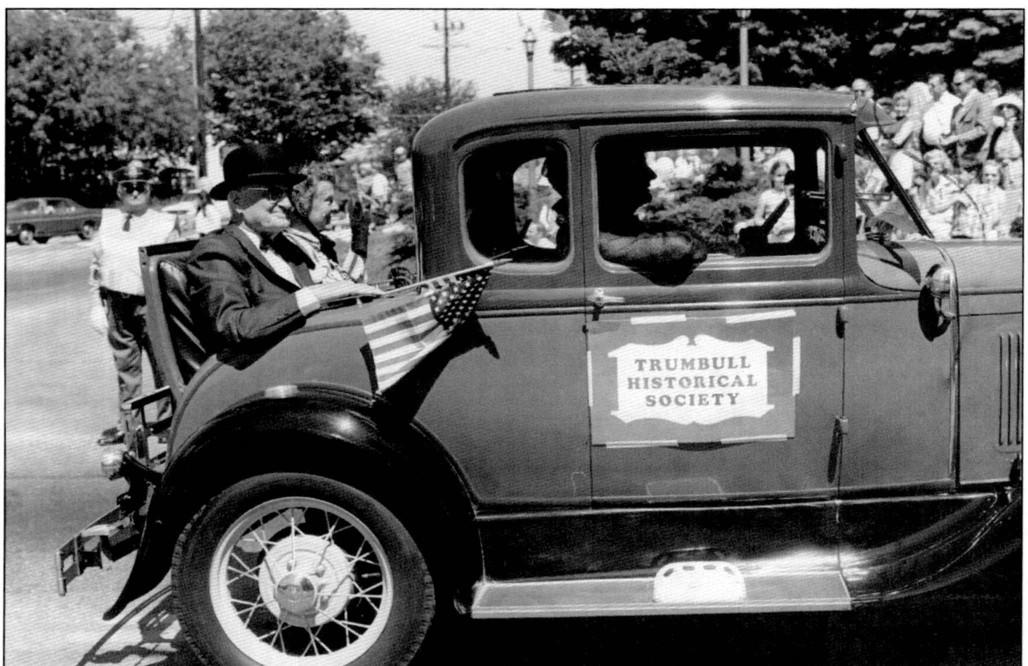

Trumbull Historical Society founder E. Merrill Beach enjoys the view from the rumble seat during the town's Memorial Day parade in 1976.

Four

The Pequonnock Valley

Encompassing the route of the Housatonic Railroad and its surrounds, the Pequonnock River Valley greenway is an Eden-like oasis that holds some of the town's most fantastic sights. Running through the center of the town, the valley was home to a popular 19th-century amusement park, early industries, and natural places considered sacred by local Native Americans. The New York, New Haven and Hartford line of the Housatonic Railway was the key to opening Trumbull to the rest of the world, providing transit of manufactured goods to a new group of consumers. Named by the Paugussett tribe, the name Pequonnock means "cleared field." Almost lost to development in the 1970s, the valley remains today as a popular hiking and biking spot with many trails to be explored and sights to be seen. The main rail trail extends from Tait Road in Trumbull Center to Whitney Avenue, where it passes under the Route 25 highway into Old Mine Park before traversing Route 111. Today, it is part of the Housatonic Rails-to-Trails greenway.

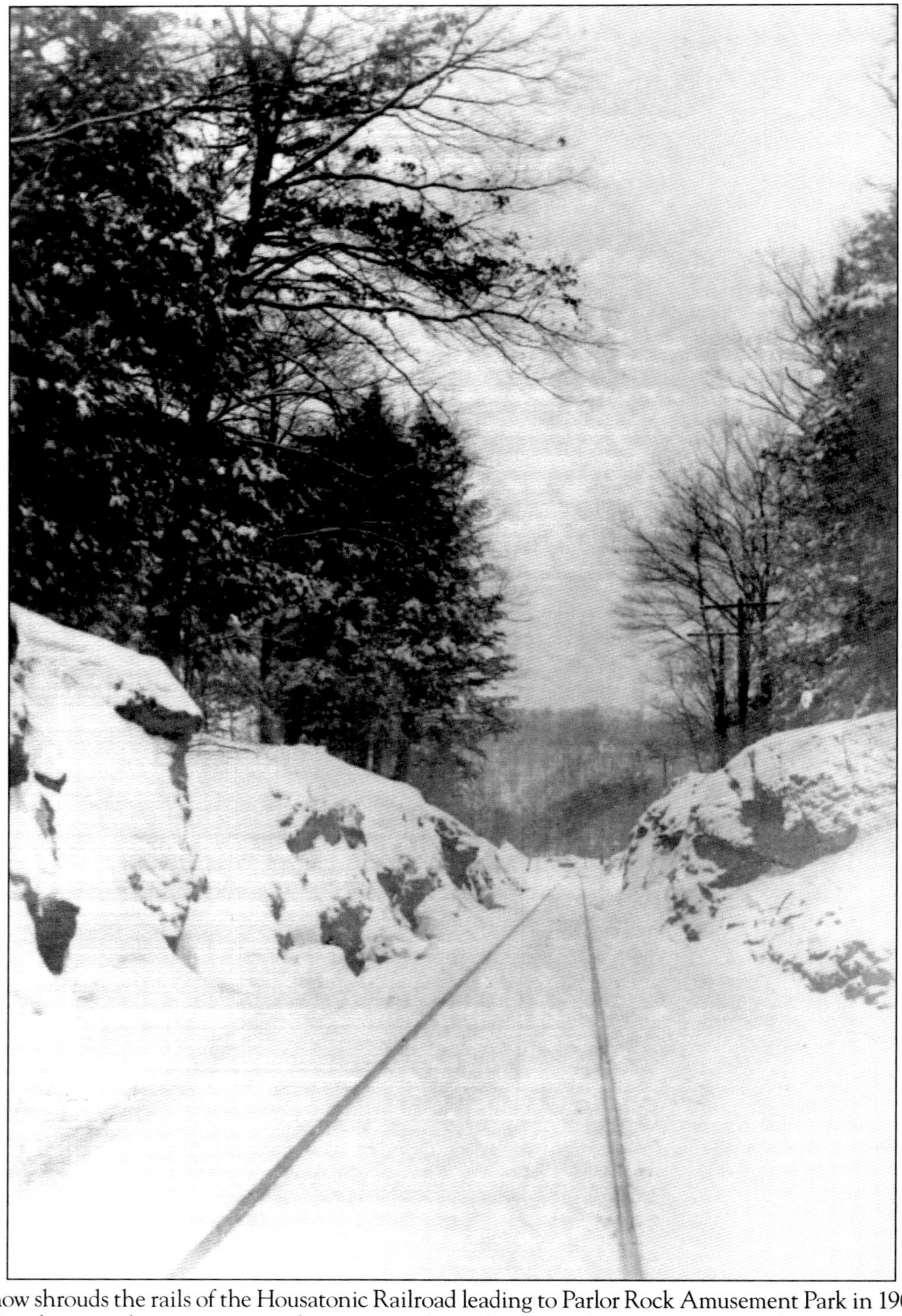

Snow shrouds the rails of the Housatonic Railroad leading to Parlor Rock Amusement Park in 1907. Already a popular summertime destination, the park attracted winter visitors with an enormous toboggan slide added in 1887. The slide was located just to the northwest of what is now Route 25. The park was lit with electric lights designed by a coworker of Thomas Edison.

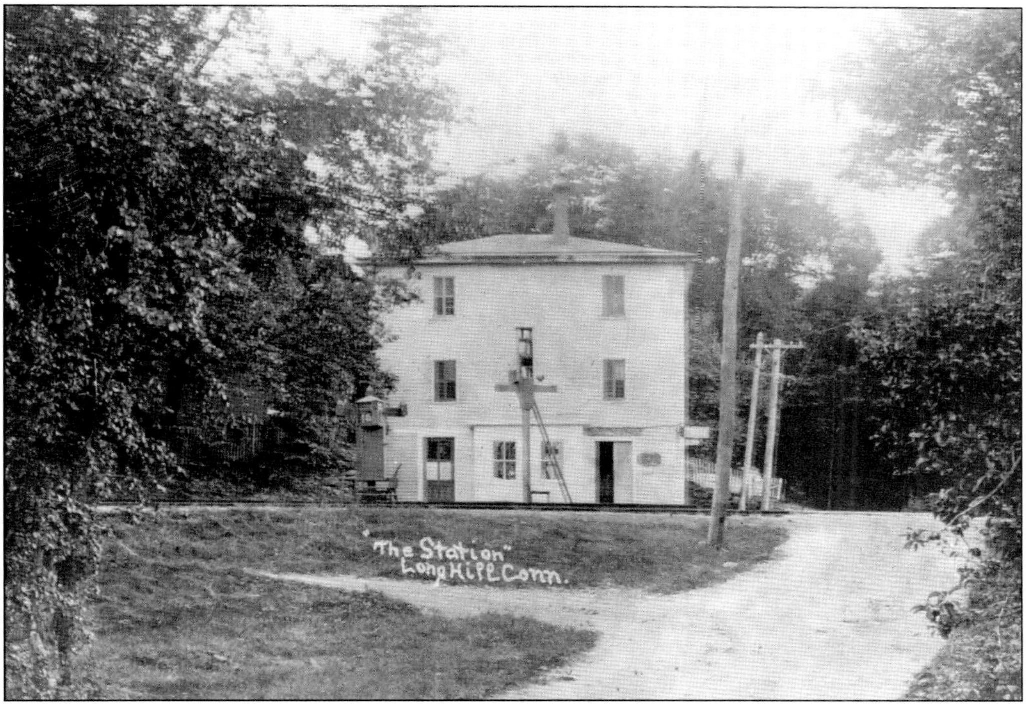

In operation from 1840 until the early 1930s, the Long Hill railroad station was an important hub for raw materials used by the area's textile factories and cigar shops.

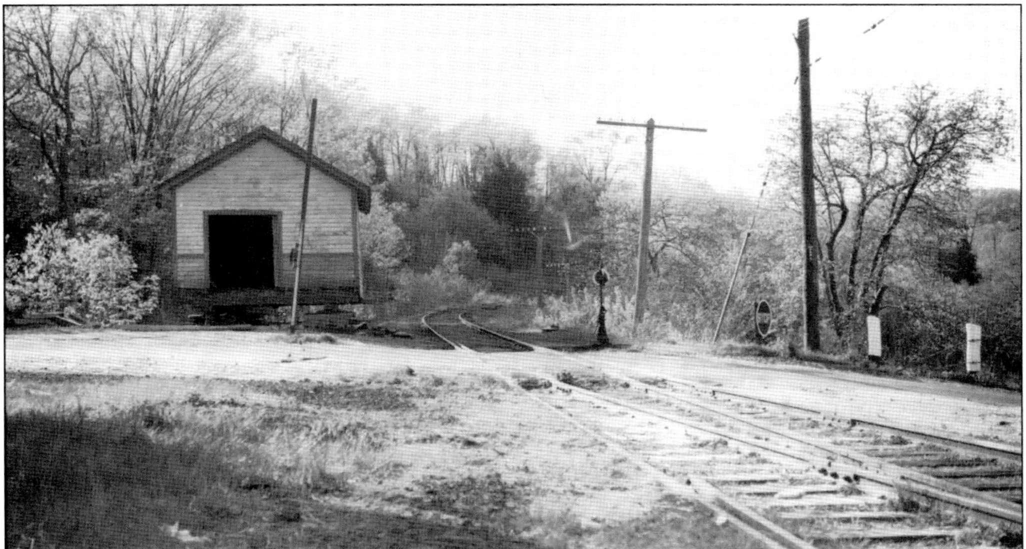

This view of the freight shed across from the Long Hill train station may not look familiar, but it shows a site traversed by hundreds of people today who hike or bike along the Pequonnock rail trail. The road seen here is Whitney Avenue, and the tracks mark the location where the rail trail now crosses it.

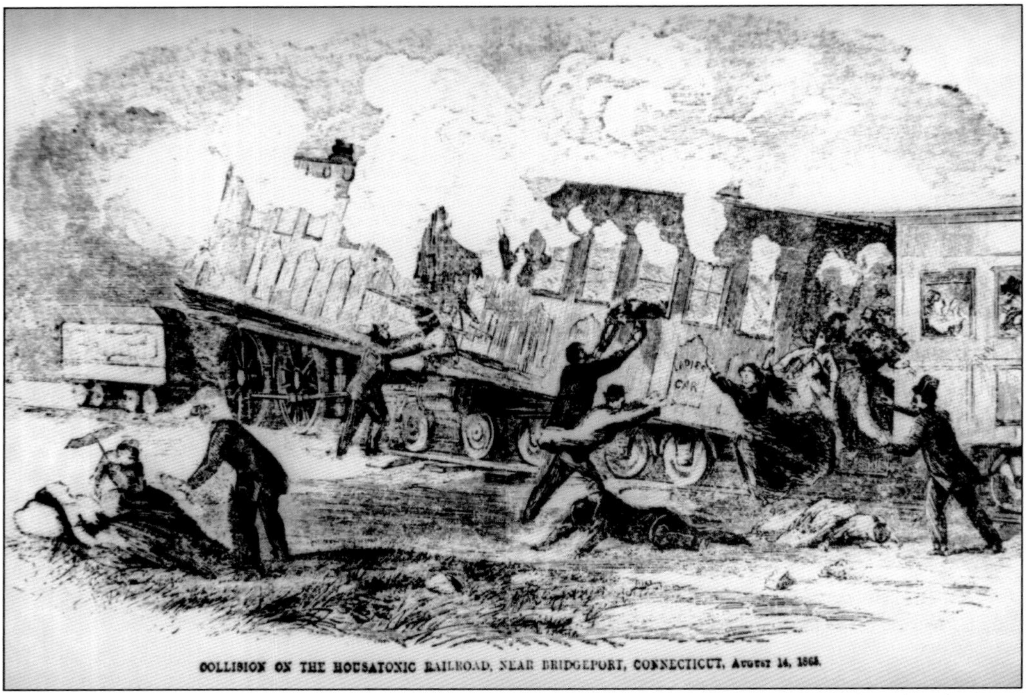

Accidents, some of them serious, were not uncommon on the Housatonic Railroad. Above, a somewhat dramatic drawing captures the chaos of a train wreck that occurred north of Bridgeport. Below, train cars lay scattered following a crash on September 30, 1901, that occurred about 1,000 yards south of the Long Hill depot on Whitney Avenue. In that incident, a northbound New York, New Haven and Hartford train rammed head-on into a southbound train that had not stopped at the siding in Stepney because its engineer had dozed off. Five people were killed, including the engineer on the northbound train. A prize ox being transported was thought to be killed but was found uninjured in a badly damaged steel car a couple of days later, waiting to be taken to the fair in Newtown.

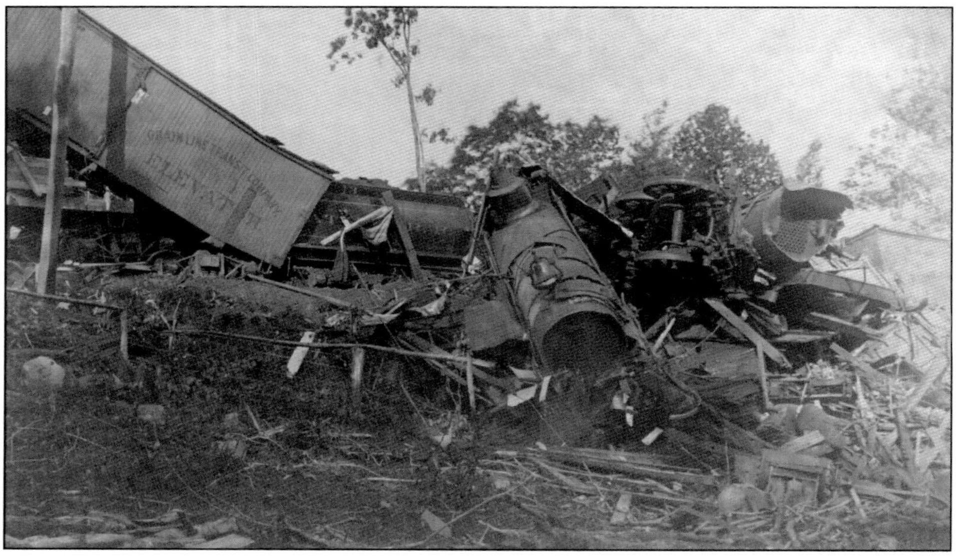

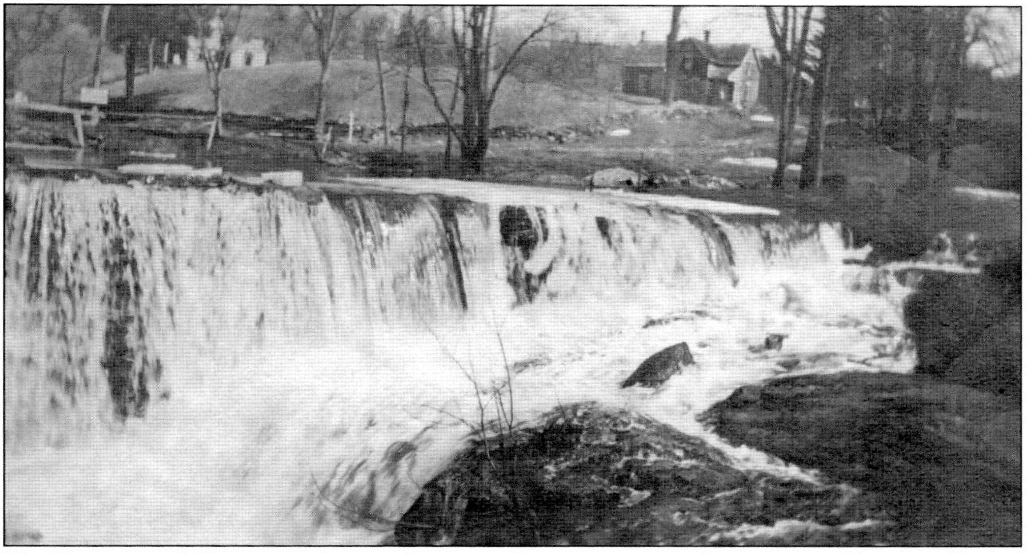

The Pequonnock River was dammed at several places so that the water could run mills and generators. One of these spots was along Whitney Avenue, where the water spilled over into a terrific waterfall. The Radcliffe Mill was located just south of Whitney Avenue. Rebuilt after a fire in 1893, the mill continued to produce knit wristlets for gloves until 1938, when it was closed and torn down.

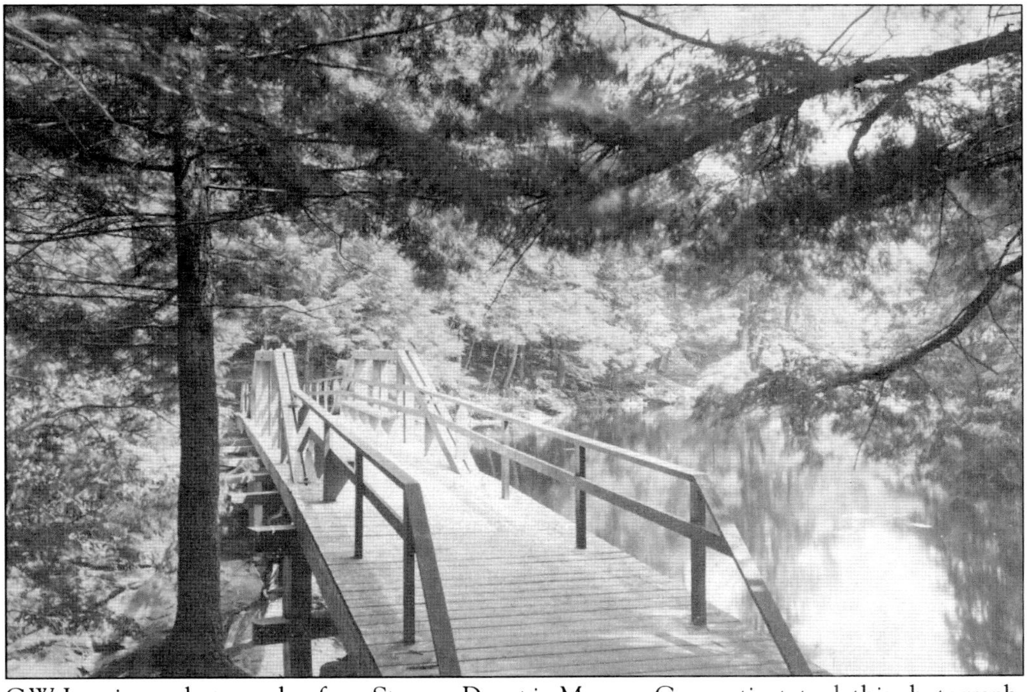

G.W. Lovejoy, a photographer from Stepney Depot in Monroe, Connecticut, took this photograph, entitled "Bridge over the Glen," in Parlor Rock Park. To the right of the bridge is Lake Hi-Hi, a popular feature of the 19th-century amusement park.

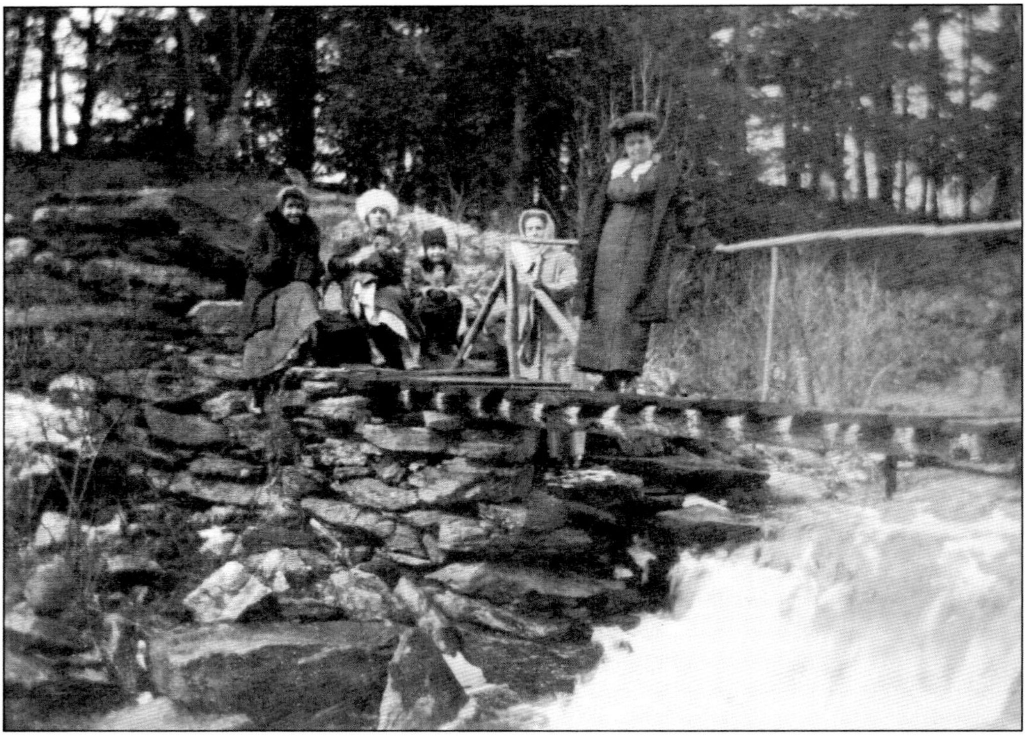

Ethel and Pauline Perry pose near the waterfall below Lake Hi-Hi at Parlor Rock. The park, which opened in 1879, drew visitors to Trumbull's Pequonnock Valley for 20 years. The remains of this bridge can still be seen on the river, just south of the Route 25 highway overpass.

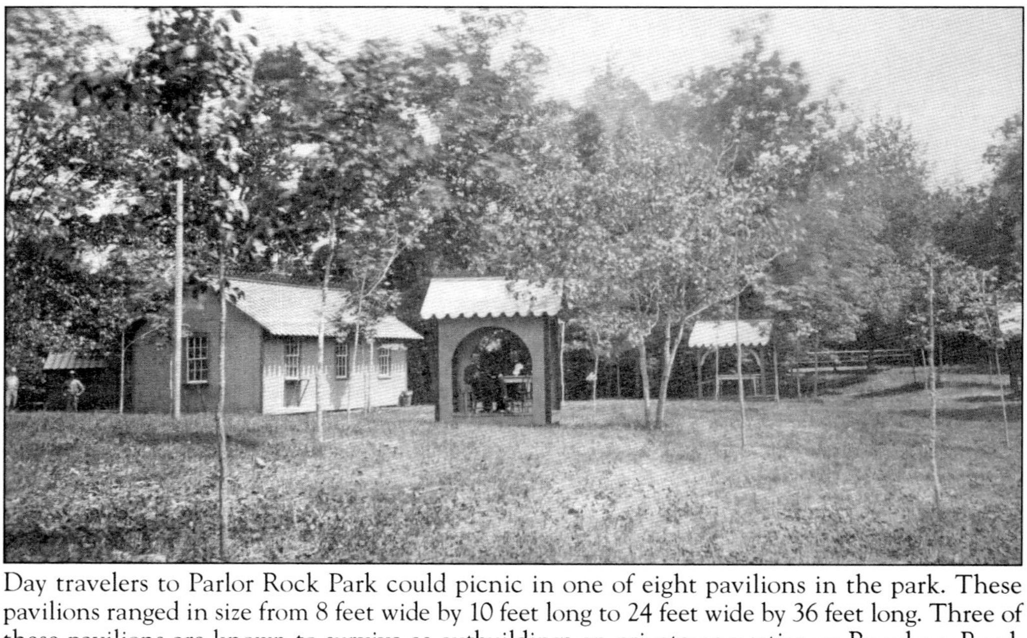

Day travelers to Parlor Rock Park could picnic in one of eight pavilions in the park. These pavilions ranged in size from 8 feet wide by 10 feet long to 24 feet wide by 36 feet long. Three of these pavilions are known to survive as outbuildings on private properties on Broadway Road, Main Street, and Riverside Drive.

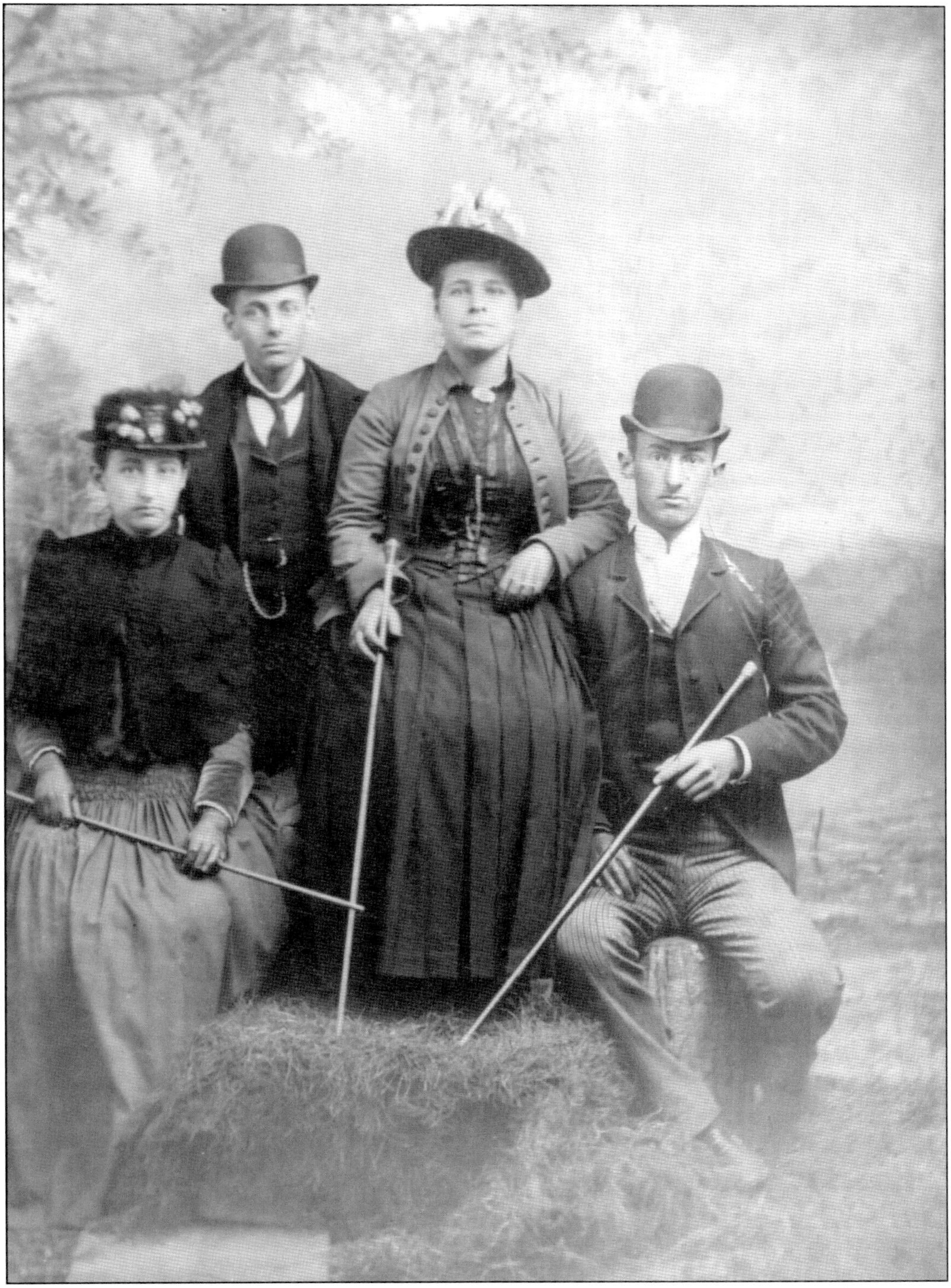

Sitting for a souvenir portrait at the Parlor Rock photographic studio was one popular activity at the park. This tintype taken at Parlor Rock is dated 1896. The man on the right is Samuel G. Seeley; the others are unidentified.

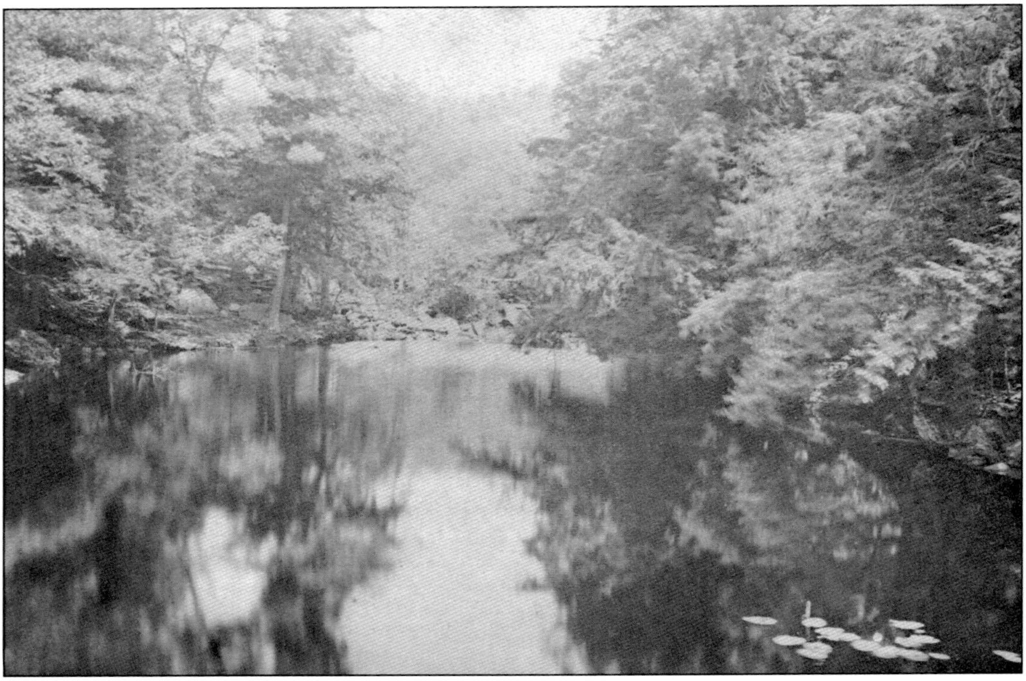

Formed by a dam across the Pequonnock River, Lake Hi-Hi provided access to boating and fishing as part of Parlor Rock Park's amenities. Paddle boats rented for 25¢ a day, and visitors could also stroll around the lake on a path known as "Lover's Lane." Both Lake Hi-Hi and Lake Lo-Lo, a small swimming hole located south of Whitney Avenue, were popular spots for visitors.

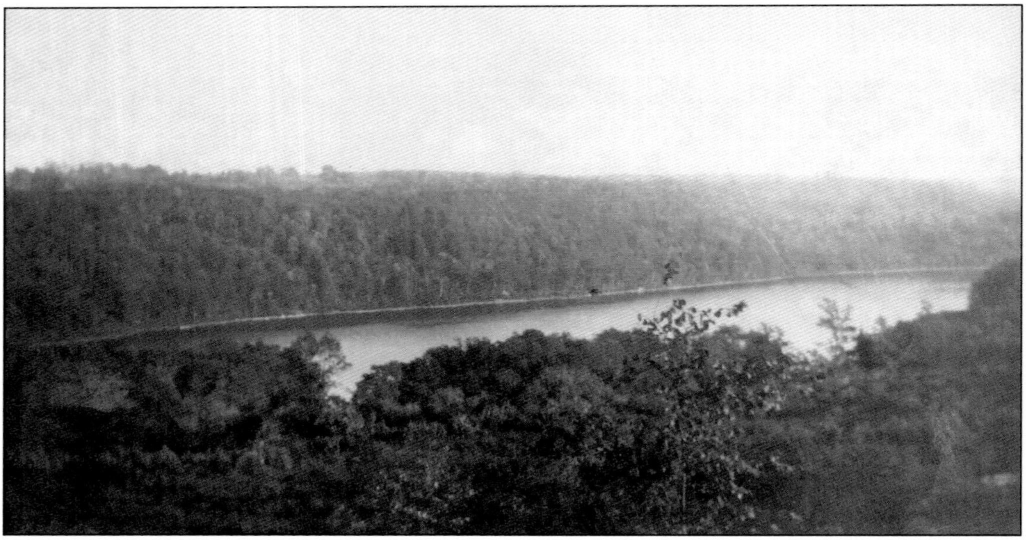

Located in the heart of the Pequonnock Valley, Trumbull Pond, also called the Trumbull Reservoir, was quite a sight in 1930. Owned by the Bridgeport Hydraulic Company, the reservoir covered 72 acres and provided water for the city of Bridgeport. As president of the Bridgeport Hydraulic Company, legendary showman P.T. Barnum was the driving force behind creation of the reservoir, which was used between the 1800s and early 1900s. The reservoir was drained in 1941 after a boy drowned in it.

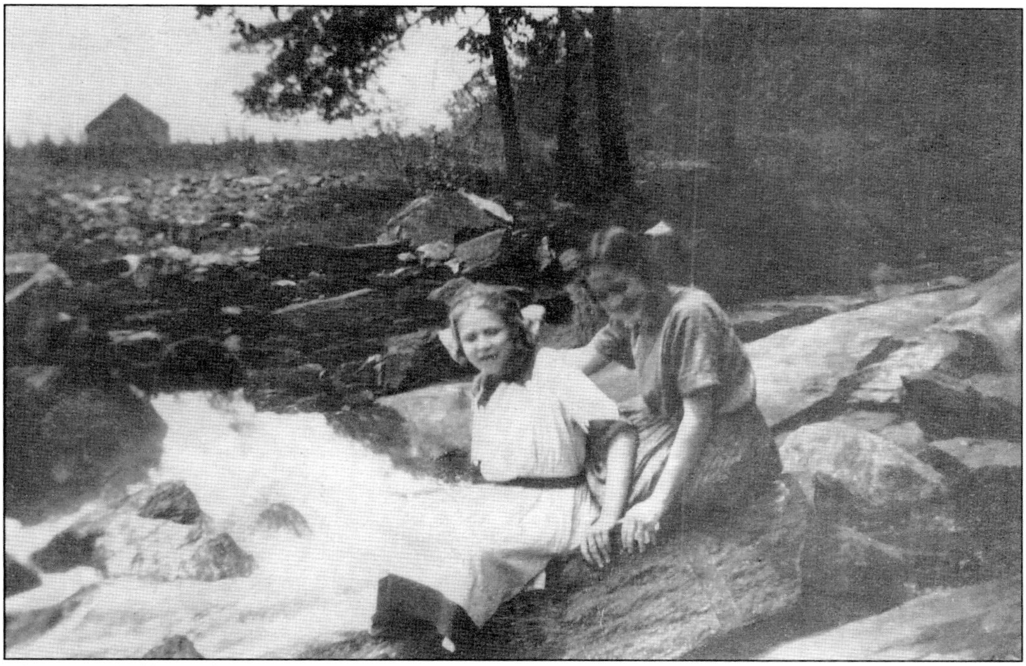

The Trumbull Pond was enjoyed by residents as a scenic spot and a great location for swimming and fishing. Local boys often skinny-dipped in it and enjoyed hailing the trains as they passed on the Housatonic Railroad on their way to Massachusetts and New York. This pastime is memorialized in a painting by William Lee that hangs on the second floor of Trumbull Town Hall. The dam that created Trumbull Pond was also a popular spot, as seen in this photograph. The drain pipe behind the girls pictured here is still in existence, poking from the ruins of the dam in the Pequonnock Valley State Park.

Trumbull's first outdoor advertisement was painted on the sheer rock cliff near the Trumbull Pond dam. The advertisement was plainly visible from any passing train. Parts of the advertisement are still visible today as a result of being sheltered by the rock overhang.

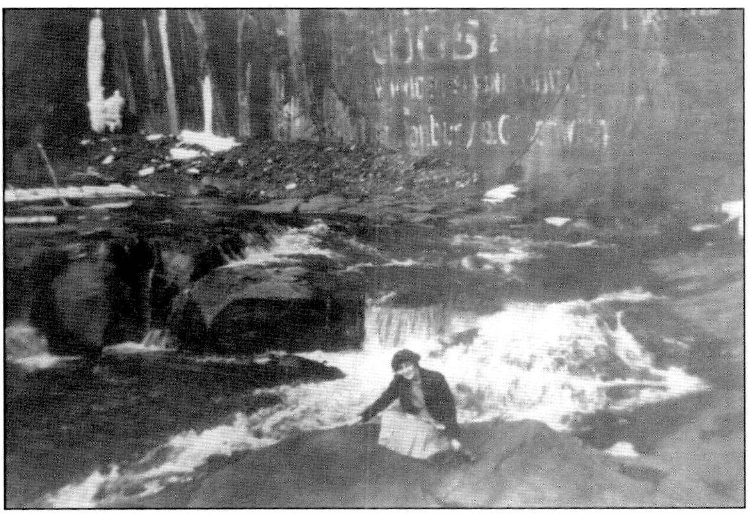

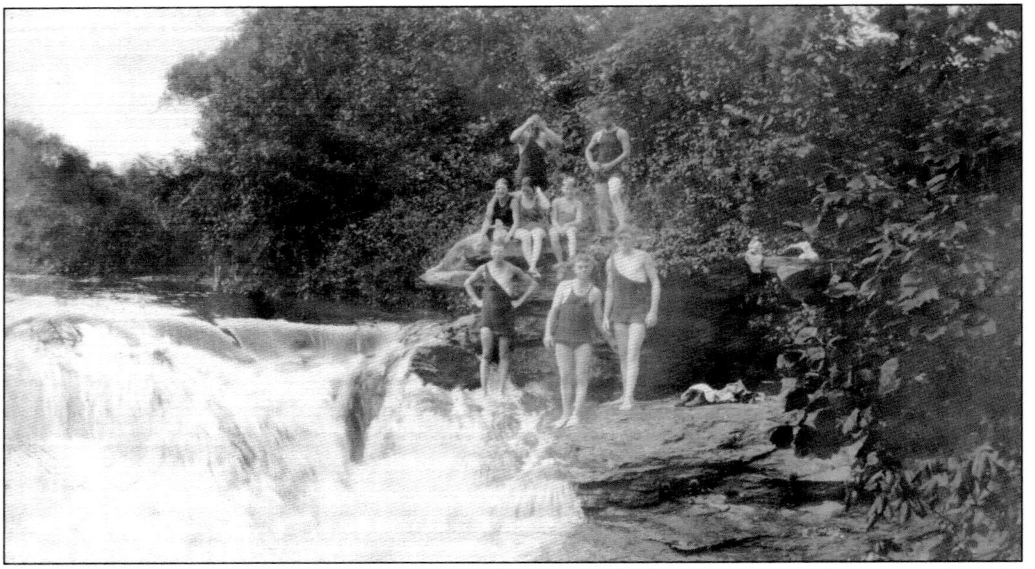

Swimming was a popular activity for young folks in Trumbull early in the 20th century, but the water in the Pequonnock River could be quite treacherous in the years before its flow was diverted to create the Easton Reservoir. This c. 1919 photograph shows the rapids that were located behind the old town hall (now the Helen Plumb Building).

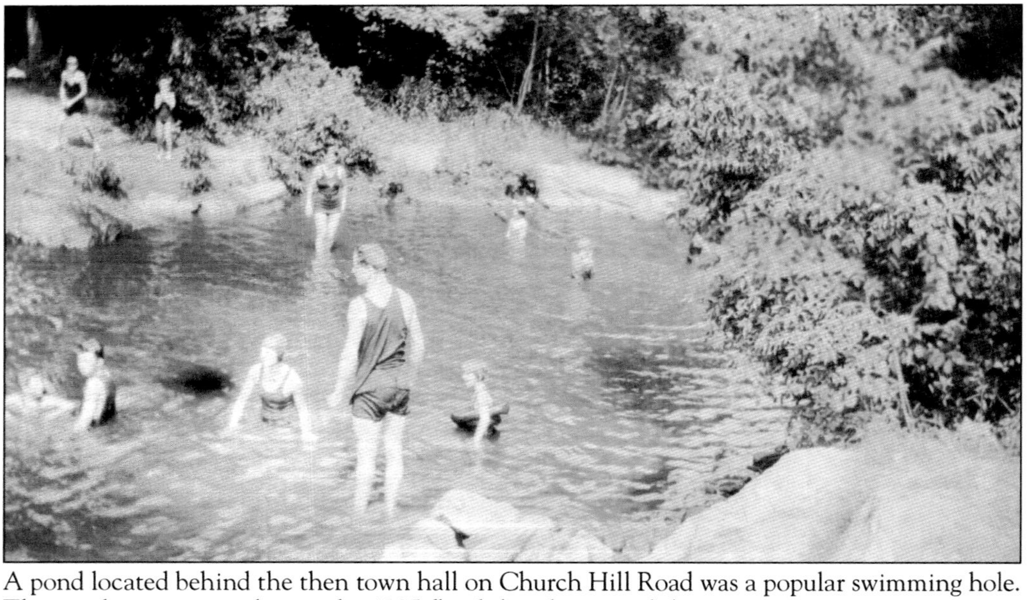

A pond located behind the then town hall on Church Hill Road was a popular swimming hole. The pond is now gone, lost in the 1905 flood that devastated the area.

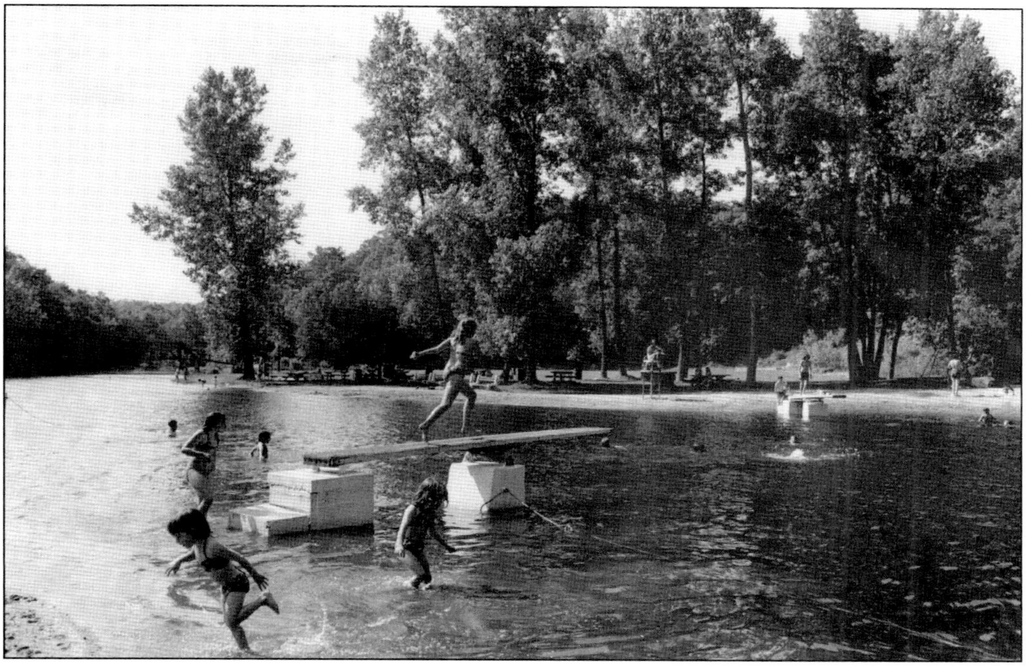

In later years, the beach at Old Mine Park, pictured in 1975, became a preferred swimming hole. Following the draining of Trumbull Pond, residents pressed for a safe place in which Trumbull youth could enjoy the river.

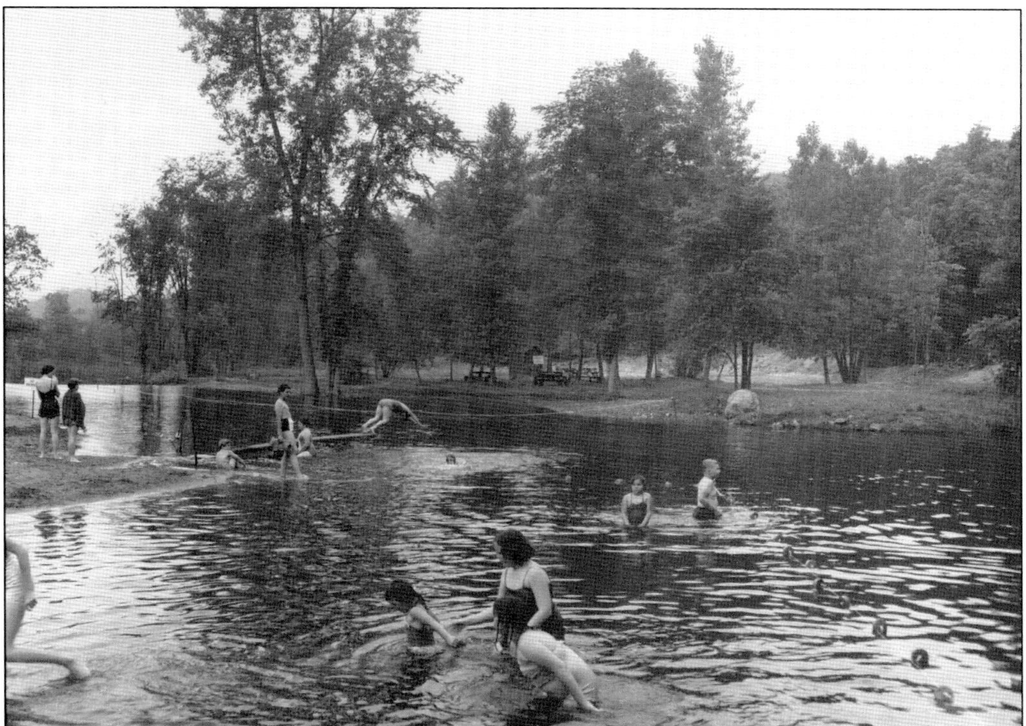

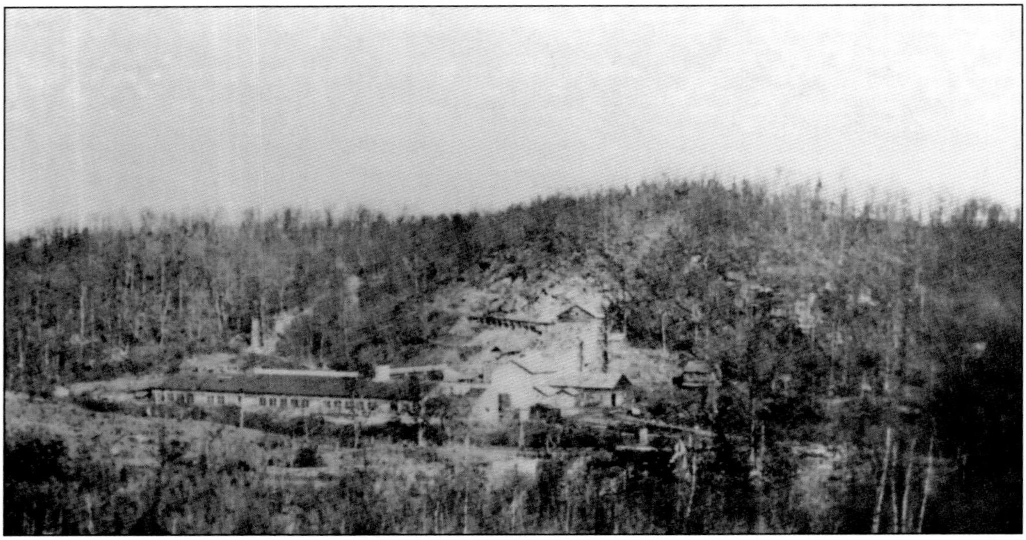

Established in 1898, the plant of the American Tungsten Mining and Milling Company sprawled across the area now known as Old Mine Park. Among the 65 minerals identified there was a massive vein of white quartz once used by local Indians to make arrowheads.

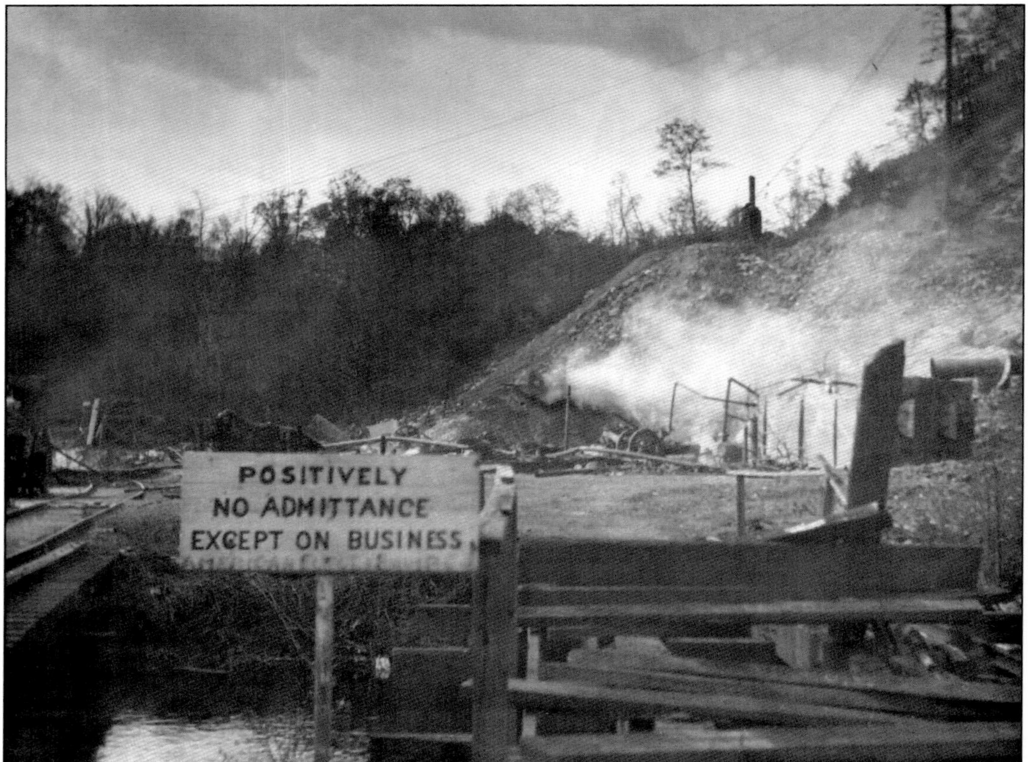

The fire at the tungsten mine on May 21, 1916, caused the mine to close. The fire caused tremendous loss and led to the mine's owner giving the land to the Town of Trumbull in lieu of back taxes. It eventually became Old Mine Park.

Evidence of mining efforts in the area of Old Mine Park remained years after operations there ceased. This 1967 photograph shows the ruins of a limekiln. To this day, hikers in the park can see remnants of repeated efforts to mine the mineral-rich hills.

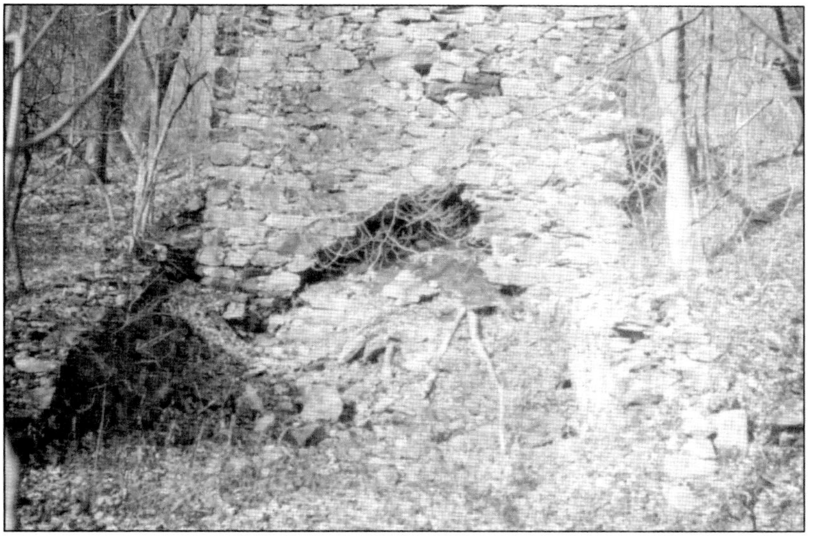

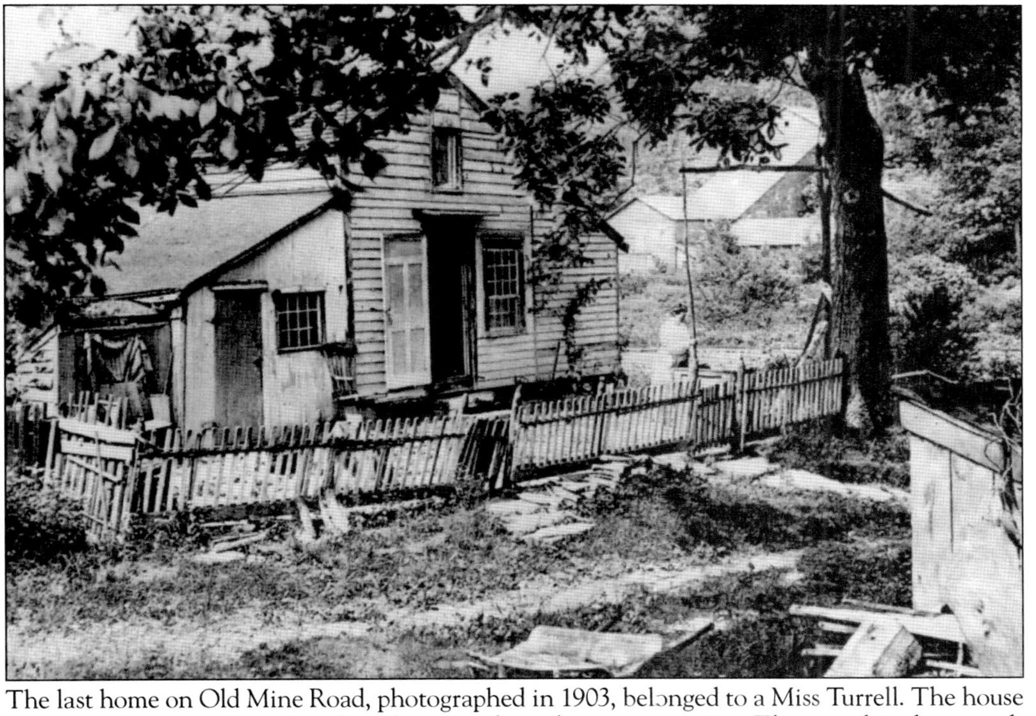

The last home on Old Mine Road, photographed in 1903, belonged to a Miss Turrell. The house was situated next to the railroad tracks across from the tungsten mine. The year this photograph was taken, Turrell was attacked in her home by a stranger believed to have been a hobo who had ridden the railway line to her home. Although Turrell was able to get to a nearby farm for help, her attacker was never caught.

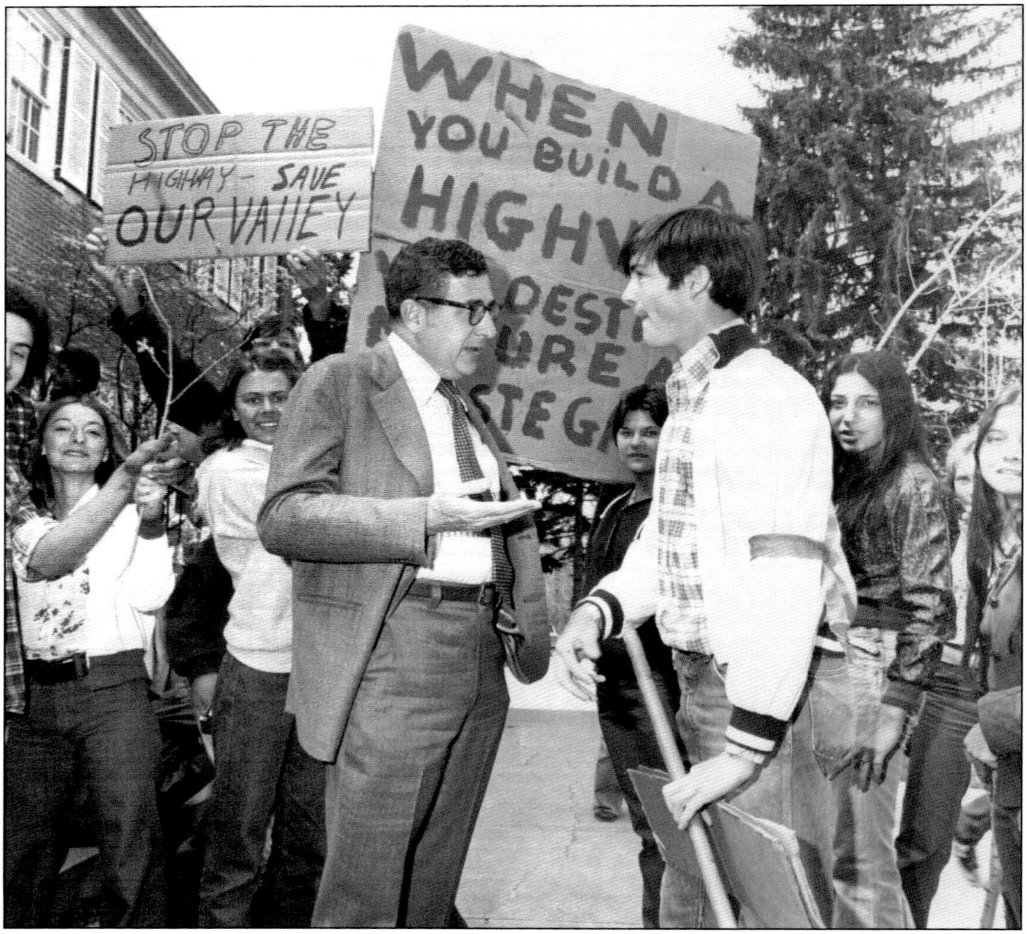

Above, Trumbull students confront first selectman Jim Butler on May 6, 1974, to protest plans to develop the Pequonnock Valley. Pictured to Butler's right is Bill Finch, who would later serve as state representative for Trumbull and as mayor of Bridgeport. Below, the protest continues on the construction site. Although part of the valley, including most of Parlor Rock, would be flattened with the construction of the Route 25 highway, the future of the rest was secured in 1989, when the town and state entered a purchase agreement that preserved the area as open space.

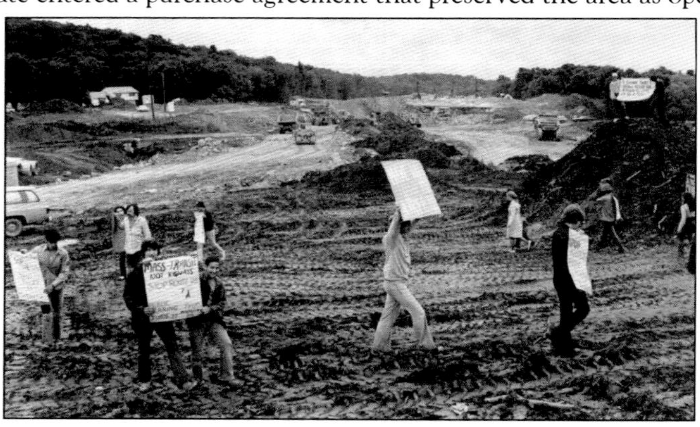

Five

TASHUA

Tashua comprises the northwest corner of the town of Trumbull. Its name is derived from Tawtashua, or Tamtashua, the Native American name for Tashua Hill, a rise 608 feet above sea level that offers a view of Long Island Sound. For this reason, the hill served as a vantage point from which American rebels watched for British warships entering Connecticut's harbors during the Revolutionary War.

The family of John Mallett was one of the first to settle at Tashua in 1710. In 1760, with more families following, the Christ Episcopal Church in Tashua was established. Although business and industry were booming in other areas of town, Tashua remained largely farmland, even through the 20th century. Evidence of these historic farms can be seen in the old stone walls and prim farmhouses in areas near Stonehouse Road and along Madison Avenue. The David Mallett Jr. House, located on Tashua Road and built around 1760, is listed in the National Register of Historic Places.

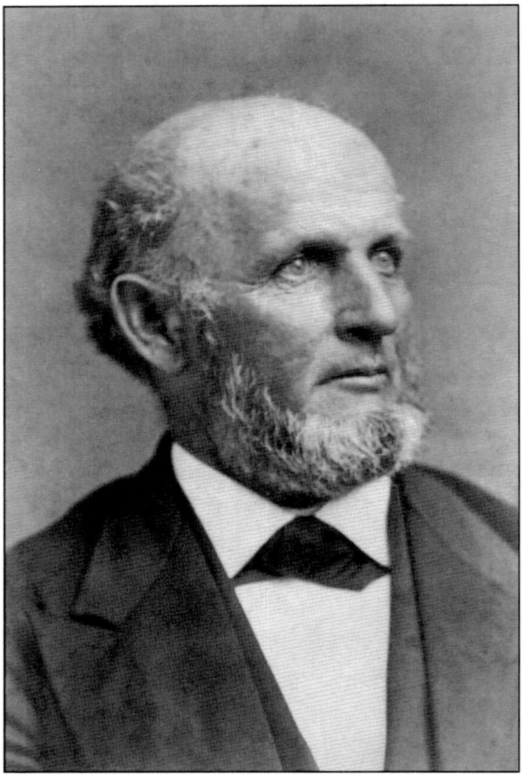

Originally from France, the Mallett family settled in the Tashua area of Trumbull in 1710. Aaron Benjamin Mallett, pictured here, was born in Tashua in 1816, the son of Aaron Mallett and Eunice Beach. In 1873, he served as Trumbull representative to the Connecticut State Assembly. He died in 1907.

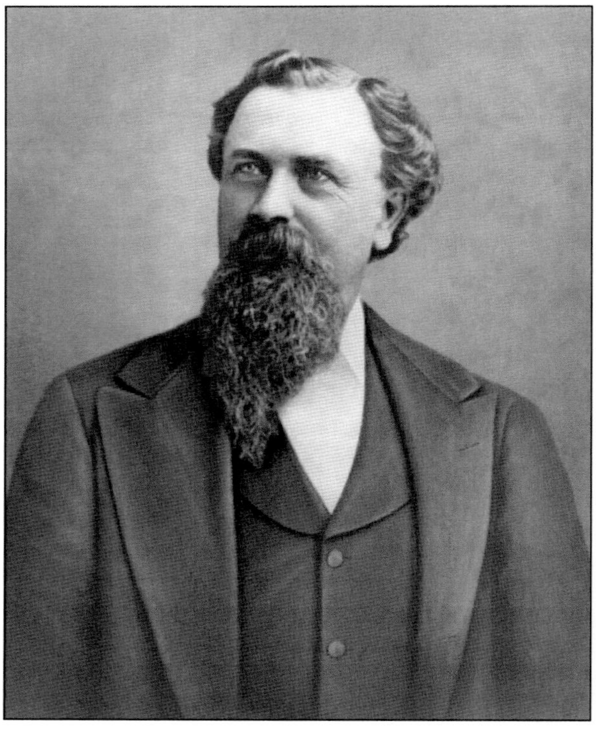

Dr. Seth Hill, born in 1837, was Tashua's only physician at the turn of the century. He charged 50¢ for an office visit and $1 for a house call. He is remembered for his home on Tashua Road, Hillsden, and for his unusually fine physique.

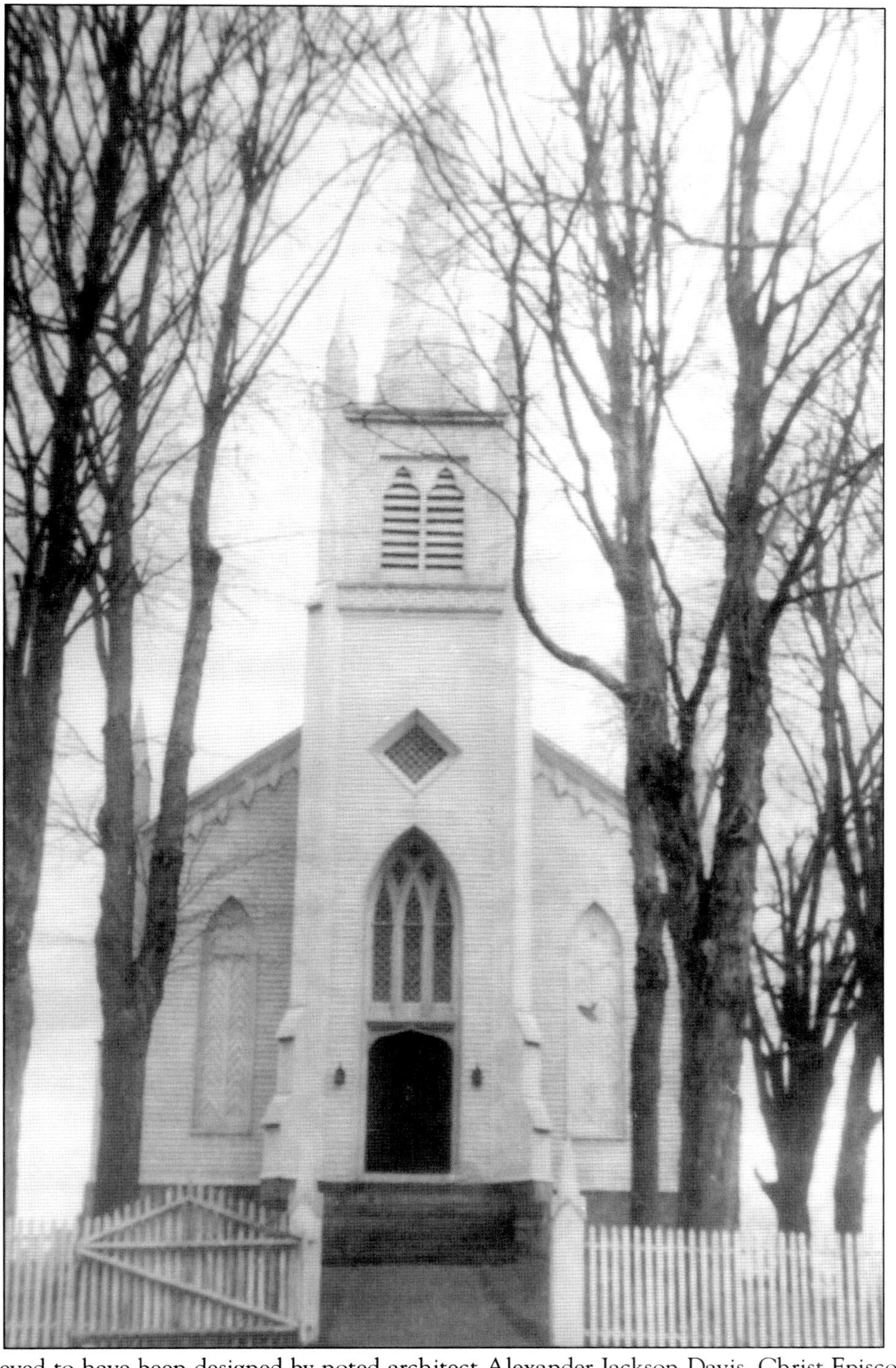

Believed to have been designed by noted architect Alexander Jackson Davis, Christ Episcopal Church Tashua stands at the corner of Madison Avenue and Tashua Road. Consecrated in 1847, it was the third church built for the parish.

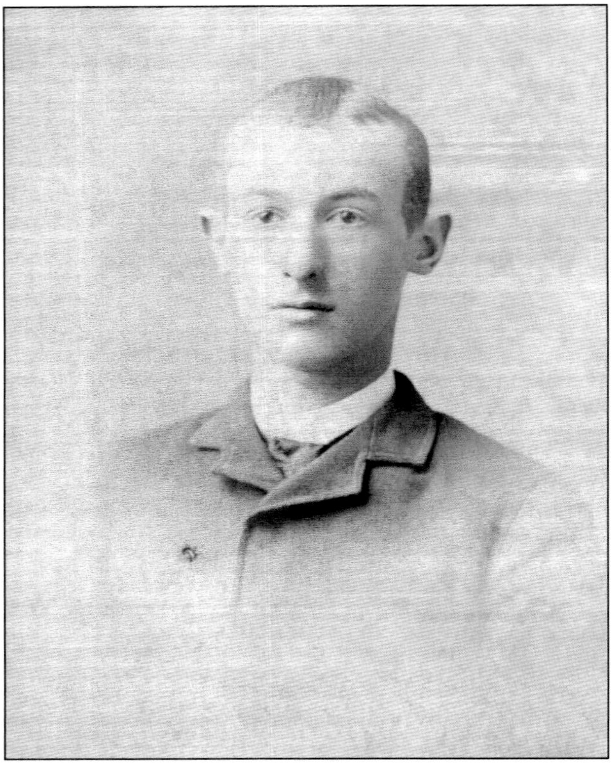

Samuel G. Seeley was 20 years old when this photograph was taken in 1890. Born to Samuel and Josephine Seeley in 1870, Samuel inherited half of the family's property and lived in an apartment inside the grand house with his bride, Fannie May Wales, of Monroe, whom he married in 1898. They were the parents of Evelyn, Dorothy, Sam, and Howard Seeley.

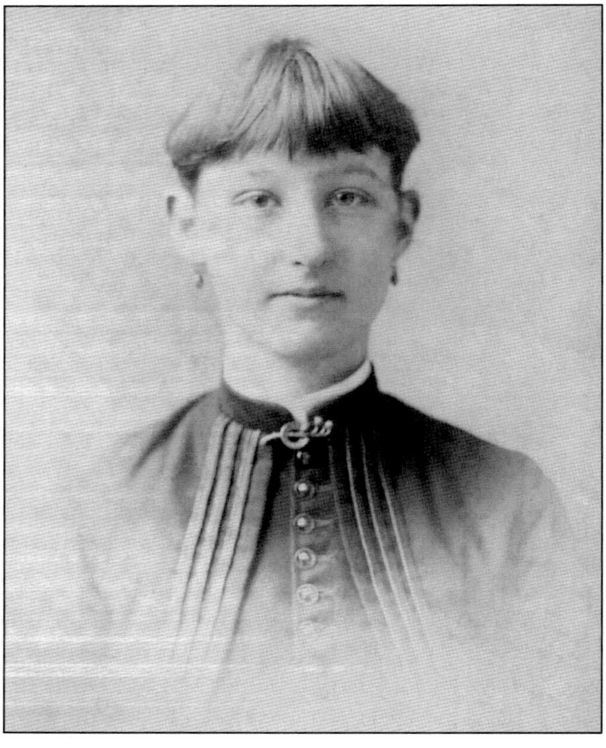

Dasie J. Seeley, born in 1872, lived at the Seeley family homestead at 106 Seeley Road. As a teenager, she attended Bridgeport High School. Each morning, she milked eight cows before being picked up for school at 7:00 a.m.

Nellie Seeley poses with daughter Mabel Augusta, who was born in 1890. Nellie was married to Charles Seeley, Sam's brother, in 1887, at which time she took over half of the family's 100-acre farm on Seeley Road. Charles built a home on the property, and it was here that Mabel Augusta was born by caesarean section, a rare procedure at the time. Her birth was written up in medical journals as one of the first successful operations of the kind in the area.

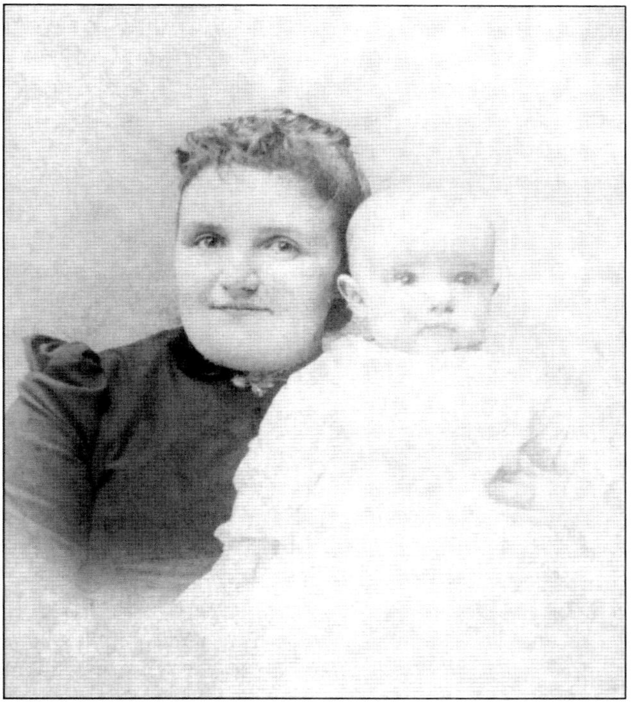

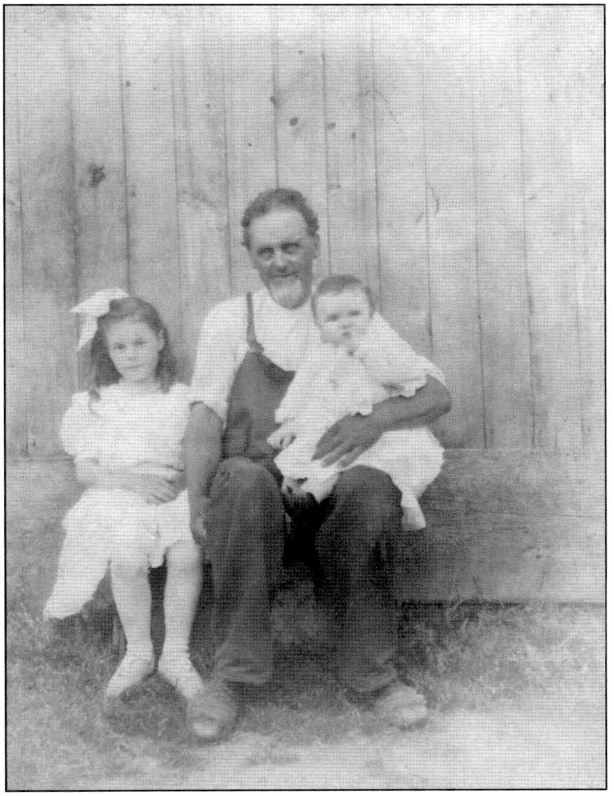

Taken in 1908, this photograph captures Grandpa Wales and Dorothy and Sam Seeley. Like the Malletts, the Seeleys were a prominent family in Tashua.

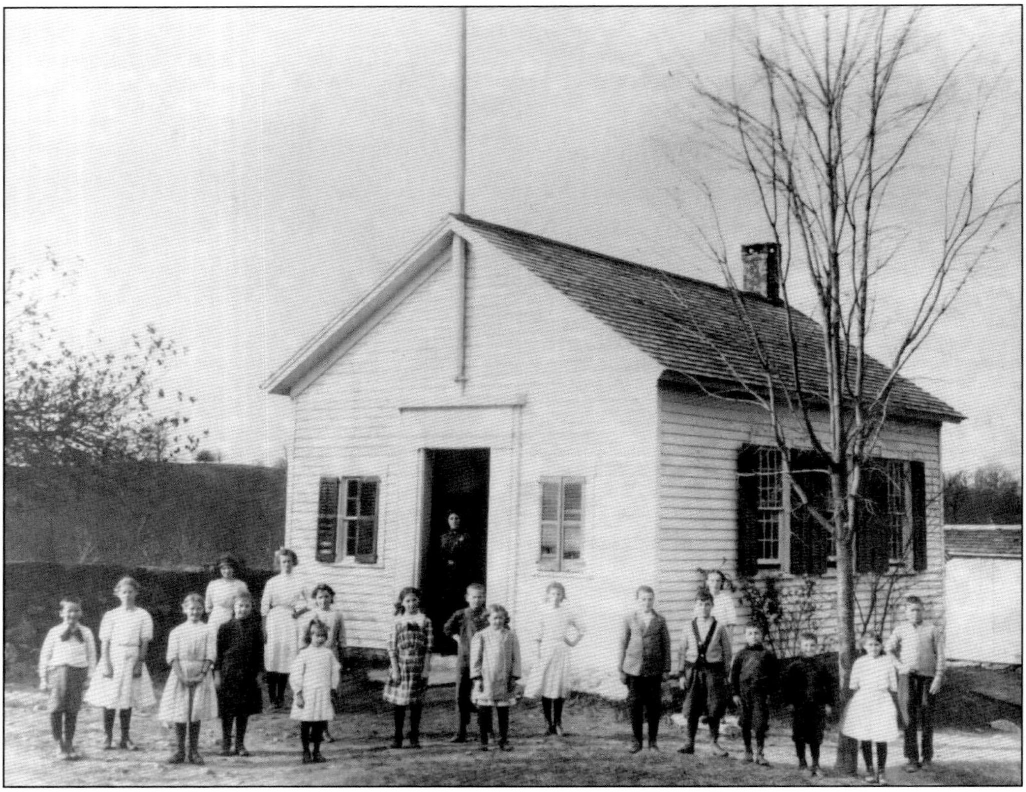

Children pose outside the Tashua schoolhouse at the corner of Fuller Road and Madison Avenue. The Tashua School District was formed in 1795, and this one-room schoolhouse, built in 1858, was used until 1920. Inside, the white clapboard building had a wood-burning stove for heat and hooks and shelves for the student's coats and lunch pails. There were separate entrances on the outhouse in back of the school for boys and girls. Former student Dorothy Seeley remembered boys throwing rocks through the half-moon cutout in the outhouse door to bother the girls.

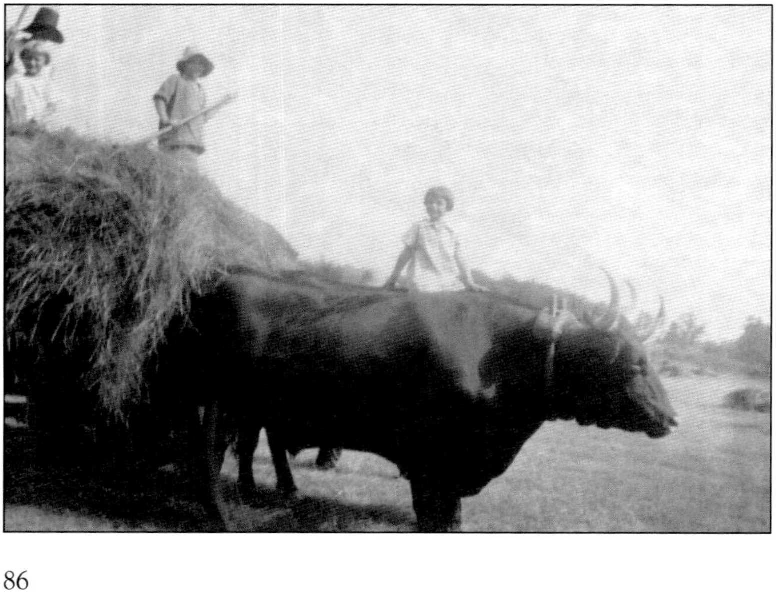

Farming was a way of life in Tashua; for children, farm life meant chores, but it also meant fun, which these children seem to be having atop a hay wagon pulled by a huge team of oxen in the early part of the 20th century.

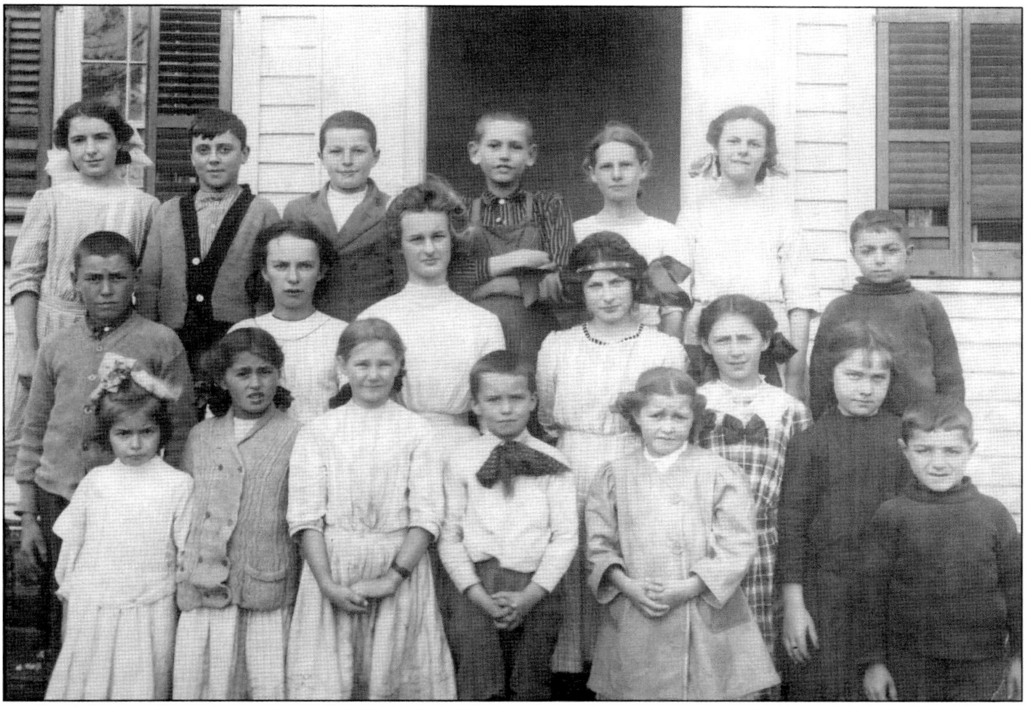

Many of the children attending Tashua School in 1914 were from the area's founding families, and their grown-up photographs appear on other pages in this book. Pictured here from left to right are (first row) Rebecca Jones, Louise Kaechele, Stella Kohler, Elbert Fuller, Mary Kaechele, and an unidentified student; (second row) Karl Kaechele, Helen Platko, Evelyn Seeley, Mildred Peck, Maud Mallett, and Jennie Mallett; (third row) Ruth Jones, George Helmerich, Harry Goldman, Walter Kaechele, Beatrice Kohler, Dorothy Seeley, and one unidentified youngster.

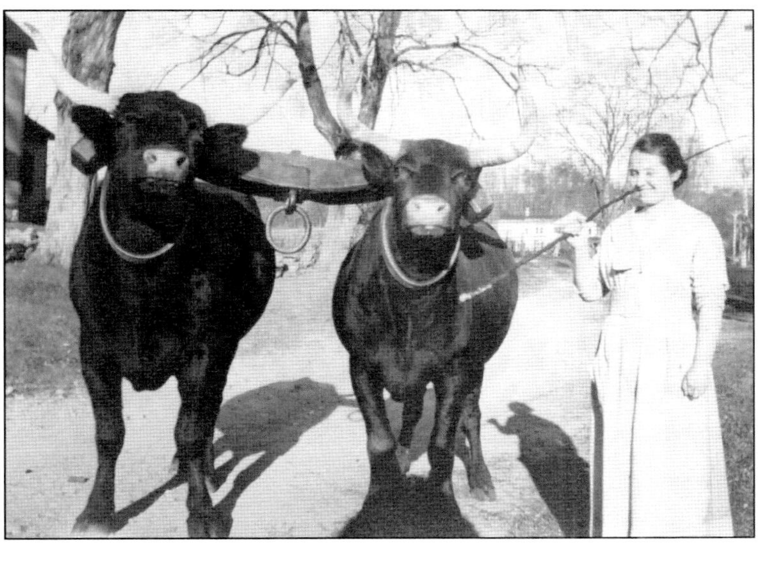

Ethel Mallett poses with her family's oxen in 1917. Oxen were valued as beasts of burden and used on many farms in Tashua and throughout Trumbull. Old-timers describe them as sure-footed and superior to horses in pulling heavy loads, particularly through snow.

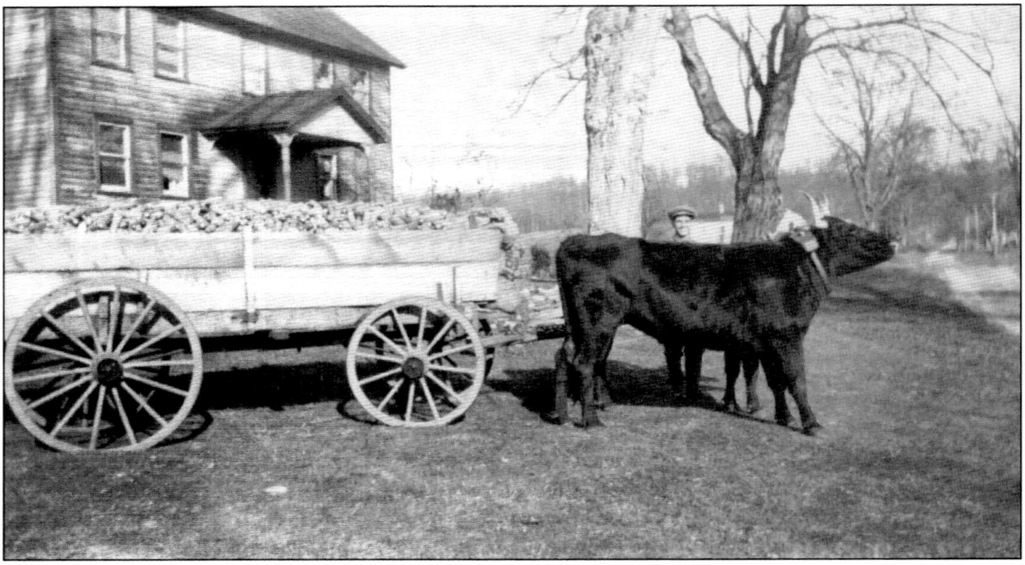

To look at these photographs, it appears the Mallett farm was very productive. Above, Percy Mallett is all smiles as he poses with a load of corn (68 bushels) in 1918. Below, a pair of oxen haul hay piled as high as the sky on the 134-acre farm, more than half of which was located in Easton. In 1923, the family decided to sell the homestead to the Bridgeport Hydraulic Company; three years later, distraught over the sale, 31-year-old Percy took his own life. The onetime homesite is now covered by the waters of the Easton Reservoir.

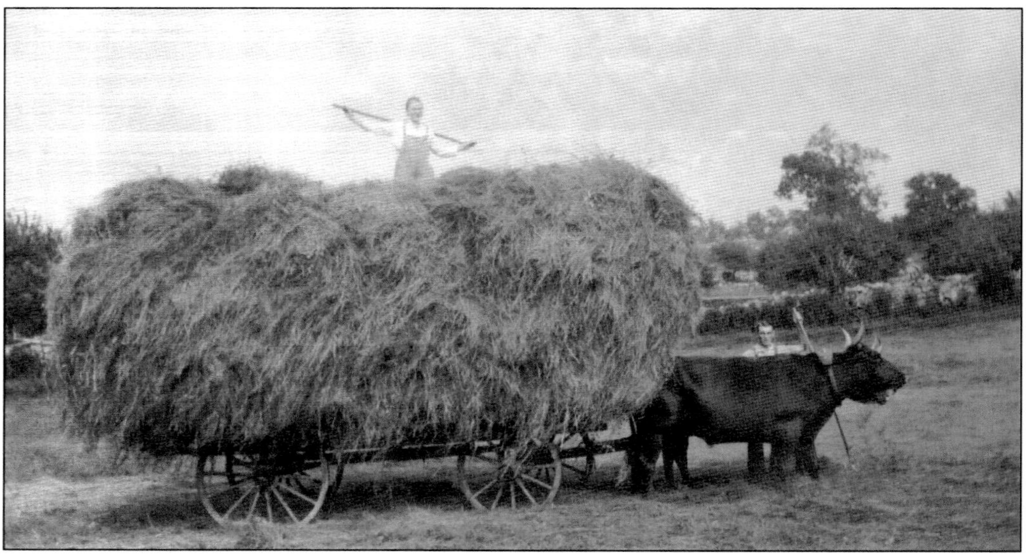

Dorothy M. Seeley appears in her graduation photograph in 1920. She was a founding member of the Trumbull Historical Society. Her book *Tales of Trumbull's Past* is a compilation of historical sketches she wrote for the society newsletter, the *Gristmill*, from 1968 to 1983.

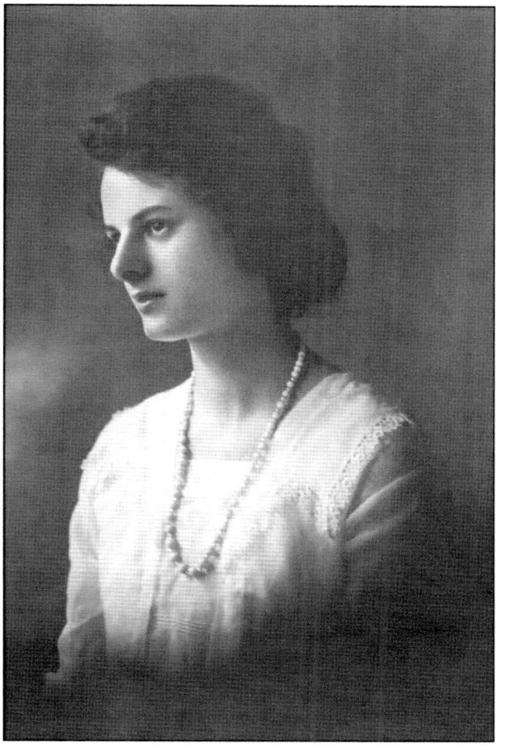

"Photobombing" is not just a 21st-century prank: a close look at the right side of this image of three Seeley women reveals a Seeley brother, probably Harold, poking his head into the composition. Sitting on the steps in this photograph is Josephine Wales Seeley, who is flanked by granddaughters Evelyn and Dorothy. At the age of 17, Josephine came from Wilton to work as a dressmaker for the Seeley family. She married Samuel Seeley and had six children. After Samuel died, Josephine had a modern new house built for herself, her children, and grandchildren.

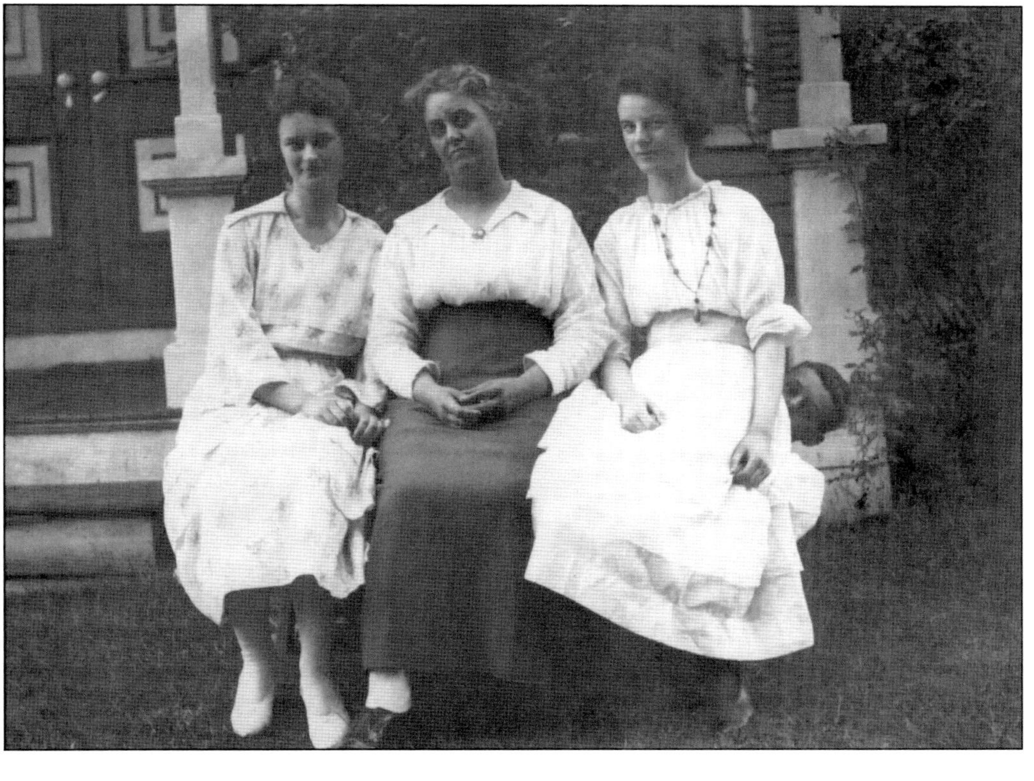

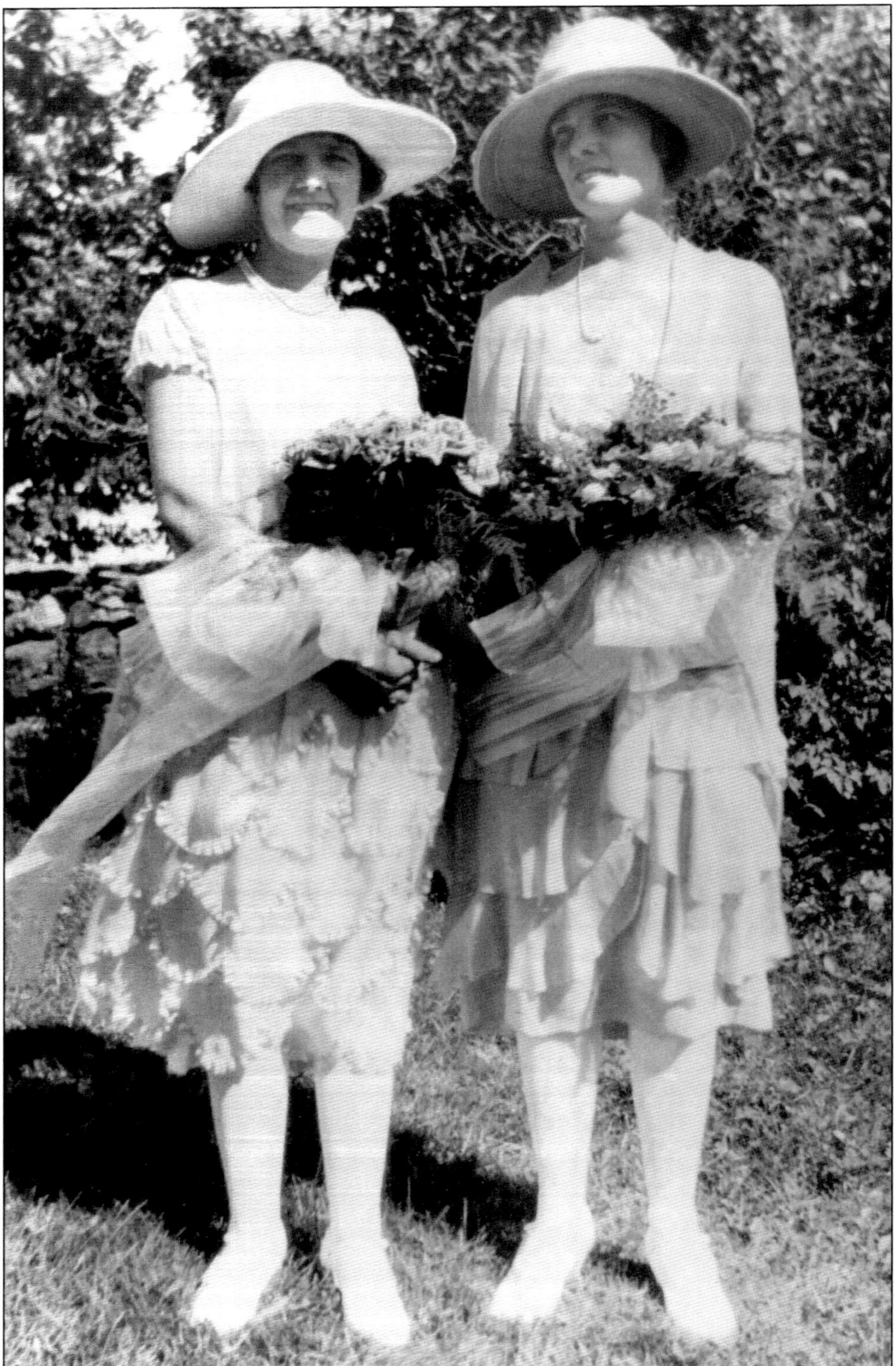

New bride Beatrice Kohler (right) poses with her sister and attendant Stella Kohler in 1926. Both girls grew up on Madison Avenue in Tashua and can be seen as children in their school photograph on page 87. Beatrice was married to Edward Corning at Christ Episcopal Church Tashua. Her sister would get married six months later.

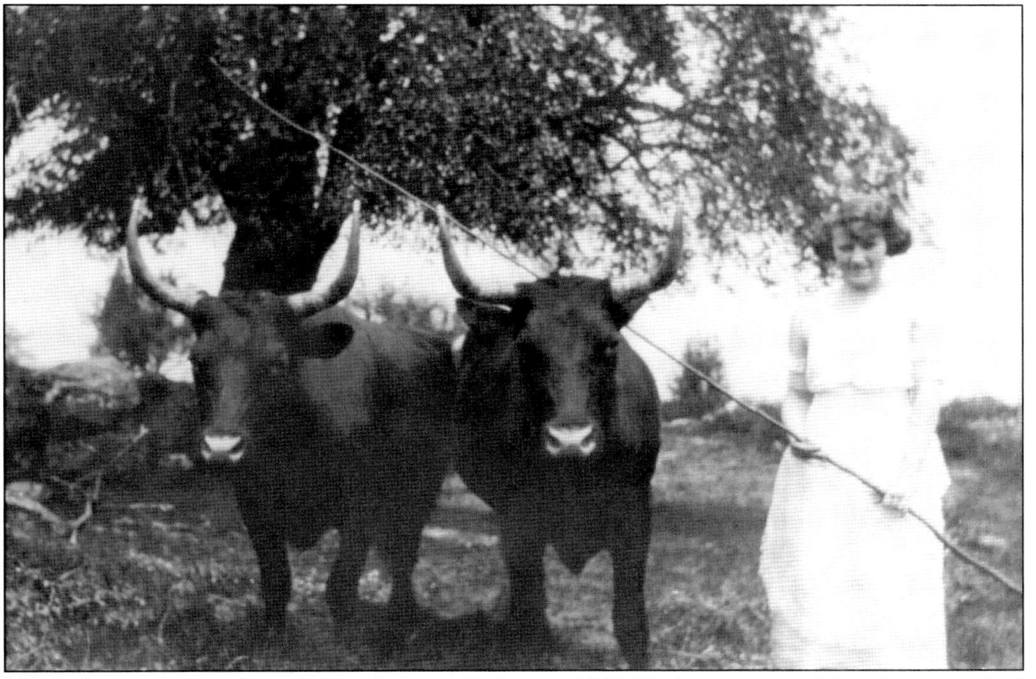

Helen Green shows off oxen on a farm in Tashua in 1920. Tashua remained largely untouched by the railroad, industry, and modernization that infiltrated the rest of the town beginning in the 20th century. Even at the time this photograph was taken, the area still consisted mostly of large farms, fields, and pasturelands.

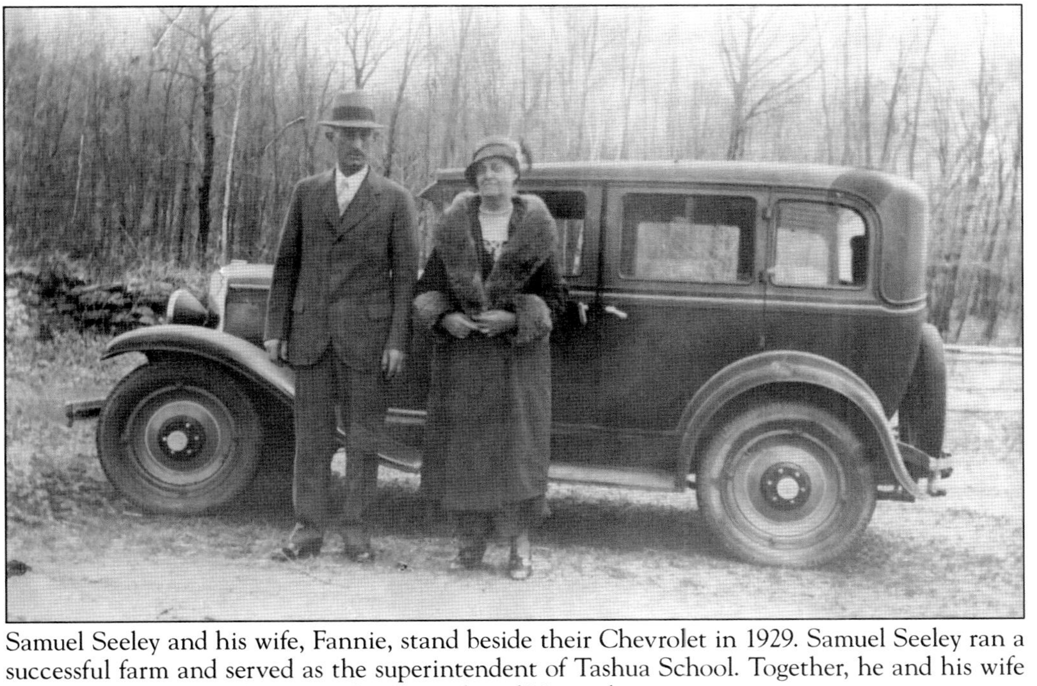

Samuel Seeley and his wife, Fannie, stand beside their Chevrolet in 1929. Samuel Seeley ran a successful farm and served as the superintendent of Tashua School. Together, he and his wife had four children, Evelyn, Dorothy, Samuel, and Howard.

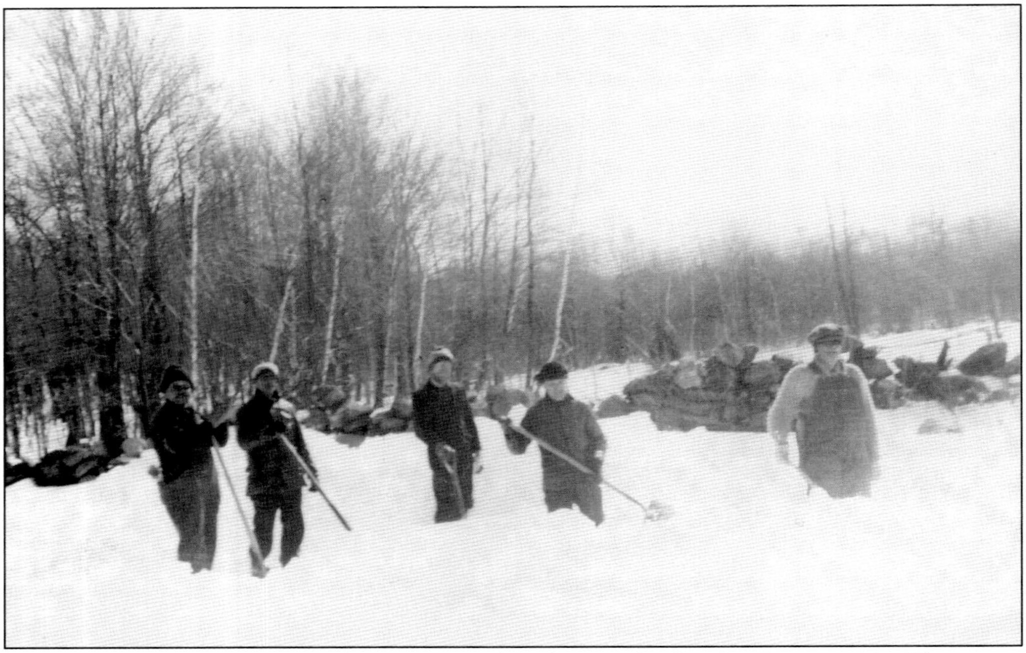

Men from the Works Progress Administration shovel out Seeley Road in January 1934. The winter of 1934 saw some of the worst blizzards to hit the East Coast since the Blizzard of 1888. Trains and deliveries were halted, and schools and businesses were closed for days at a time as everyone worked together to dig the town out from under the snow.

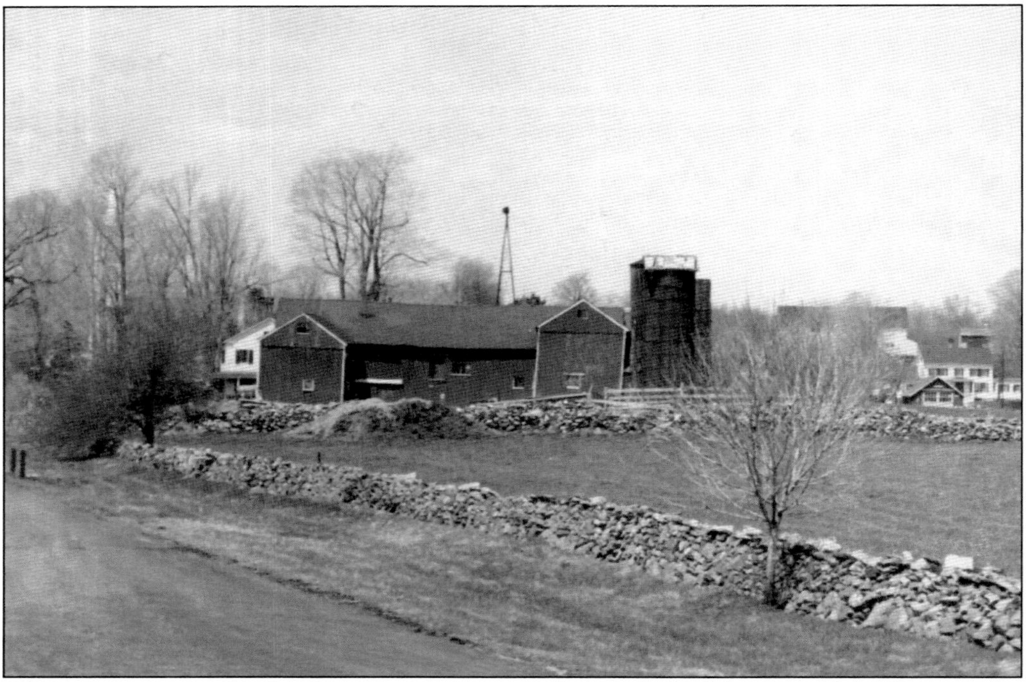

While there were still a few farms remaining in Tashua, most had disappeared by the time this photograph was taken along Madison Avenue in 1961.

Charles Kaechele Sr. kept chickens and cows at his Madison Avenue home as late as 1959, when he celebrated his 80th birthday. More than 100 relatives and friends stopped by to wish him well.

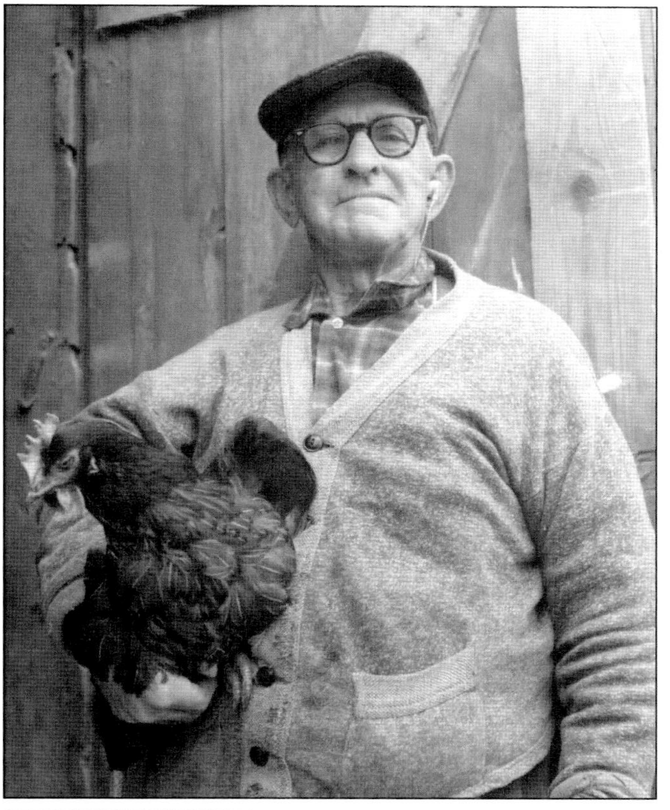

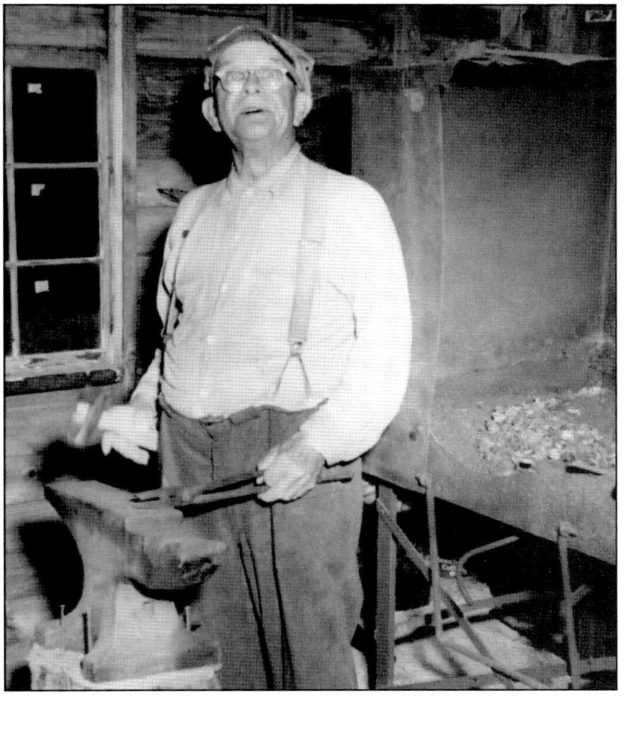

Madison Avenue blacksmith Emil Huber was 76 years old in 1961. He also worked for Bridgeport Hydraulic Company. As a farming community, Trumbull had several blacksmith shops. Among the best known was Peter Lynch's operation on Main Street in Long Hill. Horses could be shod there for $1 and oxen for $2.

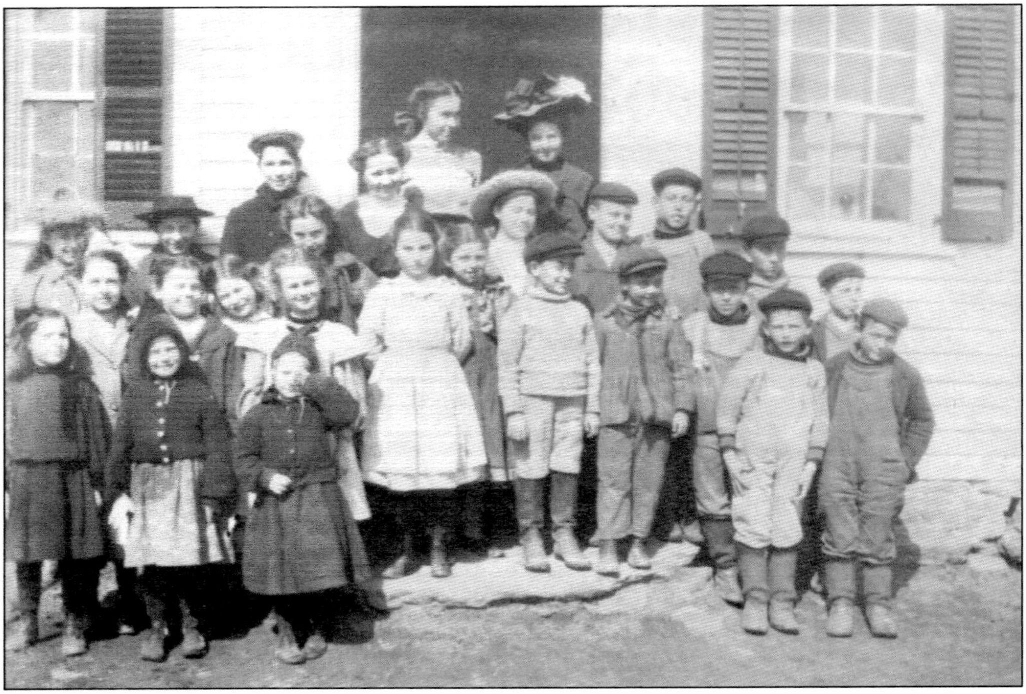

What a difference 70 years can make. Above, children pose outside Tashua's one-room schoolhouse in 1907. Below, a group of third graders at Tashua School perform *The Silver Nutcracker* in 1977. From left to right are (first row) Cathy Freiler, Gregory Papp, and Derek Meachen; (second row) Wendy Schneider, Susan Parker, Elsa Kok, Helen Nemeth, Debra Nuzzo, and Amy Schweitzer.

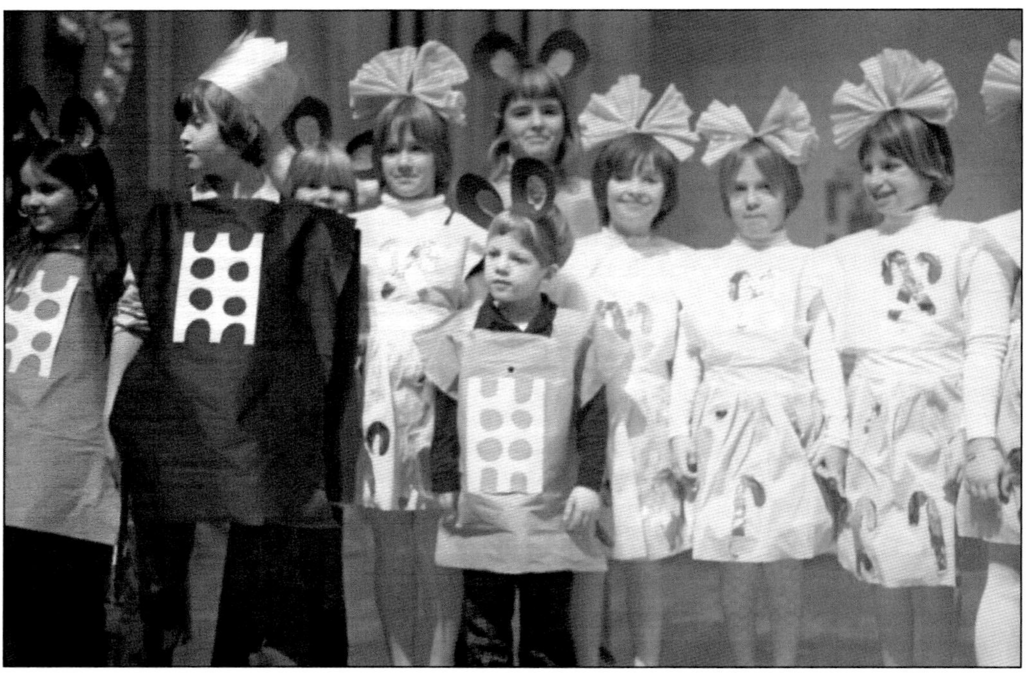

Six

Daniels Farm

There is no shortage of "Daniels" for whom Daniels Farm Road, and the northeast corner of town through which it runs, might have gotten its name. There was wealthy landowner Daniel Hawley, whose slave Nero Hawley served in the American Revolution, and Daniel Porter, whose family name was taken for another nearby street, Porter's Hill Road. But it is generally accepted that Daniels Farm Road was named for Daniel Brinsmade, who lived on Unity Road in the 1700s and who farmed the area to the north. Much of the land known as Daniel's Farm was later inherited by his descendants. Historian E. Merrill Beach recalled at least six Brinsmade families living on the road when he was growing up there in the first part of the 20th century. Beach and his wife, Florence, would later establish one of the Daniel's Farm area's favorite recreation spots. The 180-acre Beach Memorial Park was gifted to the town by the family in memory of their son Pfc. Robert Browning Beach, who was killed in England by a German bomb while en route to France in 1944. Located on the border with Nichols, the park features a unique sloped swimming pool and wooded hiking trails. In its early days, the land that is now Beach Park was a sheep meadow and woodlot from which locals cut wood for fireplaces and timber for their houses and barns. Evidence of those wood trails still exist, as do several charcoal circles possibly used more than a century ago for the conversion of wood into charcoal.

Daniels Farm Road still retains several homes dating from those early days, including the c. 1740 home of Theoplis Nichols, the 1756 home of Daniel Hawley, and the 1810 home of Daniel Porter. Once located on Daniels Farm Road, the Eliakim Beach Tavern gained fame as the birthplace, in 1779, of noted Yale professor and scientist Benjamin Silliman. Silliman's mother, the wife of Revolutionary general Gold Selleck Silliman, had fled to the tavern to escape the burning of Fairfield by the British. The historic building was dismantled and moved to Darien in the 1960s.

True to its name, Daniel's Farm was dotted with farms through the 1940s. When development caught on in the late 1950s, the transformation was swift. Barns came down virtually overnight as farms were carved up to make room for new houses, streets, and schools.

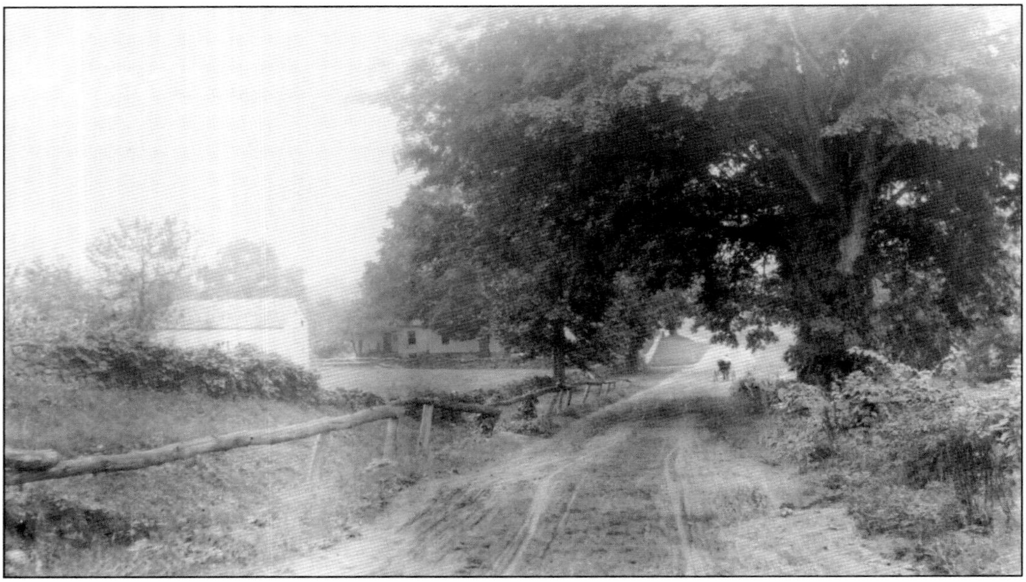

A horse-drawn cart makes its way toward Trumbull Center in this early photograph of Daniels Farm Road.

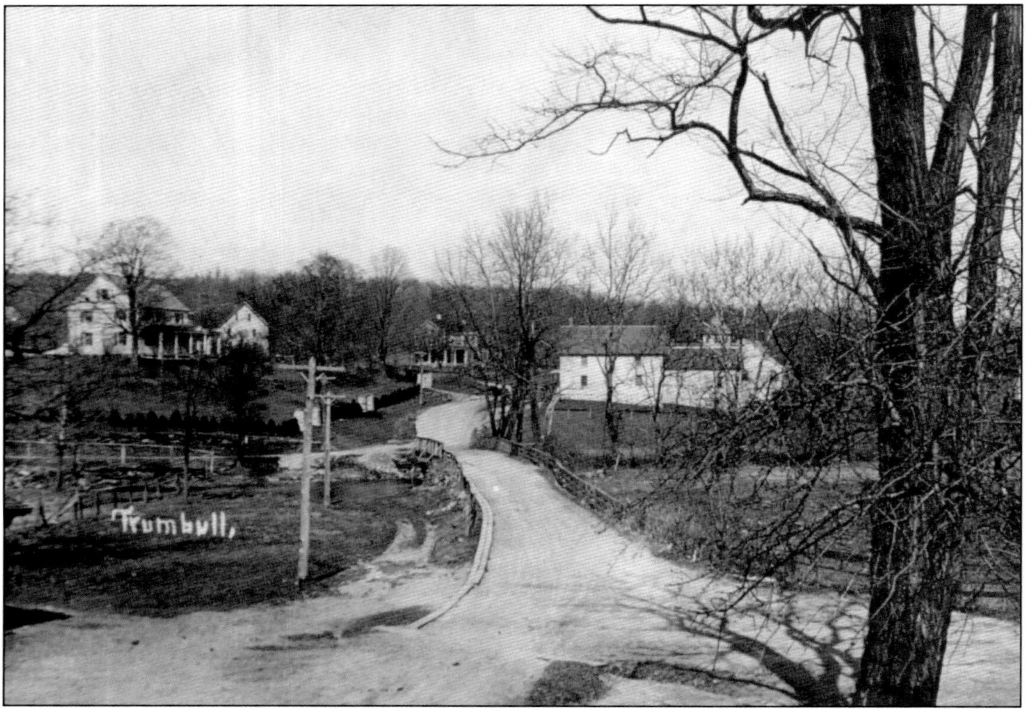

This photograph takes in a view of Daniels Farm Road from its intersection with White Plains and Church Hill Roads. The bridge over the Pequonnock River can be seen, as well as the Daniel Hawley house on the left. On the right is a former mill.

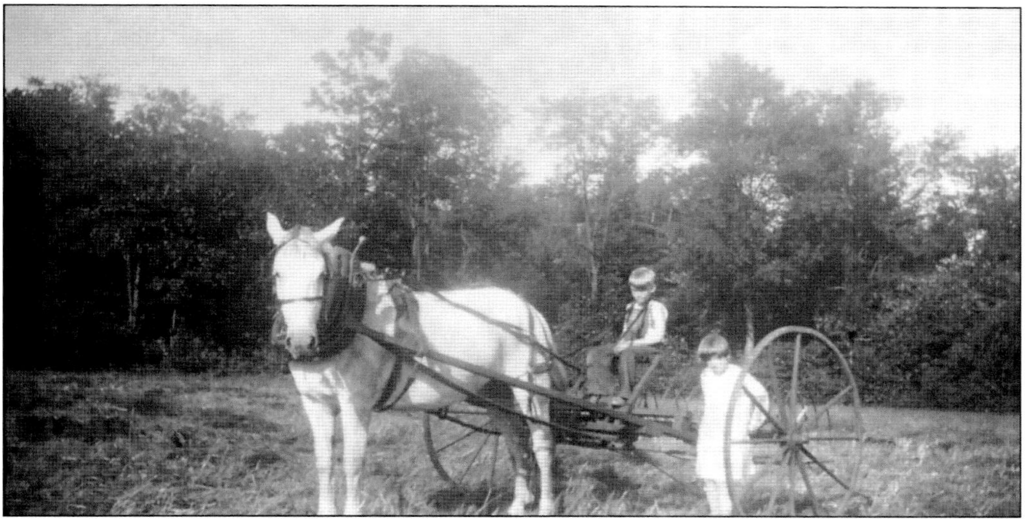

Jane and Art Claud-Mantle are photographed in 1928 with a hay rake hitched to Susie, the horse their family acquired along with their Daniels Farm Road farmhouse in the 1920s. Jane taught at Long Hill School in the early 1940s and was a special education teacher in Trumbull through the 1970s. Art survived the sinking of the USS *Oklahoma* at Pearl Harbor and was awarded the Purple Heart. (Courtesy Cindy Hall Arendt.)

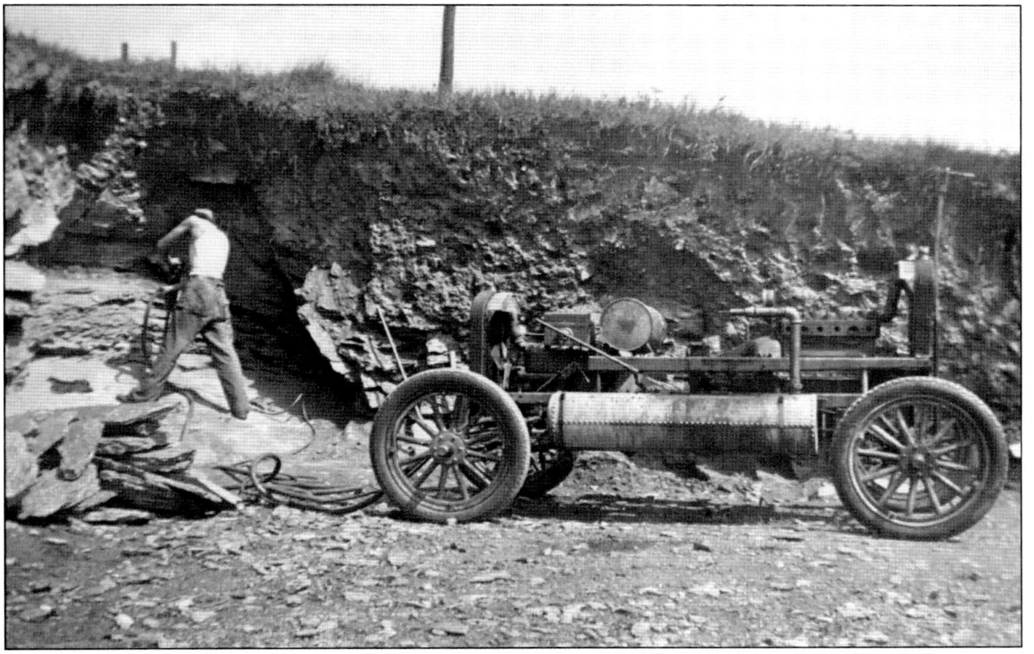

Walter Mantle works to clear a rock ledge to construct Little Plain Road in 1929. Beside him is an air compressor, which he converted from an automobile. In addition to farming, Walter and his brother Arthur, who was a tool designer at the Bassick Company in Bridgeport, ran a machine shop behind their house. The road he built took its name from the flood plain that existed along the nearby Pequonnock River. (Courtesy Cindy Hall Arendt.)

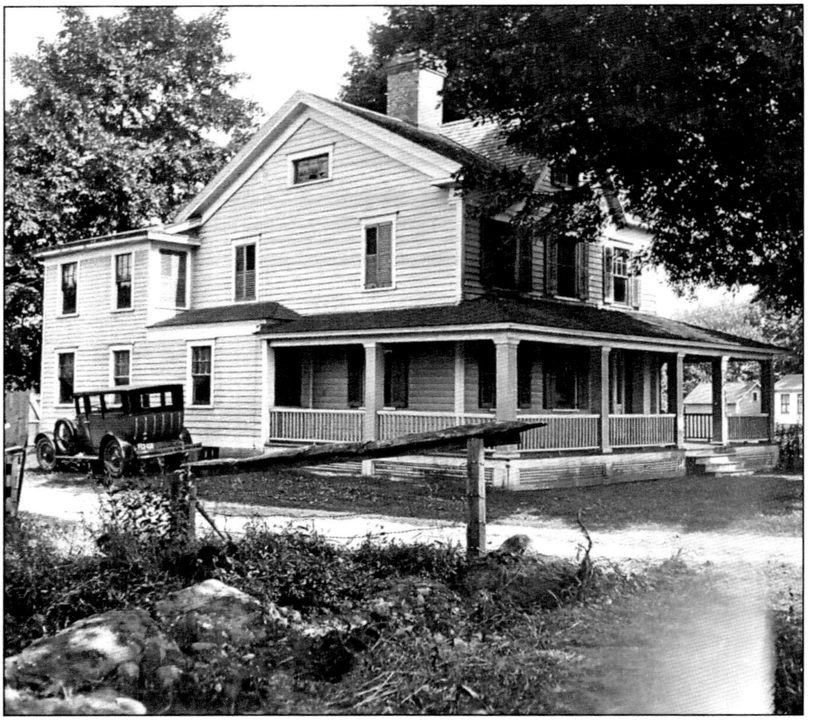

The house at 92 Daniels Farm Road had neither central heat nor indoor plumbing when it was purchased by Arthur and Walter Claud-Mantle in the 1920s. The home is still located on Daniels Farm Road at the intersection of Little Plain Road. (Courtesy Cindy Hall Arendt.)

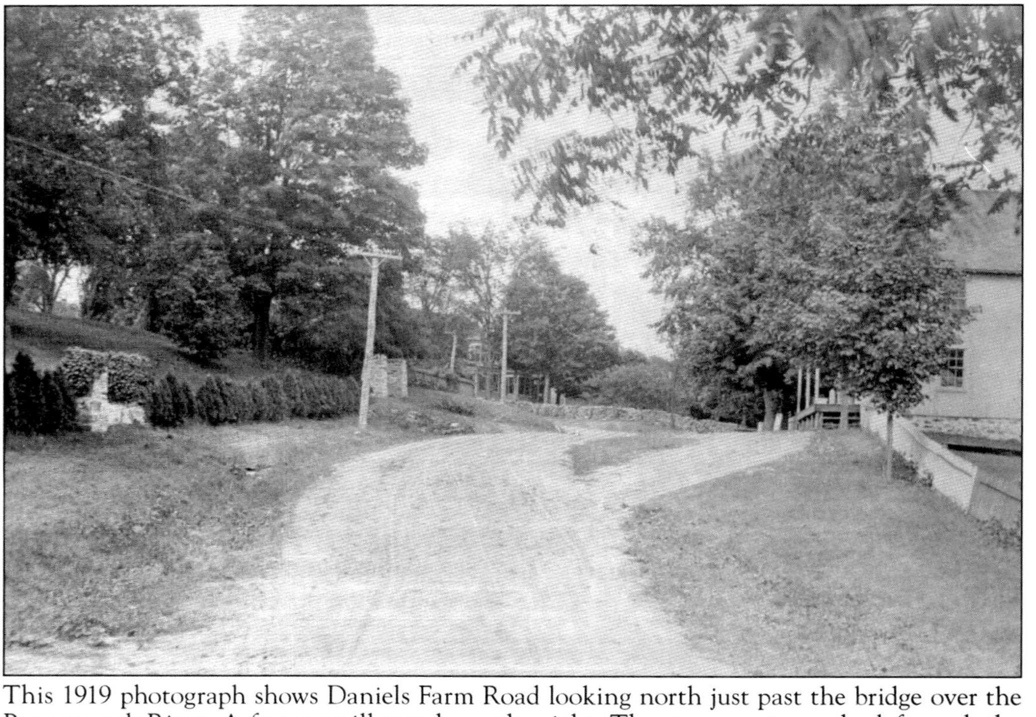

This 1919 photograph shows Daniels Farm Road looking north just past the bridge over the Pequonnock River. A former mill stands on the right. The stone posts on the left mark the driveway of the Daniel Hawley house and remain there today.

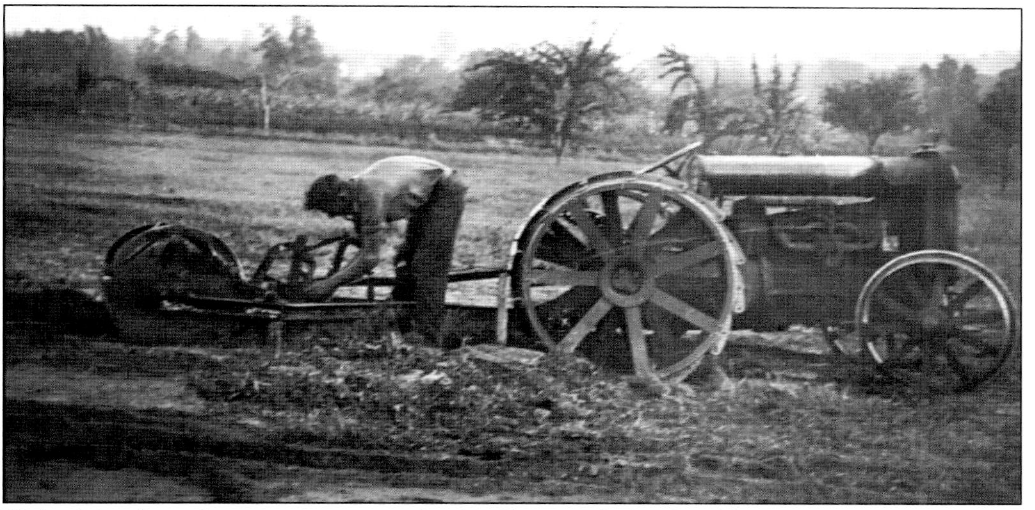

Walter Mantle works on his farm around 1930. The Mantle family sold vegetables to local markets but had started to subdivide the farm into building lots by the 1940s. To the right is a Fordson tractor with steel wheels. (Courtesy Cindy Hall Arendt.)

Joseph Claud-Mantle, his daughter-in-law Gladys, and Joseph's granddaughter Frances Ferrera inspect chicks on the family farm in 1920. Raising chickens was not terribly successful, and the family's large chicken coop eventually became a woodshop and, later, a machine shop. Another part of it was converted into a house. (Courtesy Cindy Hall Arendt.)

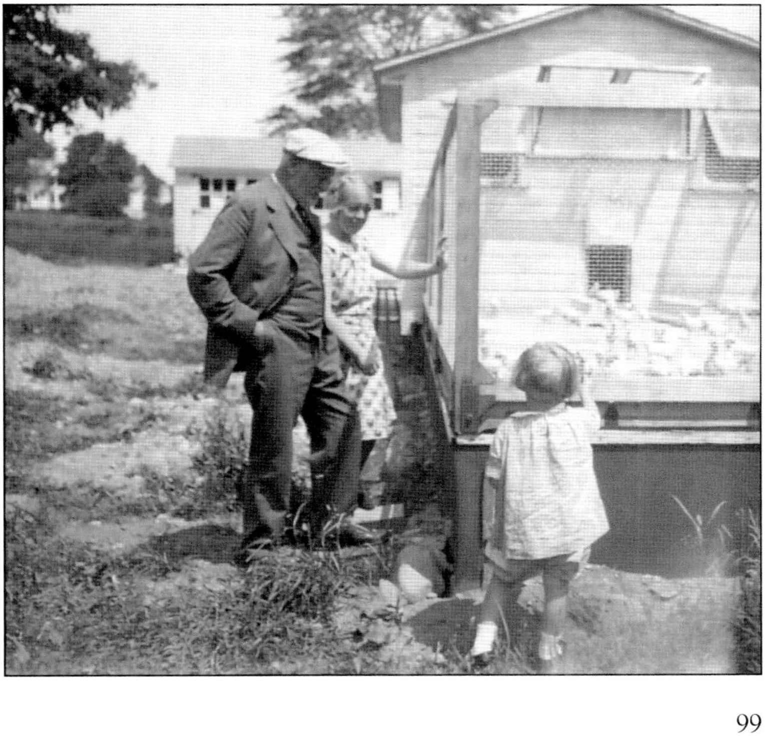

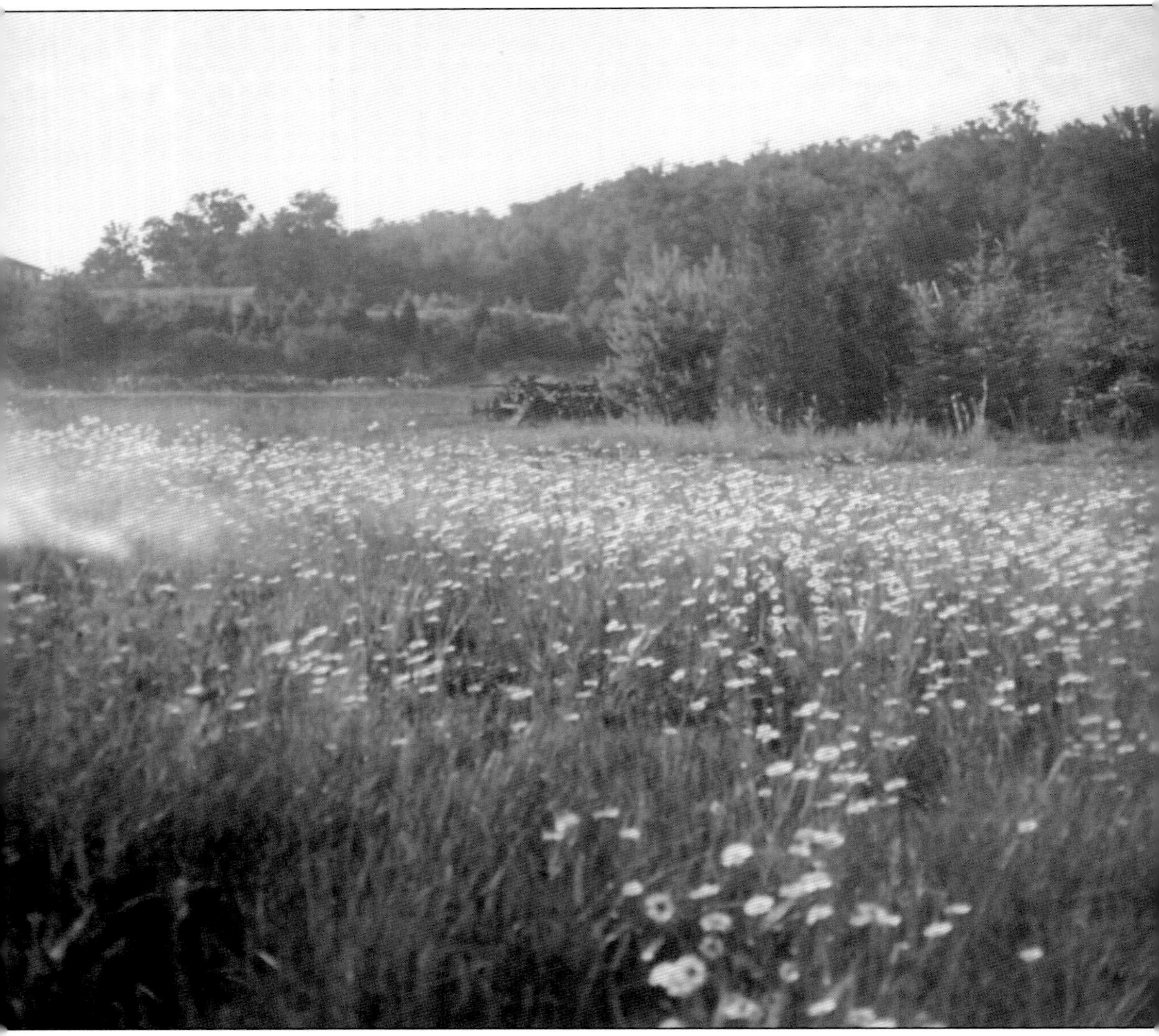

This c. 1930 photograph captures a daisy field just north of what was then the end of Laurel Street. Most of the field and the buildings in the distance were taken down to make way for the Route 25 highway. (Courtesy Cindy Hall Arendt.)

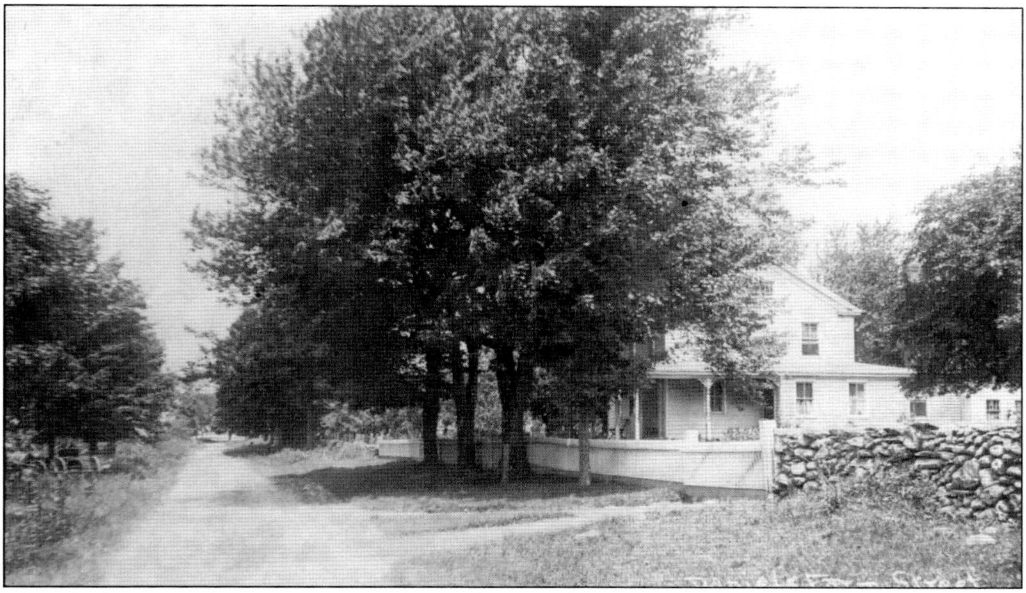

Identified as Daniels Farm "Street," the roadway in front of the Henry A. Smith homestead at 1174 Daniels Farm Road was unpaved when this photograph was taken. The house was built around 1830.

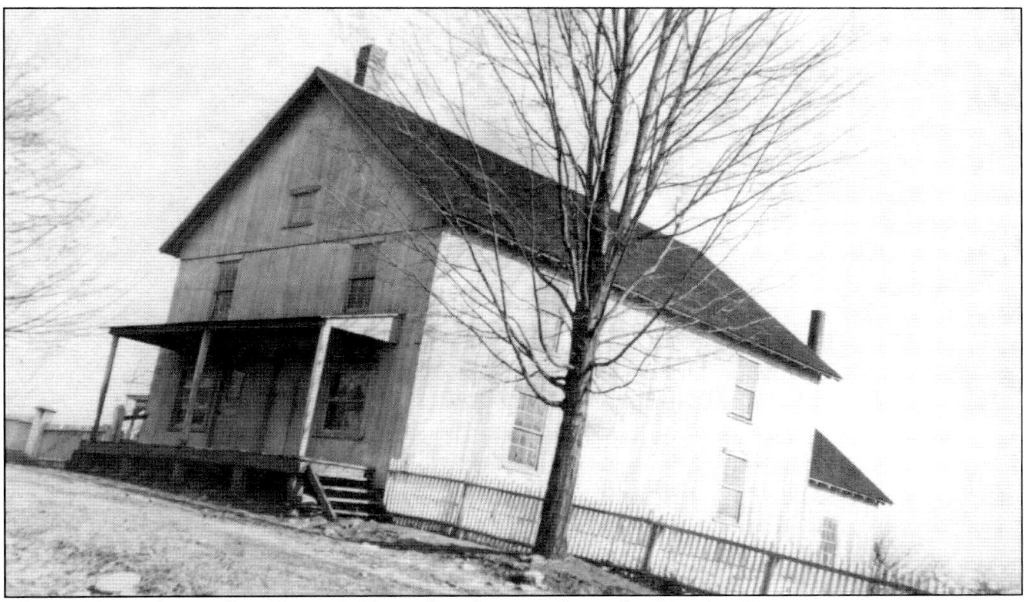

This mill was located on Daniels Farm Road across from the Hawley House.

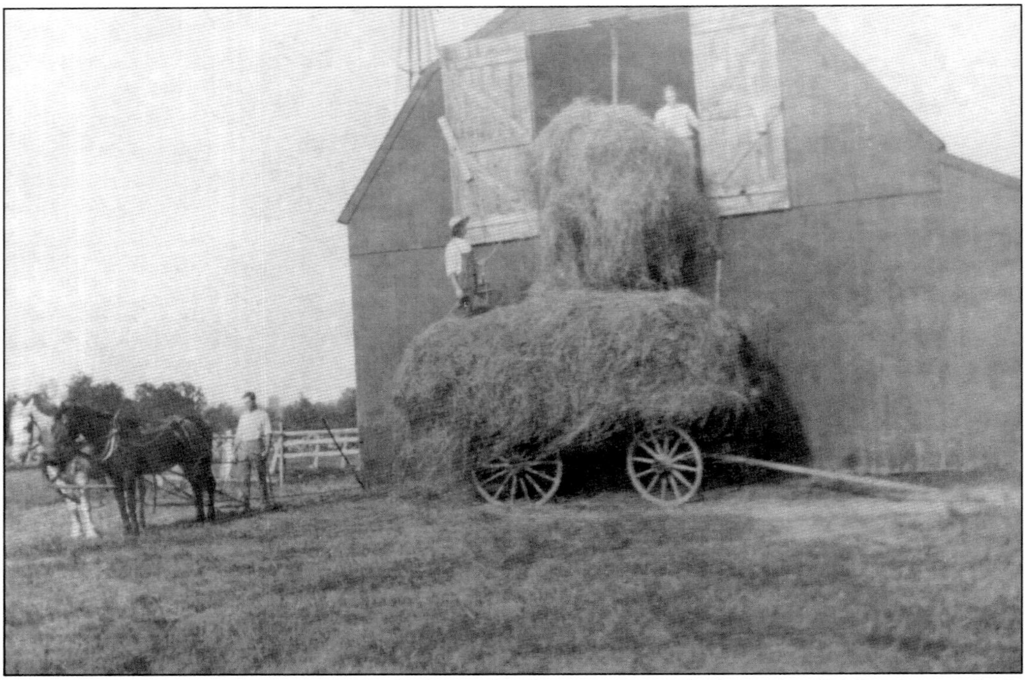

Hay is hoisted into the barn at Banford Beach's farm on Daniels Farm Road. The farm, which Beach purchased in 1892, was located near the site of the former Hillandale Country Club. In addition to being a farmer, Banford Beach served as the first selectman of Trumbull from 1920 to 1928. His son E. Merrill Beach would become a banker and noted town historian.

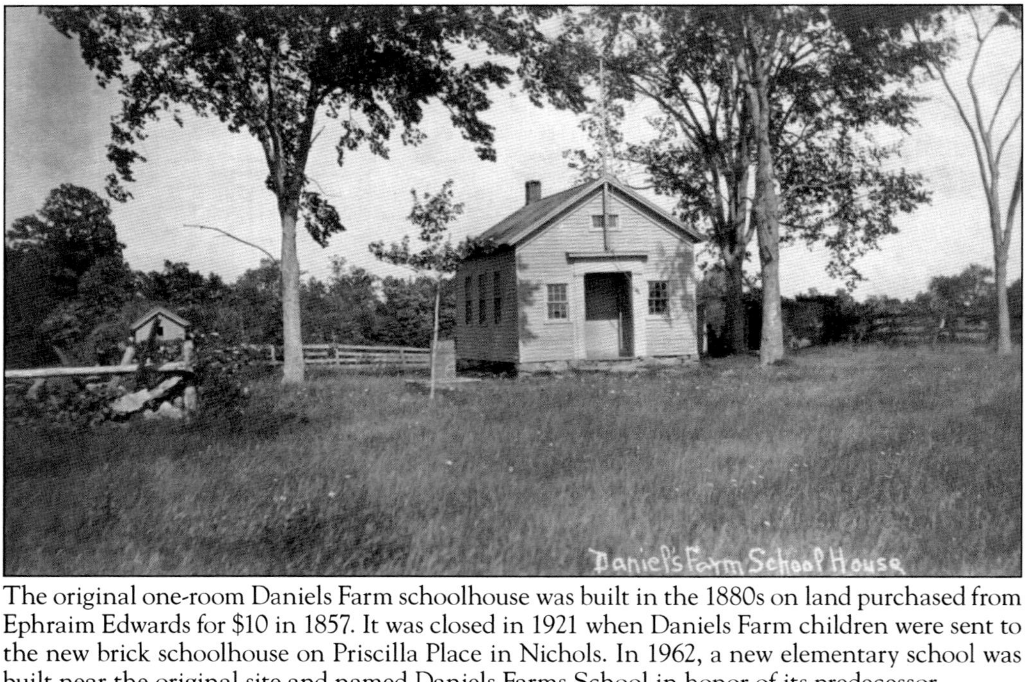

The original one-room Daniels Farm schoolhouse was built in the 1880s on land purchased from Ephraim Edwards for $10 in 1857. It was closed in 1921 when Daniels Farm children were sent to the new brick schoolhouse on Priscilla Place in Nichols. In 1962, a new elementary school was built near the original site and named Daniels Farms School in honor of its predecessor.

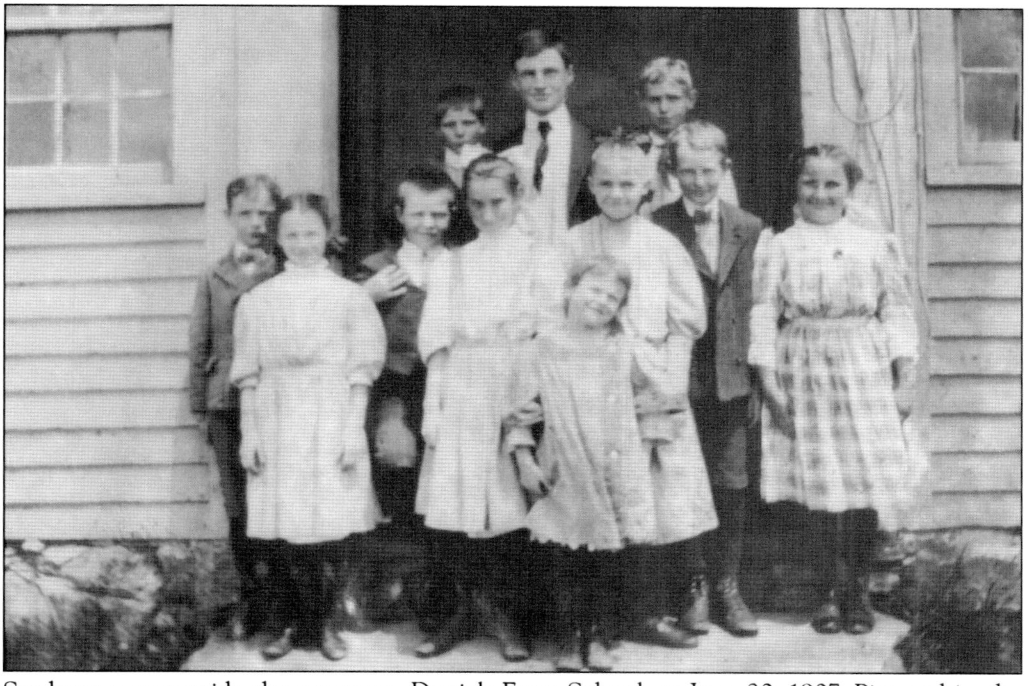

Students pose outside the one-room Daniels Farm School on June 20, 1907. Pictured in the photograph are, from left to right, John Schlottman, Dorothy Beach, Edward and Herman P. Strobel, Ida Belden, E. Merrill Beach, Elfreda Schlottman, Mable B. Beach, Charles Osborne, Harry P. Burr, and Mable Wildman. The teacher at that time was Miss C.A. Reitter, who does not appear in this photograph.

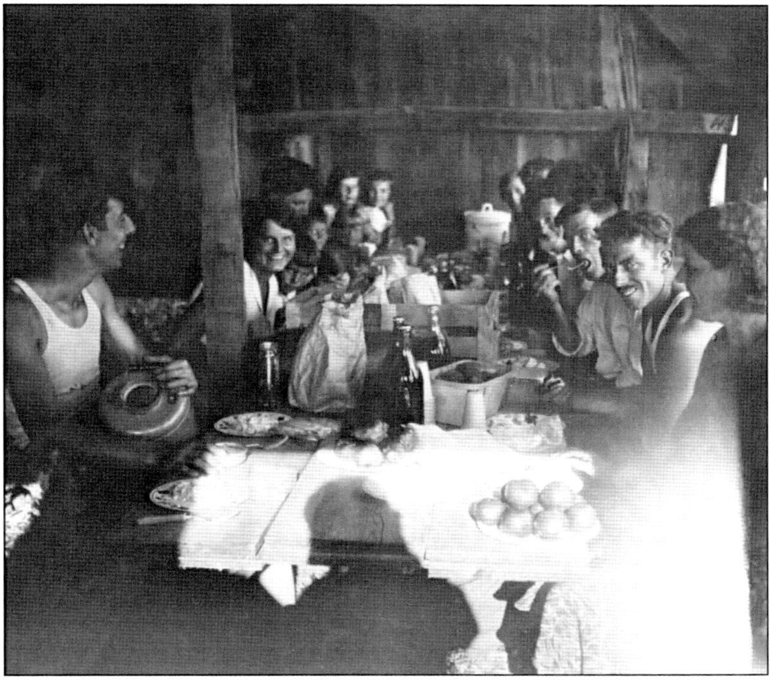

Friends and family gather for a barn party at the Daniels Farm Road farm of Arthur, Gladys, and Walter Mantle. The three can be seen on the far right. Mildred Ferrera, Arthur and Walter's sister, is smiling next to the post. Extended family often visited the farmhouse, and younger cousins sometimes spent summers there. (Courtesy Cindy Hall Arendt.)

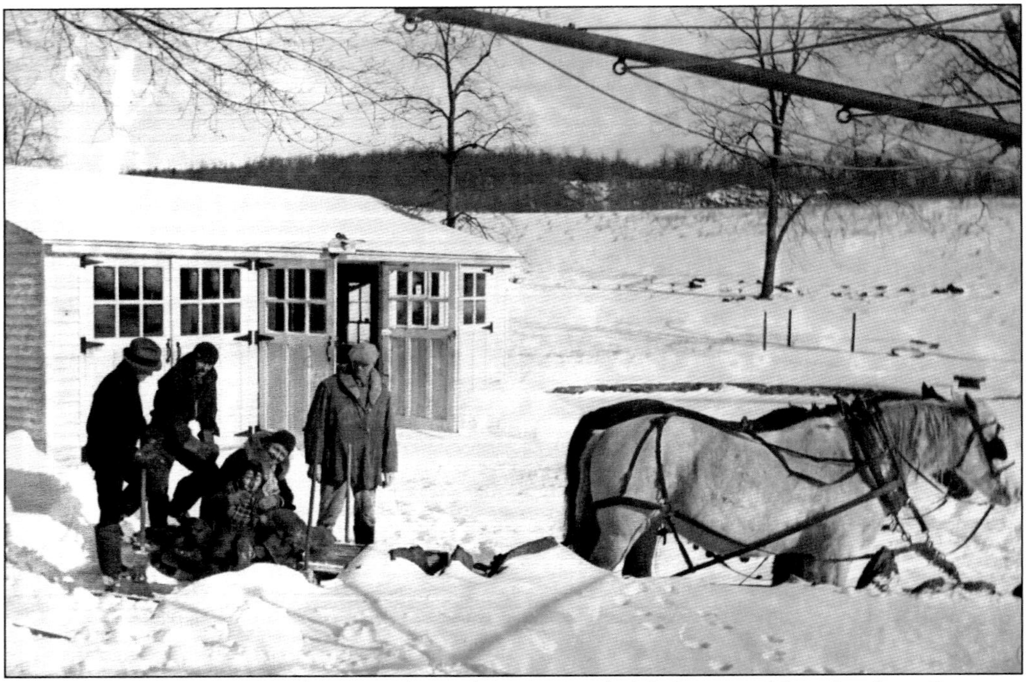

Fred Reynolds, Art and Walter Mantle, and Lucy Mantle McCann and her daughter Patty get ready for a ride on a horse-drawn sledge during the snowy winter of 1934. The garage seen in the background is still located on Little Plain Road. (Courtesy Cindy Hall Arendt.)

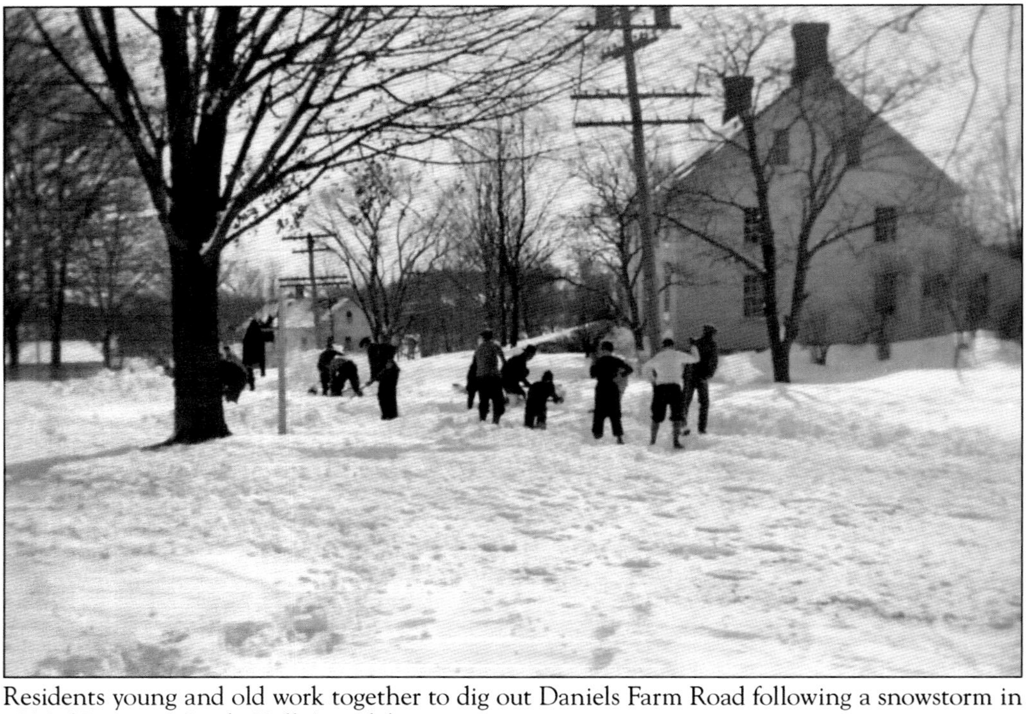

Residents young and old work together to dig out Daniels Farm Road following a snowstorm in 1936. (Courtesy Cindy Hall Arendt.)

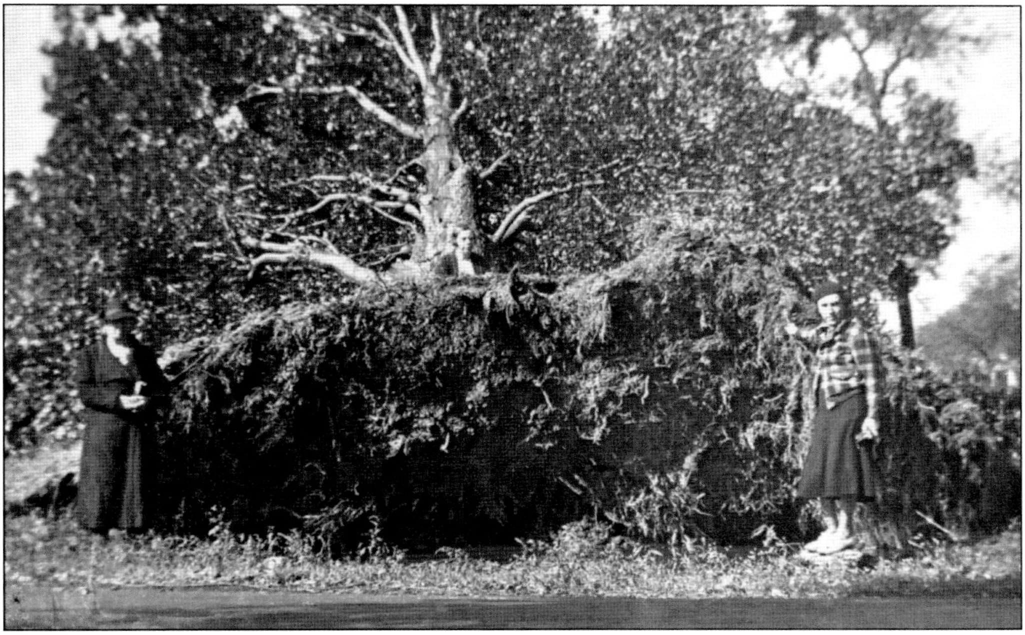

Three women pose with an uprooted tree following the devastating hurricane of September 21, 1938. The storm, which took the Northeast by surprise, was responsible for 564 deaths and damaged and destroyed more than 57,000 homes in southern New England. Wind speeds exceeding 100 miles per hour were recorded. (Courtesy Cindy Hall Arendt.)

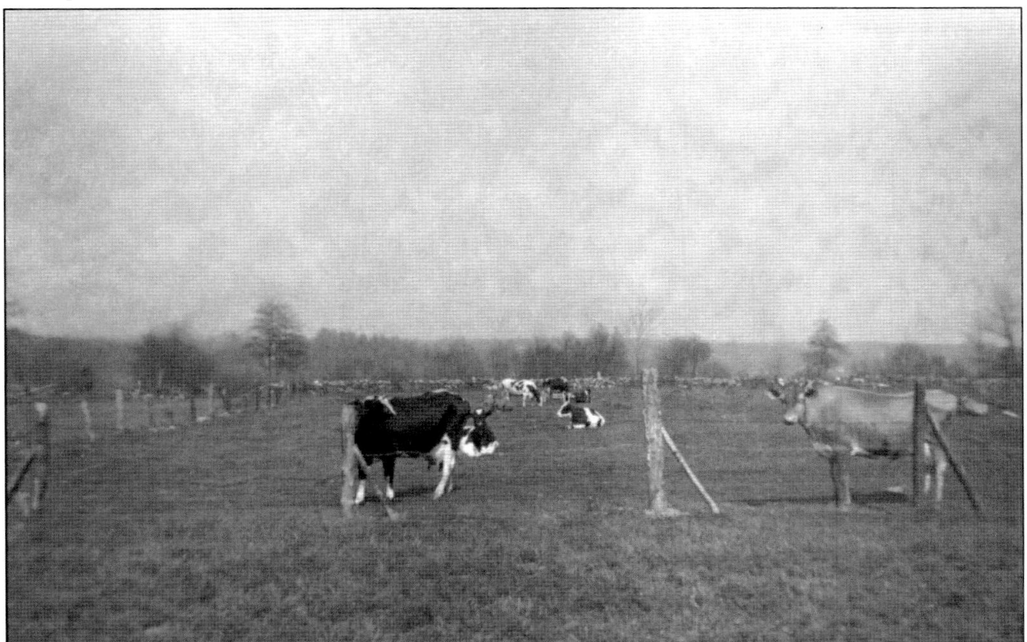

Photographed in 1946, this cow pasture was part of the Kollar farm on Strobel Road. The area is now developed as residential streets, including Midland Road and Cardinal Circle. (Courtesy Kollar family.)

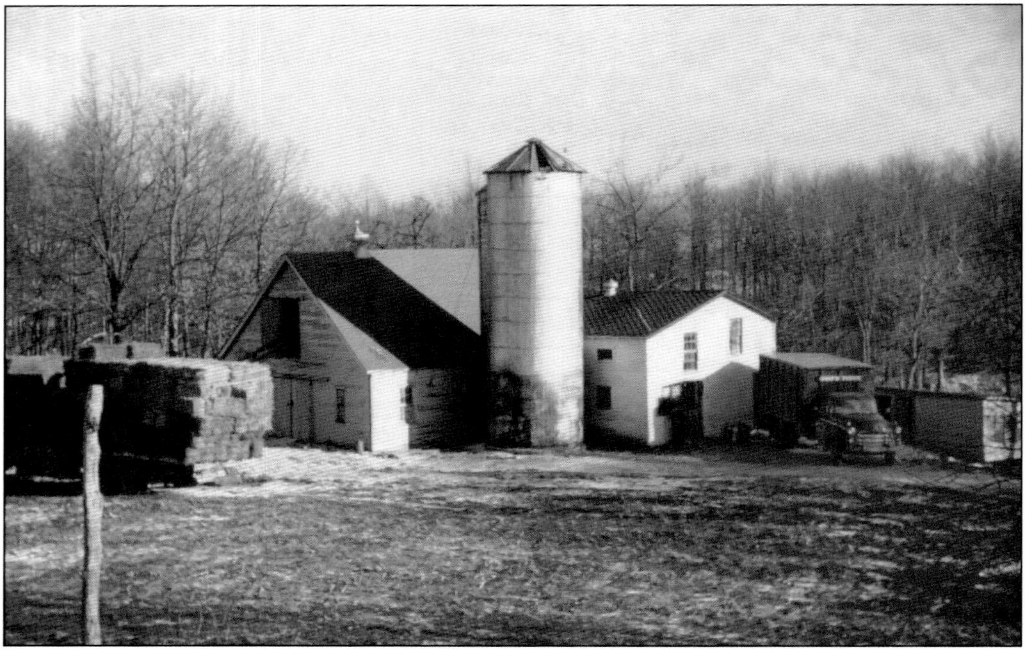

Pictured here in 1958 is the Kollar family's cow barn as viewed from the backyard of their home at 112 Strobel Road. The barn had more than 30 stalls, a loft, a silo, and a milk room. (Courtesy Kollar family.)

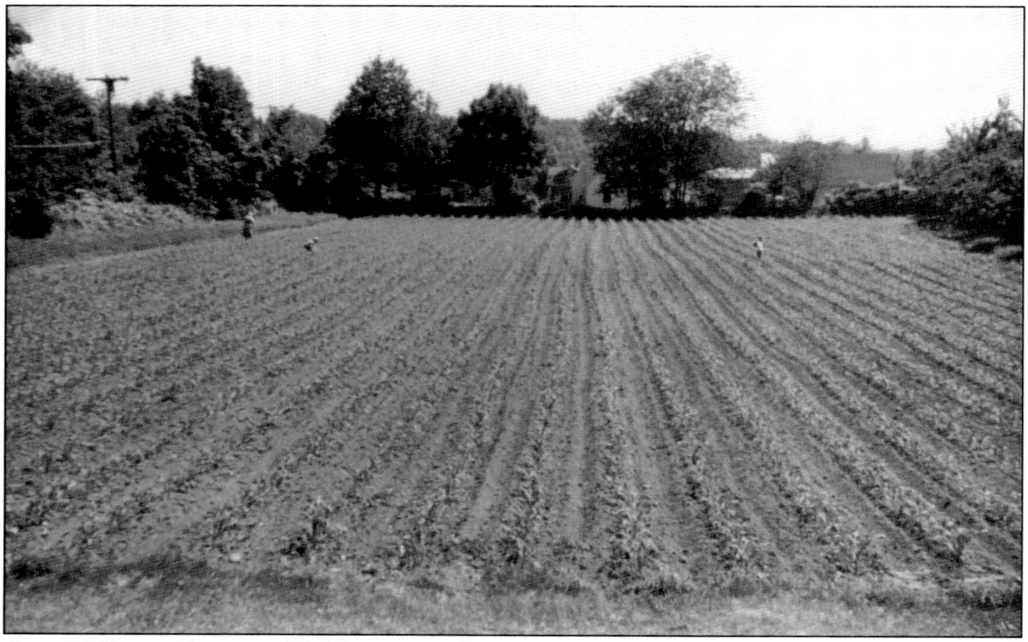

Anna Kollar and her grandchildren Jim and Rick Henrietta weed the cornfield alongside Strobel Road in 1958. (Courtesy Kollar family.)

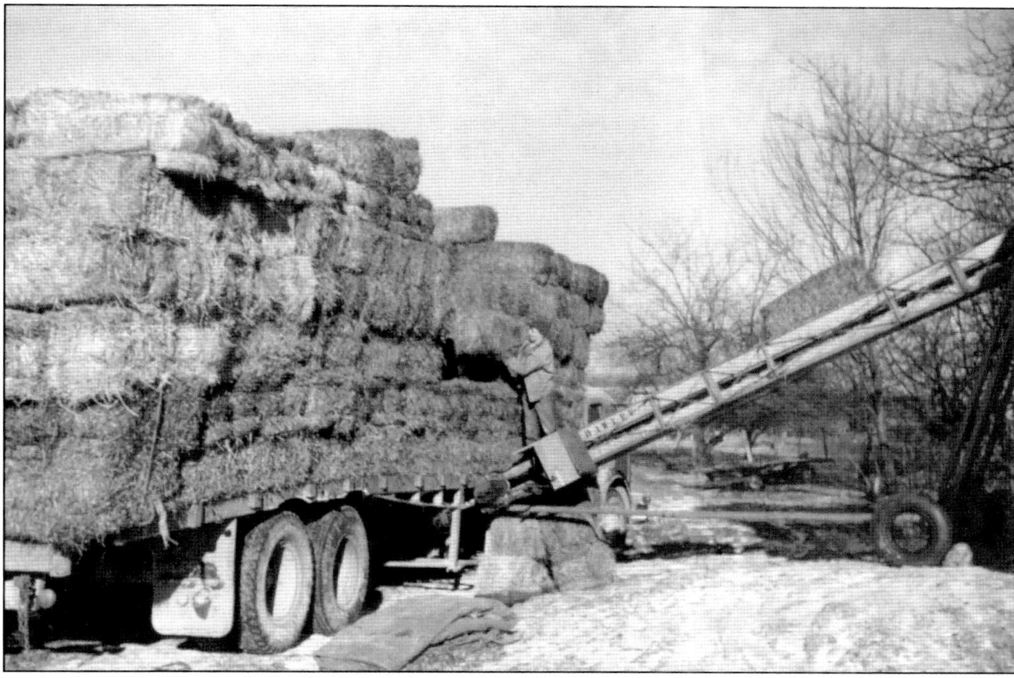

A worker unloads hay at the Kollar farm in the 1950s. Though many local farms grew their own hay, some, like the Kollars, had it trucked in from Canada. (Courtesy Kollar family.)

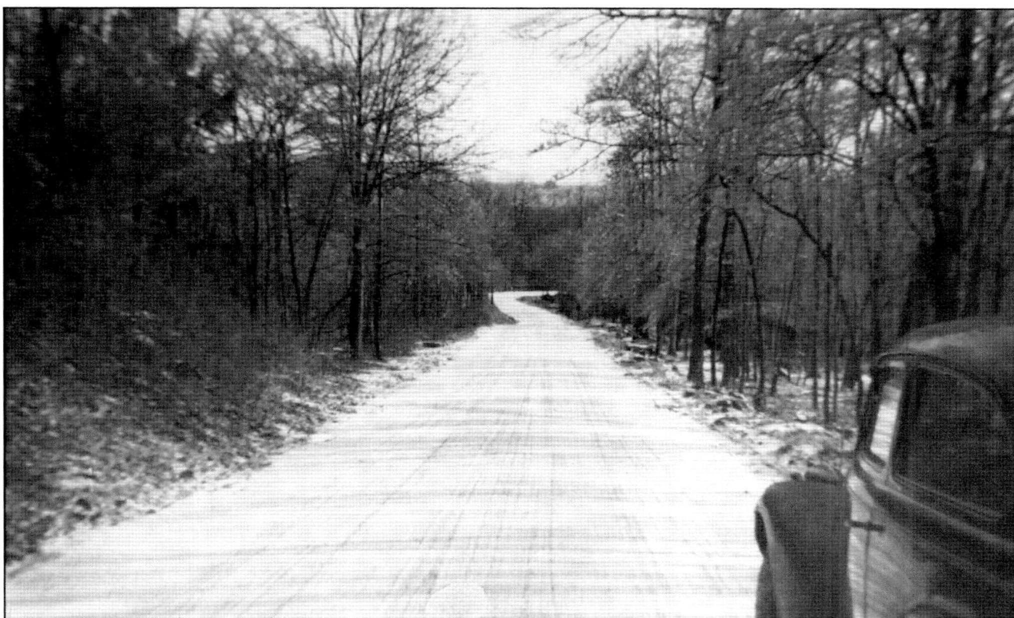

A slick Strobel Road winds downhill after an ice storm in 1946. Today, Hemlock Trail would be on the right in this photograph, and Shelter Rock and Grayrock Roads would be on the left. (Courtesy Kollar family.)

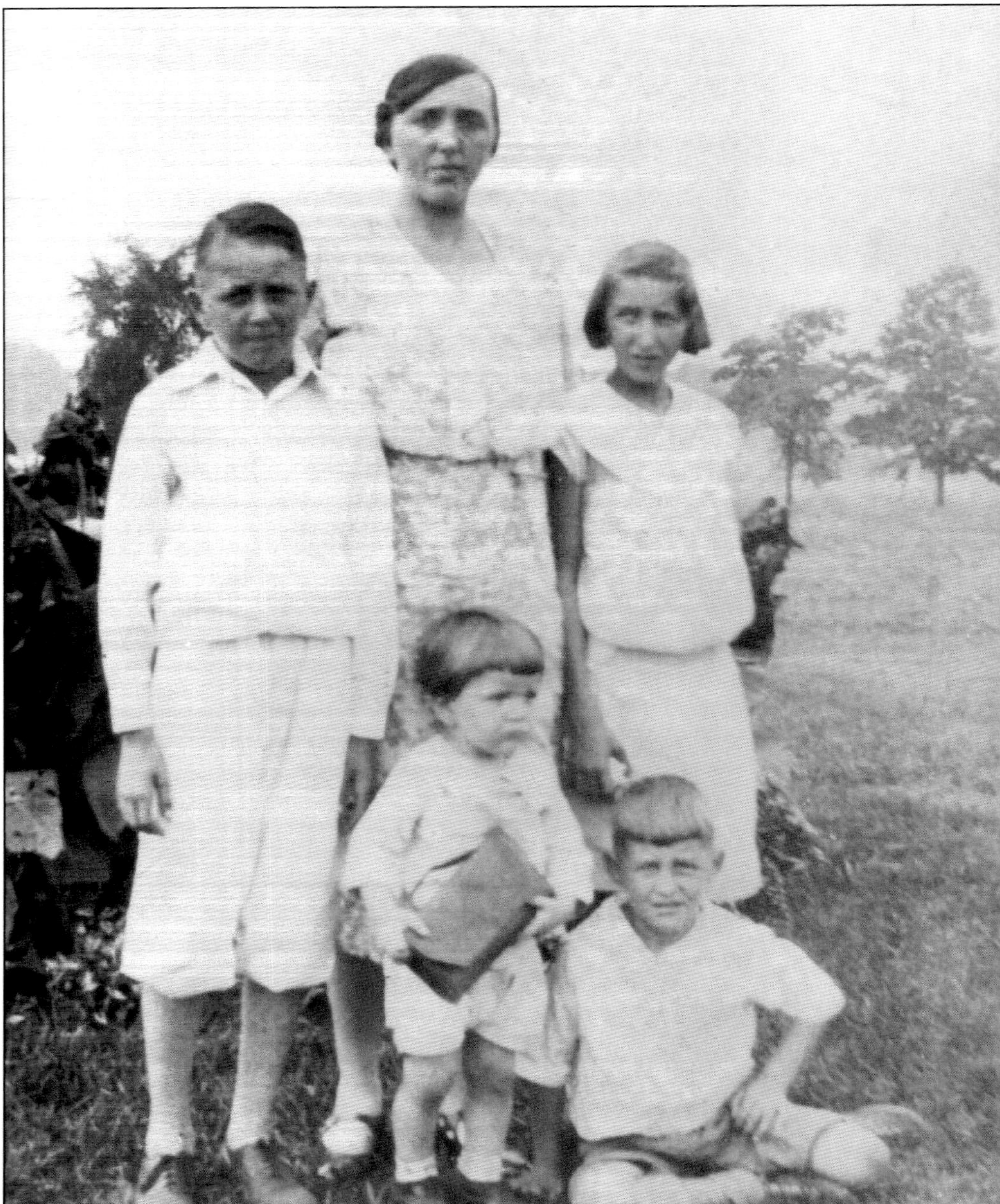

Members of the Kollar family pose for a portrait. Pictured from left to right are (first row) brothers John and Tom; (second row) Joseph, Anna (Joseph's mother), and Mary. (Courtesy Kollar family.)

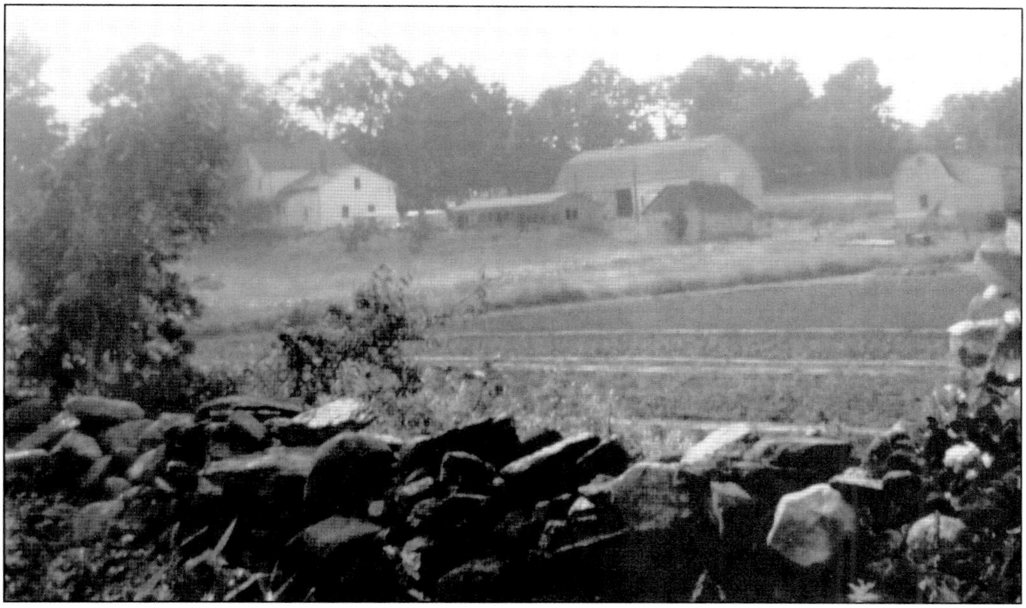

The Tomek family farm was located at the intersection of Daniels Farm and Strobel Roads. The vegetable and dairy farm was established in 1914 by Stephen Tomek and his wife, Mary. By 1948, the farm stretched over 100 acres and boasted 40 cows. Management of the farm was later taken over by Frank, one of the Tomek's 11 children. In 1966, the town bought the land for a new educational campus comprising Trumbull High and Hillcrest Middle Schools. (Courtesy Phil Kollar.)

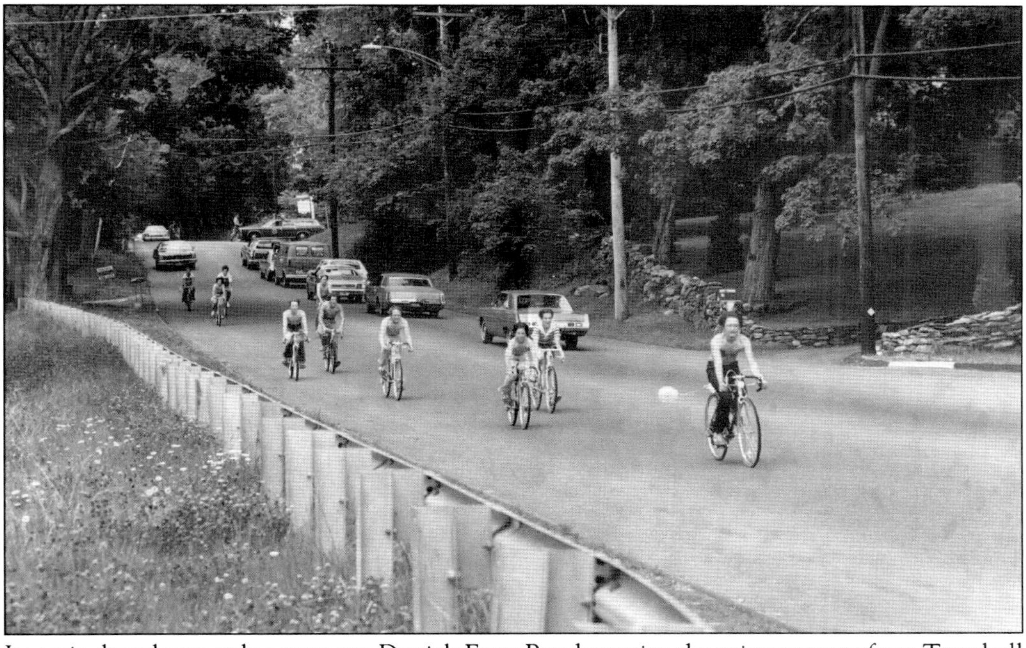

Its agricultural past only a memory, Daniels Farm Road remains the primary route from Trumbull Center to the northeast part of town. Here, a group of cyclists cruises down the hill toward Trumbull Center in 1977.

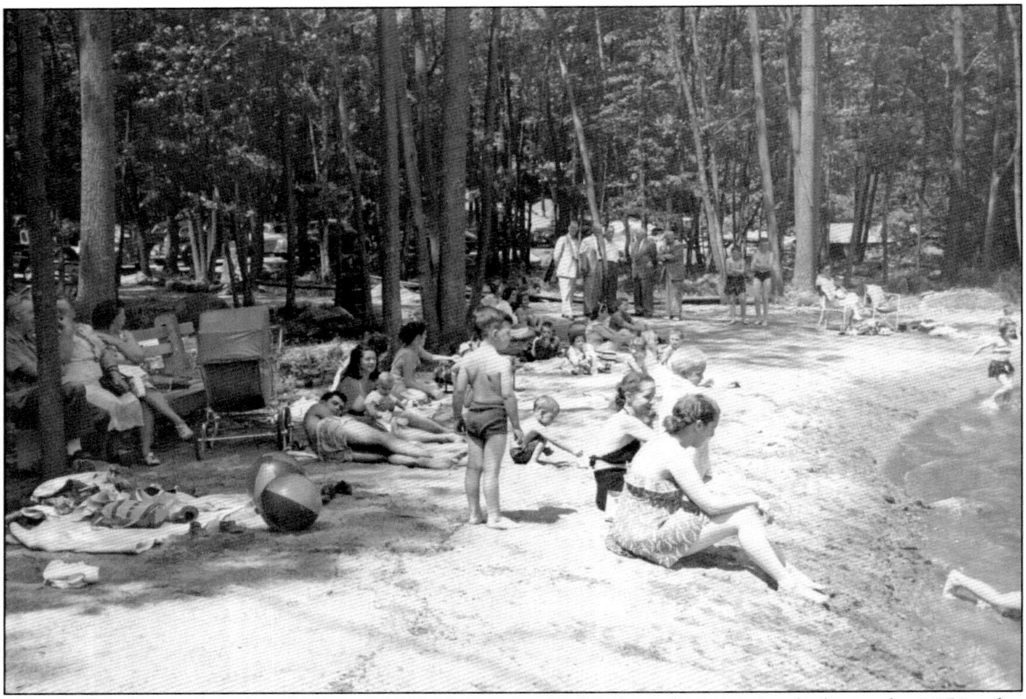

Originally, the pool at Beach Memorial Park was an old-fashioned swimming hole. In the 1950s, the popular cooling-off spot was improved with concrete walls. The new pool was designed, however, with a unique sloped side that mimicked the bank of the old pond. To this day, there are residents who believe the name "Beach Park" comes from this beach-like feature of the pool.

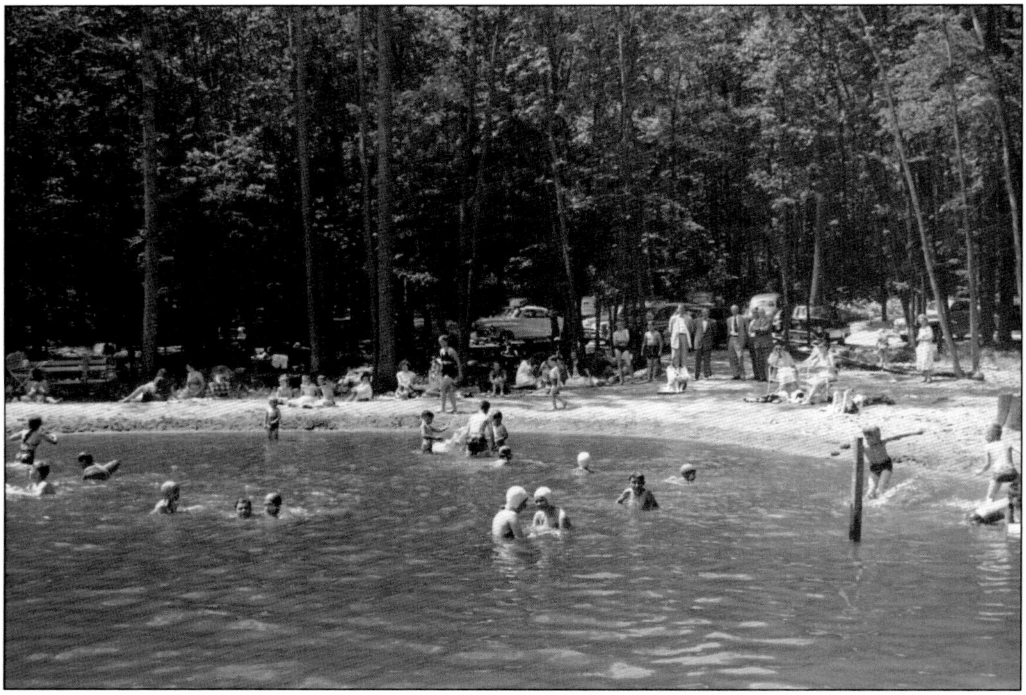

Families enjoyed the original Beach Memorial Park pool into the 1970s, when this photograph was taken. By 1990, the pool's deteriorated condition required it be rebuilt. Although new codes in force at the time would have prohibited the pool's beach-like slope, the town was permitted to retain it in the new facility.

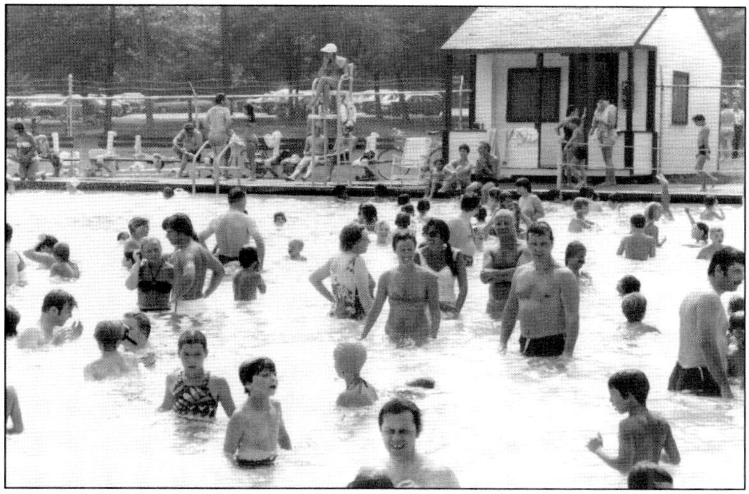

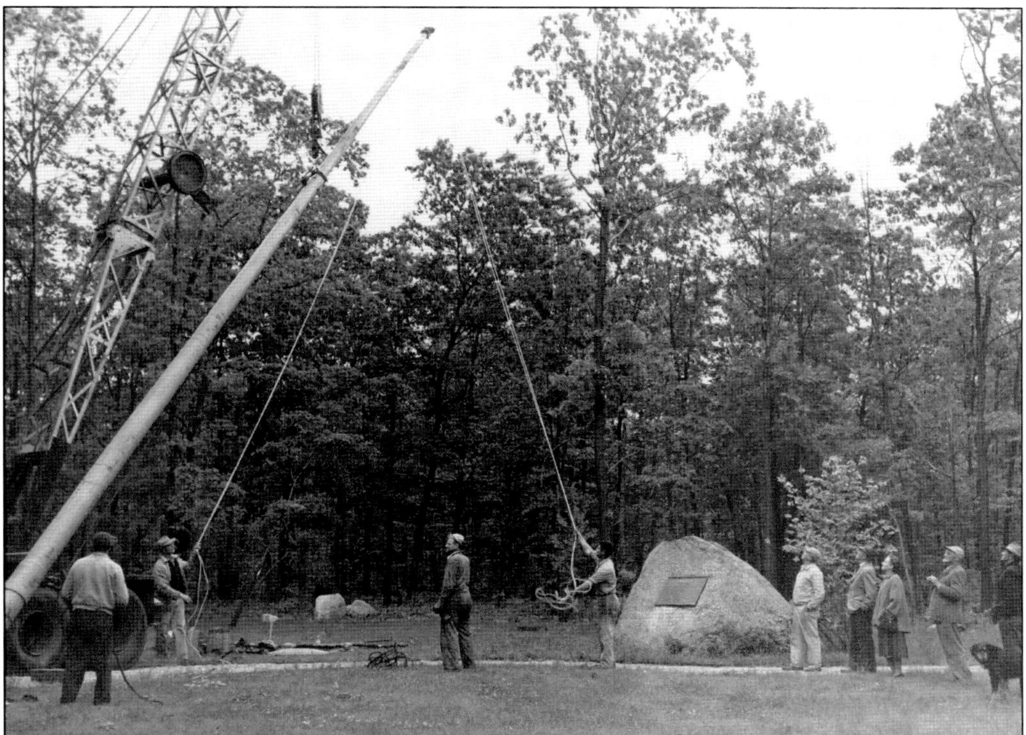

Workers lift the memorial flagpole at Beach Park into place on Memorial Day in 1951. The 50-foot flagpole was dedicated to Richard F. Moore Jr., a US Army Air Corps lieutenant who was shot down over Germany in 1944. It was placed 22 feet away from the park's memorial rock, the distance symbolizing the 22 Trumbull men who lost their lives in the war. Their names are inscribed on the bronze plaque on the boulder. For several years, Memorial Day ceremonies were carried out at the park's circle. The ceremony included the recitation of each soldier's name as Girl Scouts marched to the memorial rock and placed a plant at its base. The ceremony was continued until Trumbull initiated a Memorial Day street parade on Main Street, with ceremonies at town hall.

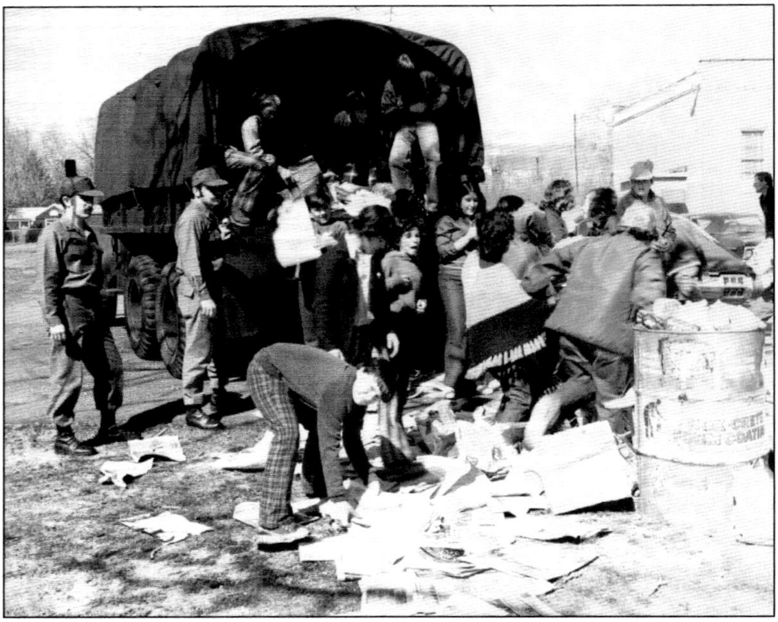

Trumbull students collect discarded newspapers during a paper drive at Hillcrest School in 1974. They were among young people across the country who took an active role in the environmental movement that began in the late 1960s.

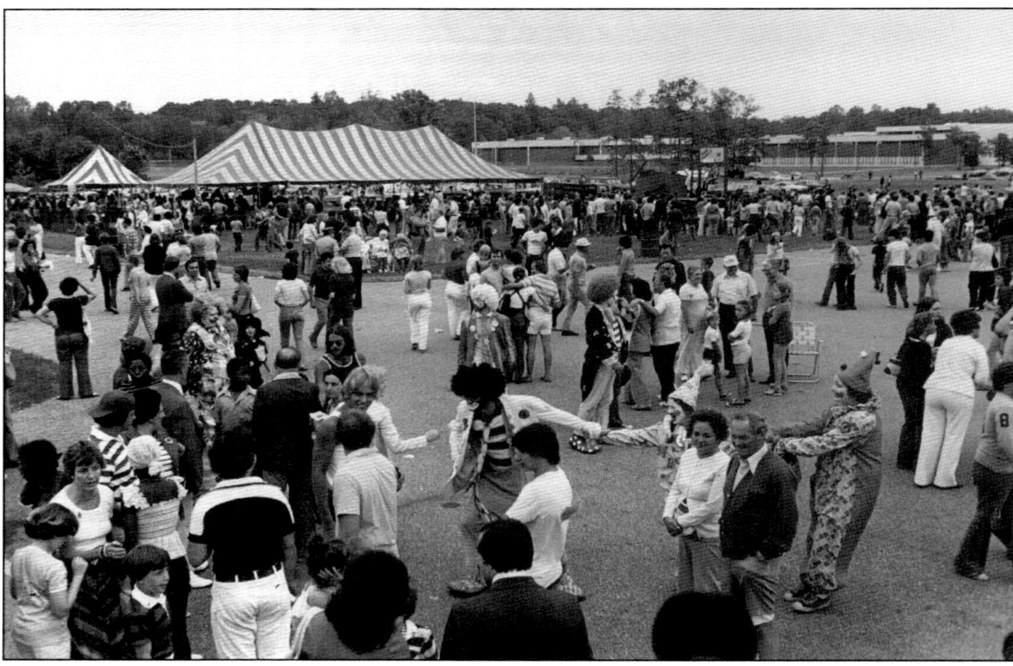

Trumbull Day, pictured here in 1977, has been a much-anticipated summer event since its establishment in 1972 as part of the town's 175th anniversary celebration. In its heyday, the celebration held behind Hillcrest Middle School drew as many as 40,000 people and featured helicopter rides, a midway, and a signature fireworks display.

Seven

Chestnut Hill

Centered on the area of Plattsville Road, Trumbull's Chestnut Hill area borders the city of Bridgeport to the south and the town of Easton to the west. Unlike Nichols, whose early settlers came from Stratford, the early settlers of Chestnut Hill came primarily from the village of Stratfield, which was located between the towns of Stratford and Fairfield. Stratfield was established in 1701 after a separate ecclesiastic society was formed to satisfy farming families that lived too far away to attend church and meetings in either Stratford or Fairfield.

The Chestnut Hill section of Trumbull was first settled in 1719 by John Edwards. Edwards was an officer in the Scottish army who rebelled against the government and was sentenced to be shot. He escaped and secretly got passage on a ship bound for Black Rock Harbor. He decided to hide out and built his home in the Chestnut Hill wilderness. Historical records show that in 1724, Edwards built and operated a wool-processing mill in nearby Ox Hill. Soon, others settled the area, with family names such as Beardsley, French, and Wakelee (or Wakeley). In 1740, Chestnut Hill became part of Long Hill Parish, which led to the inclusion of this area when Trumbull was incorporated in 1797.

Chestnut Hill remained mostly farmland prior to Trumbull's post–World War II population explosion. With more than 100 acres, the Wakeley dairy farm on Madison Avenue was one of the largest, producing milk, apples, and peaches. The Beach and French families also operated farms in the area.

However, Chestnut Hill suffered a loss of identity during the 20th century. The construction of the Merritt Parkway in the late 1930s, which bisected Chestnut Hill, and the construction of the Trumbull Shopping Park in the early 1960s dramatically changed the character of this small corner of Trumbull.

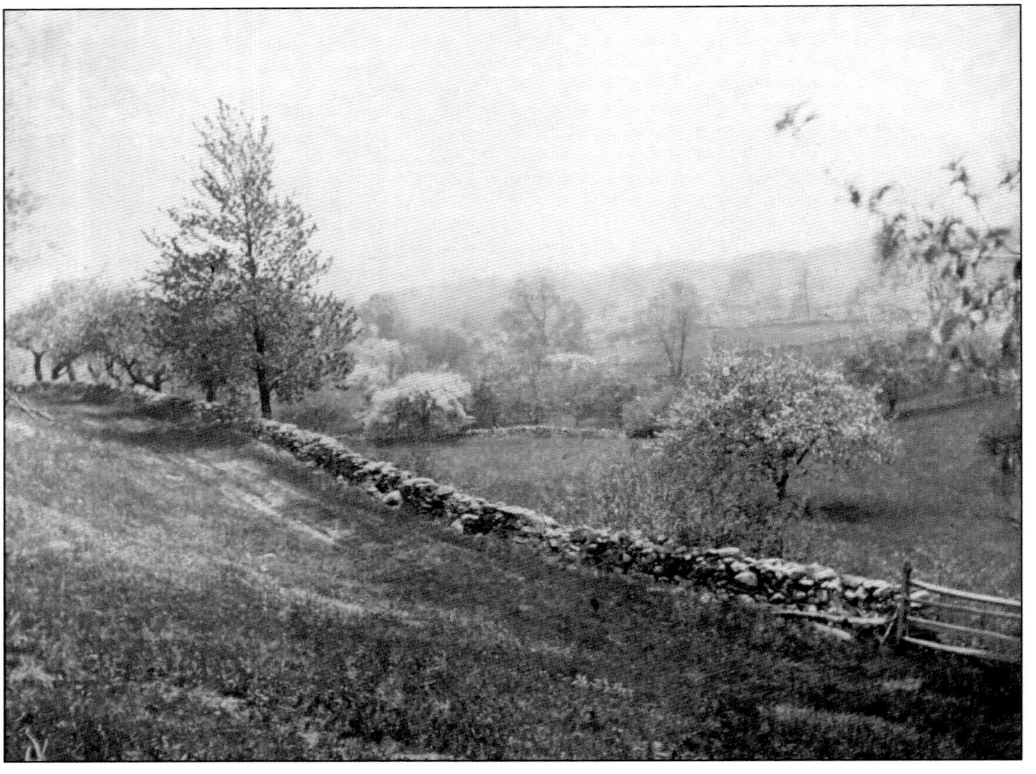

These photographs capture one of the most picturesque places in town: Agur Beach's farm, known as Natures Garden, on Plattsville Road. The Beachs' apple orchard is shown below.

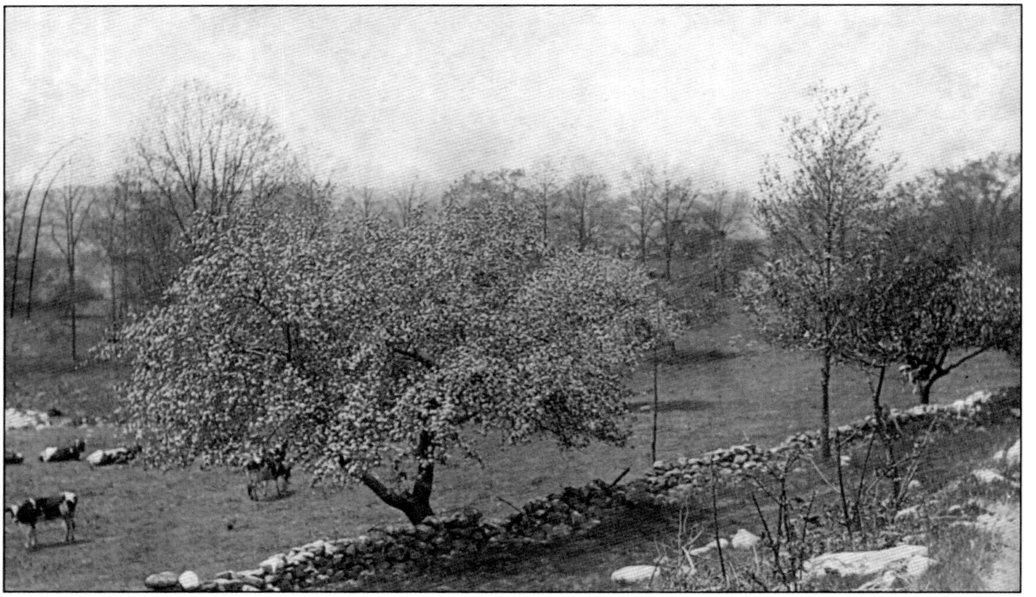

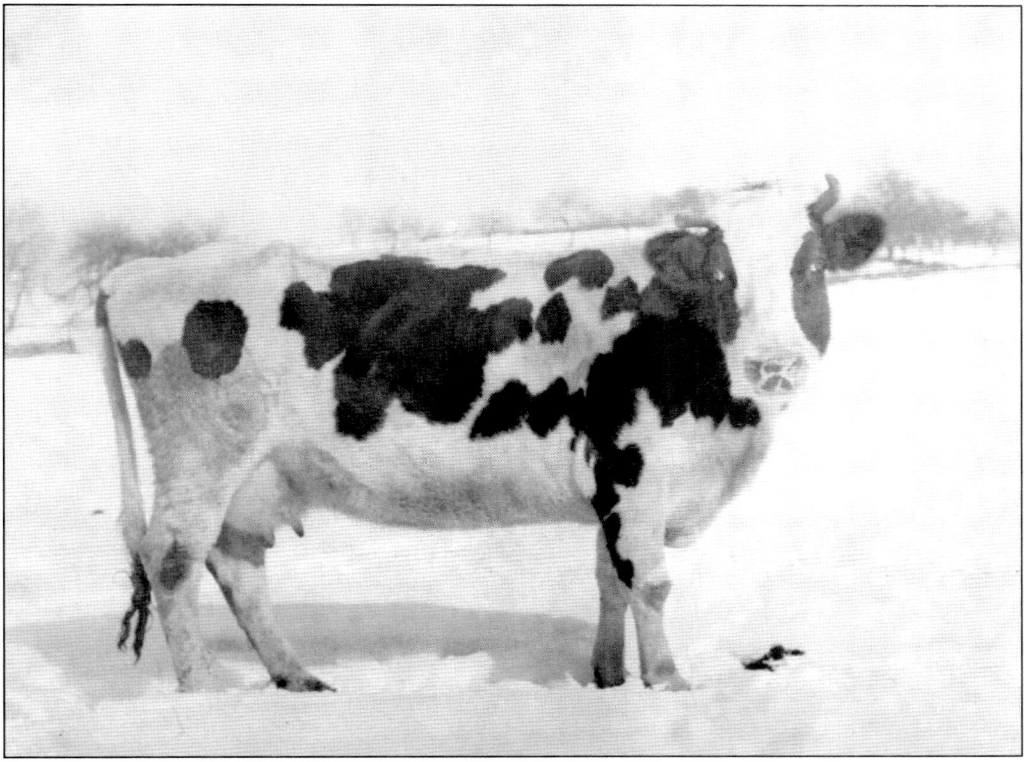

The cow in this photograph belonged to Agur Beach and is identified as "Hattie." Dairy farms were common throughout Trumbull well into the mid-20th century. Parker's Dairy in Nichols was the last to close when it was sold to a developer in 1973. Each of Parker's glass milk bottles was embossed with a homespun rhyme, usually extolling the virtues of their cows. "I'm not Elsie, I'm not Molly, I am one of Parker's cows, by golly," read one milk bottle.

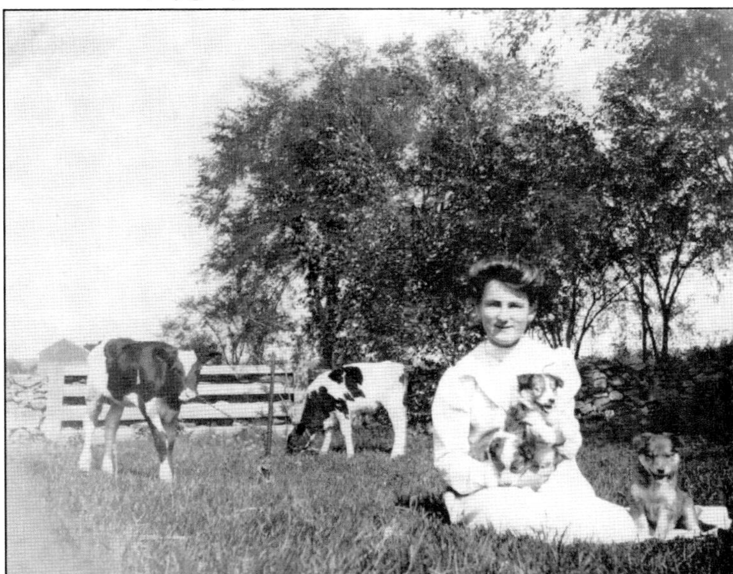

Born in 1884, Laura Hall Beach was the second wife of Agur Beach. The Halls had long been established as a Trumbull family. Laura Hall married Agur Beach in 1925 after the death of his first wife. He was 75 years old, and she was only 41. Laura Hall Beach died in 1955.

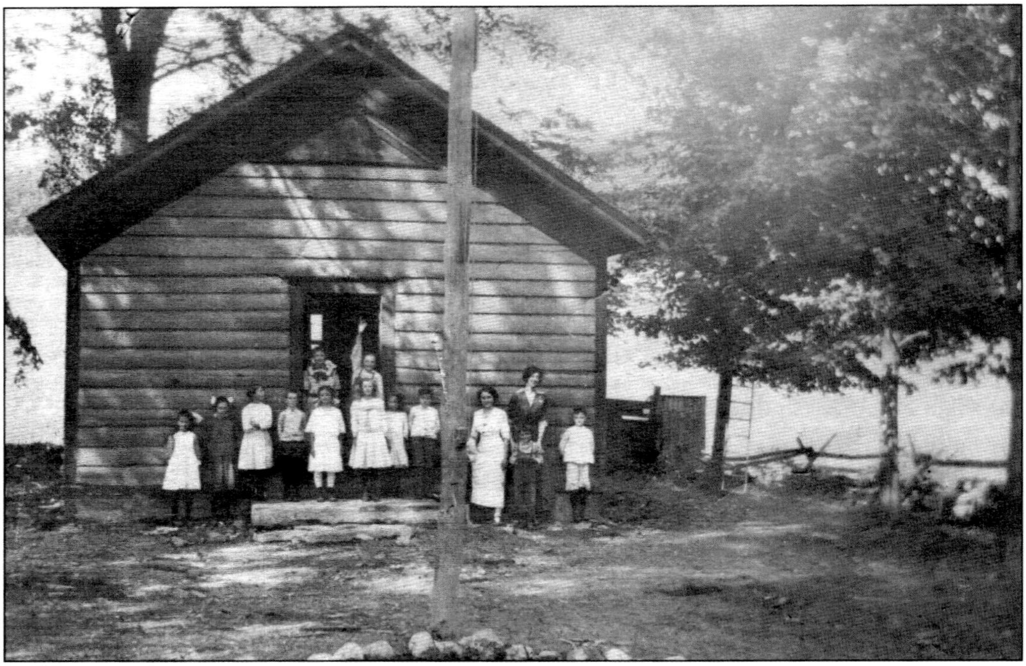

Chestnut Hill School had a difficult history. The original school, which was moved to a new site by oxen, burned to the ground the next night. It was then rebuilt but burned down again, the result of improperly disposed ashes. The third structure, below, lasted until the one-room schoolhouse was obsolete.

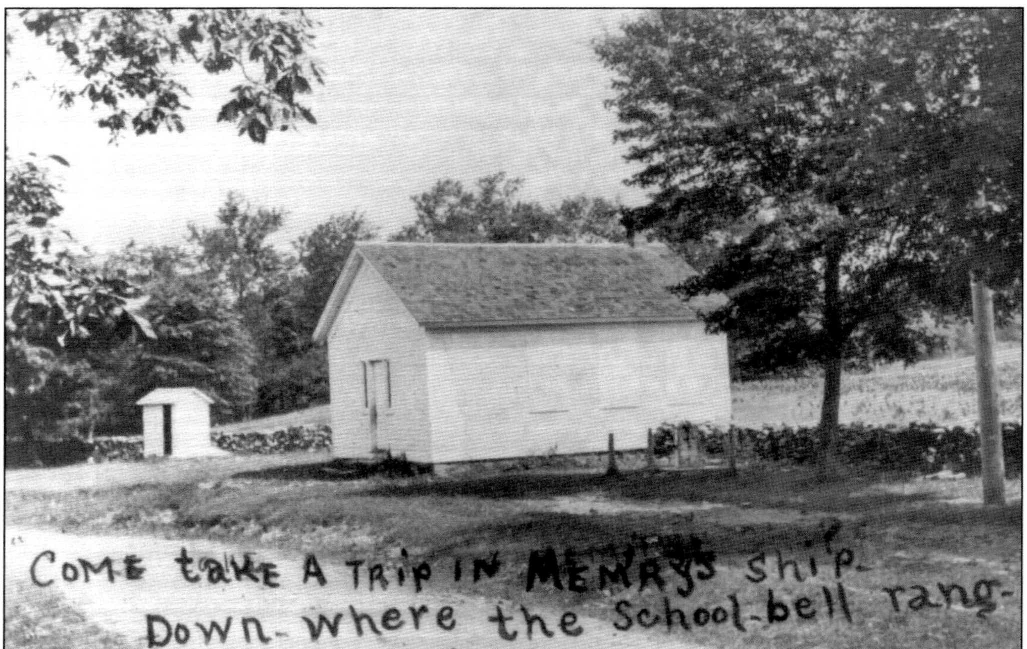

Born in Bridgeport, Elsie F. Hall taught at Chestnut Hill School as well as White Plains and Upper Long Hill schools. Never married, she died in 1967 at the age of 94. Her photograph was donated to the historical society by a handyman who came to live with Hall in 1921.

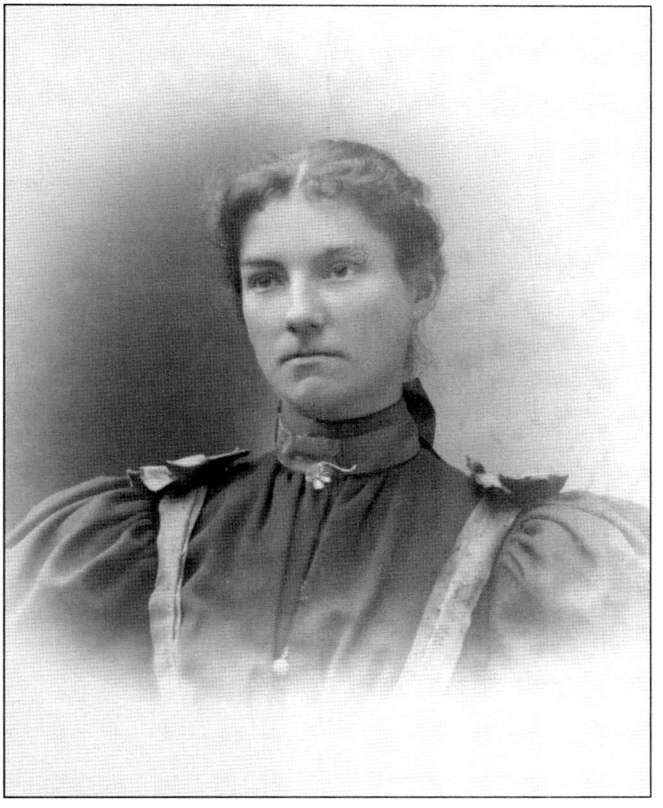

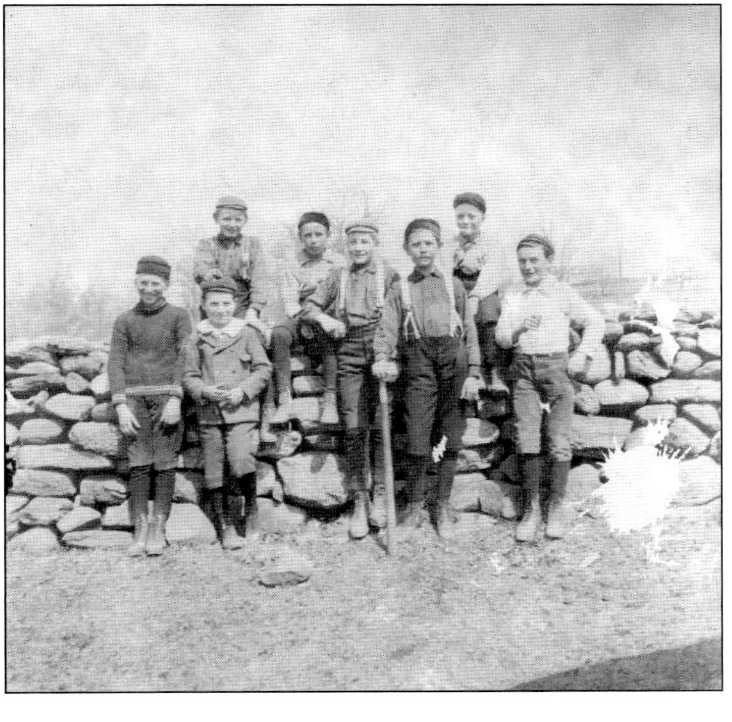

The one-room schoolhouse at Chestnut Hill had one teacher for multiple grades. The teacher often made school more enjoyable by establishing contests and games. In the spring, students competed to bring in the first flowers of the spring, which the teacher then looked up in her flower book.

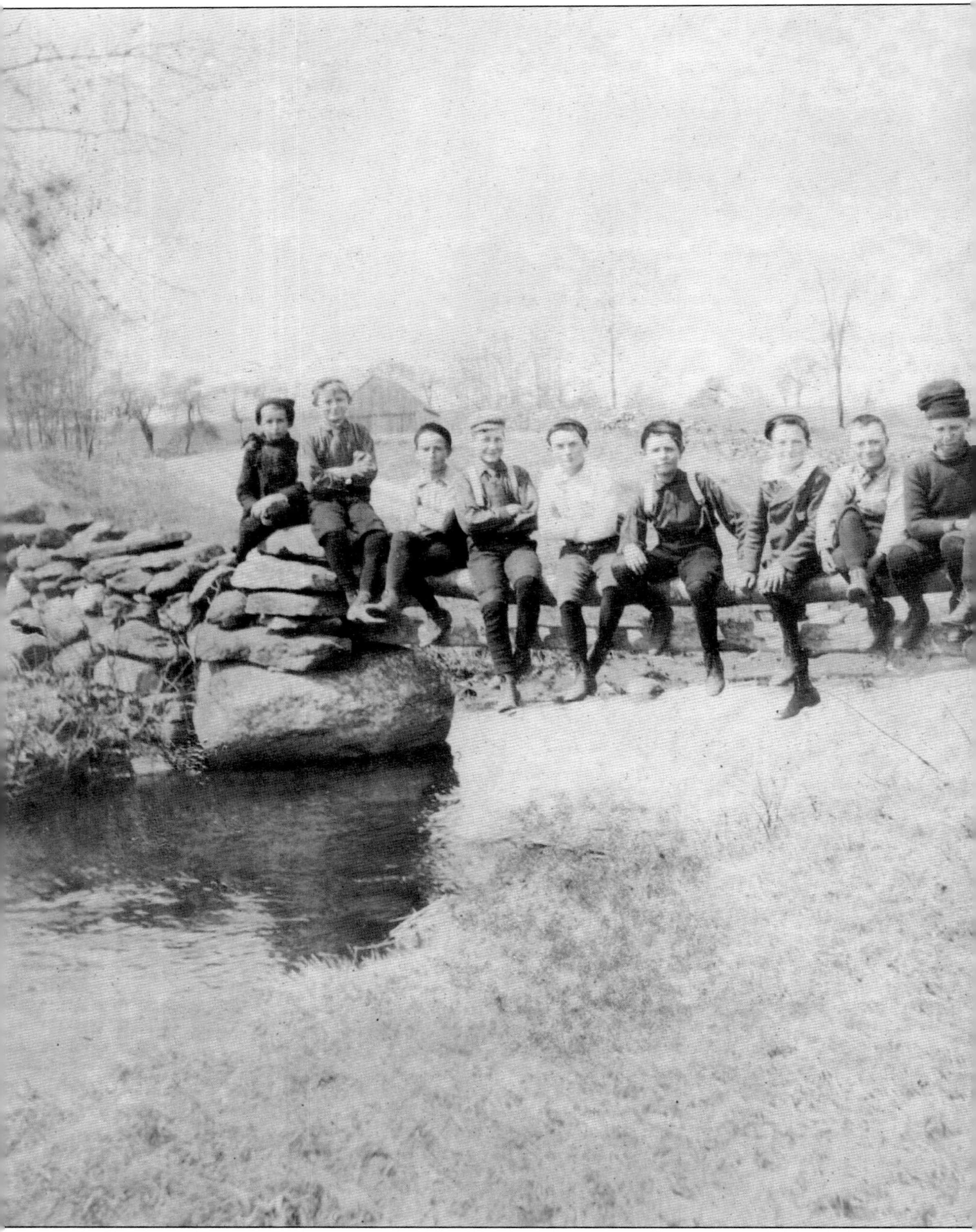

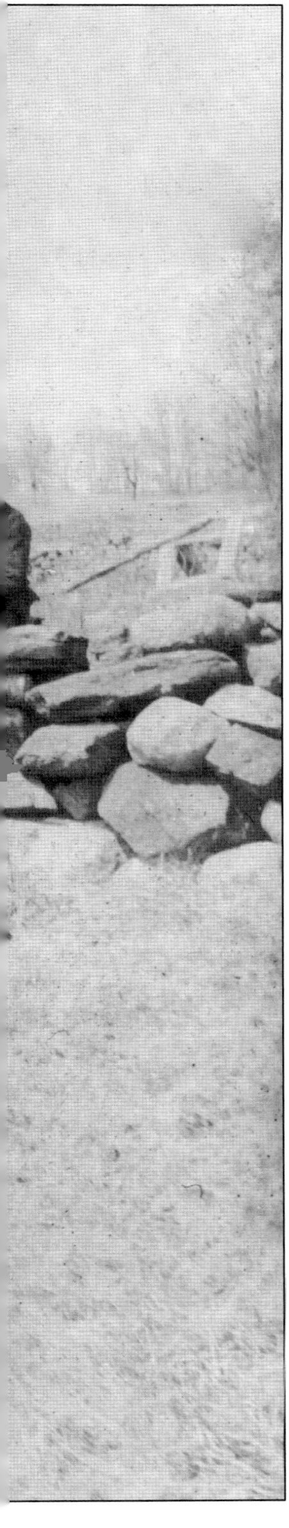

This photograph shows a group of boys from Chestnut Hill School. Former student David Miles Wakeley recalled a pump in the schoolyard with a dipper that was shared by both the students and the teacher. Mischievous boys often threw turtles, frogs, and lizards into the well for fun, thinking nothing of taking a drinking from the same well later. Children who did not behave were turned over to "Old Man Waller," a committeeman who gave troublemakers a few whacks with a hosepipe.

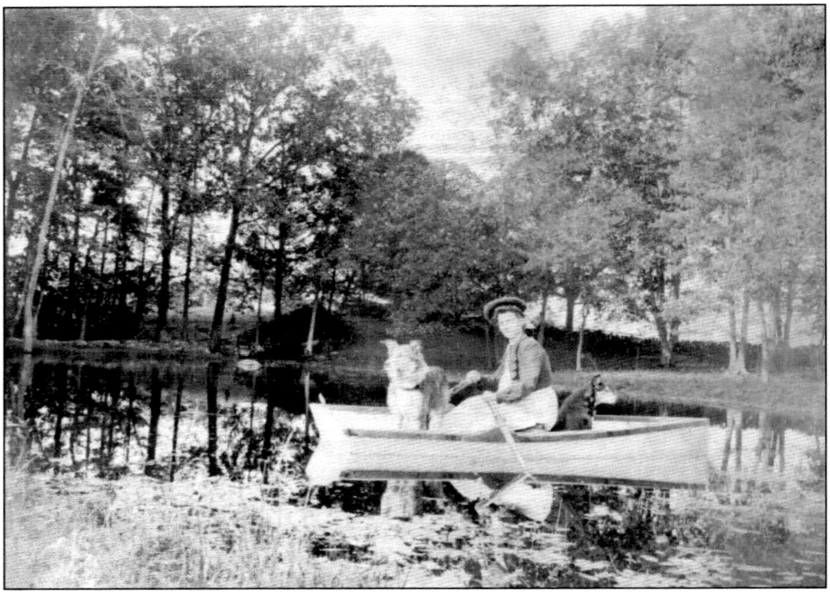

Laura Hall Beach enjoys a boat ride with her dogs on Buck Hill Pond, part of her husband's farm. While the pond was used for cutting large blocks of ice in the winter, it provided relief from the heat in the summer for both animals and humans alike.

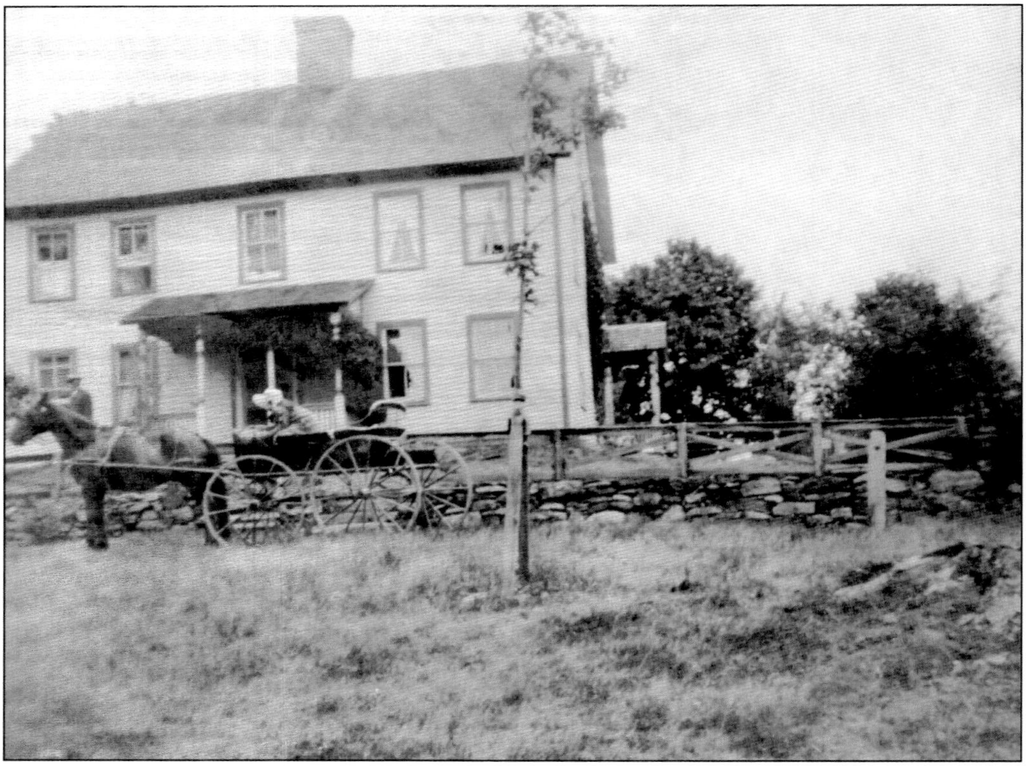

Ormel Hall's homestead was located on Plattsville Road (later Waller Road). The house, built in 1795, now faces Campbell Road. Hall served as Trumbull's first selectman from 1896 until 1897. In 1902, as Trumbull's representative to the Connecticut Constitutional Convention, he returned from Hartford with a seedling from the Constitution Oak, which he planted in his yard. The tree remained until it was damaged by Hurricane Gloria in 1985.

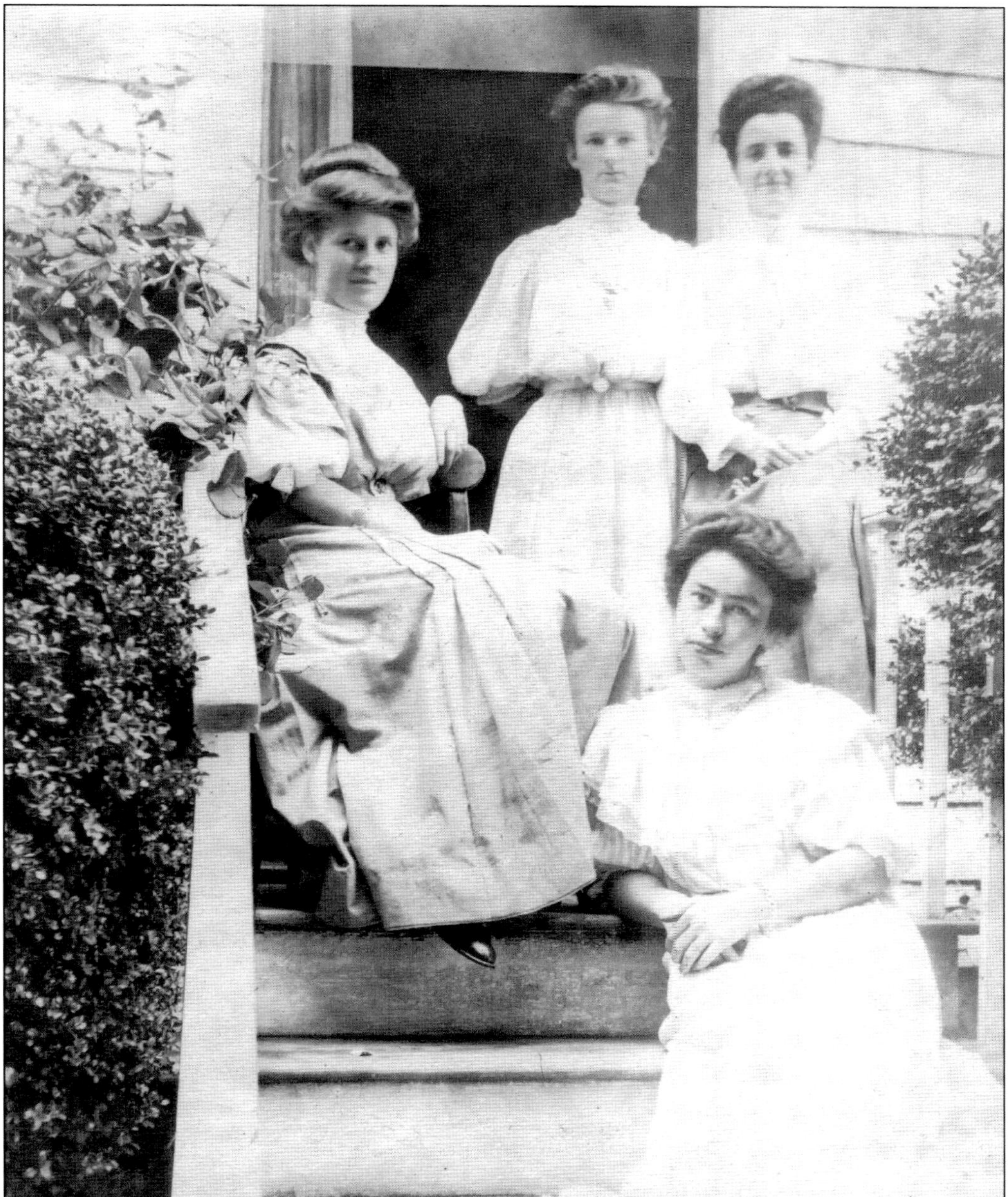

Photographed here as a young woman, Laura Hall, born in 1884, stands among friends dressed in typical Edwardian fashion. Women in this era saved hair from their hairbrushes to create natural rats, adding volume to their Gibson-girl hairstyles. Their loose, light afternoon dresses were perfect for enjoying outdoor activities popular at the time, including croquet, bicycling, boating, and tennis, or spending the day at Parlor Rock Amusement Park.

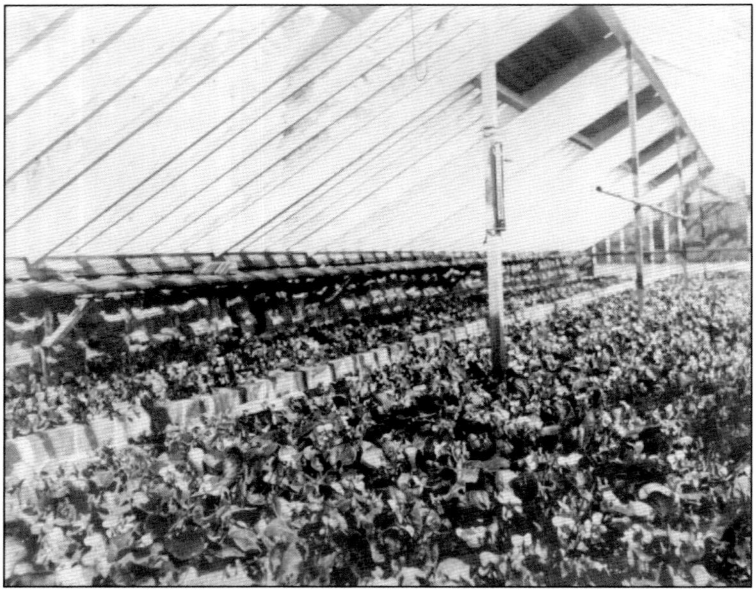

This greenhouse full of blooms belonged to William E. Waller—the "Old Man Waller" who struck fear in Chestnut Hill's misbehaving schoolboys. Waller's greenhouse was one of several in the area. His home on Plattsville Road was removed in the 1930s to make way for the Merritt Parkway.

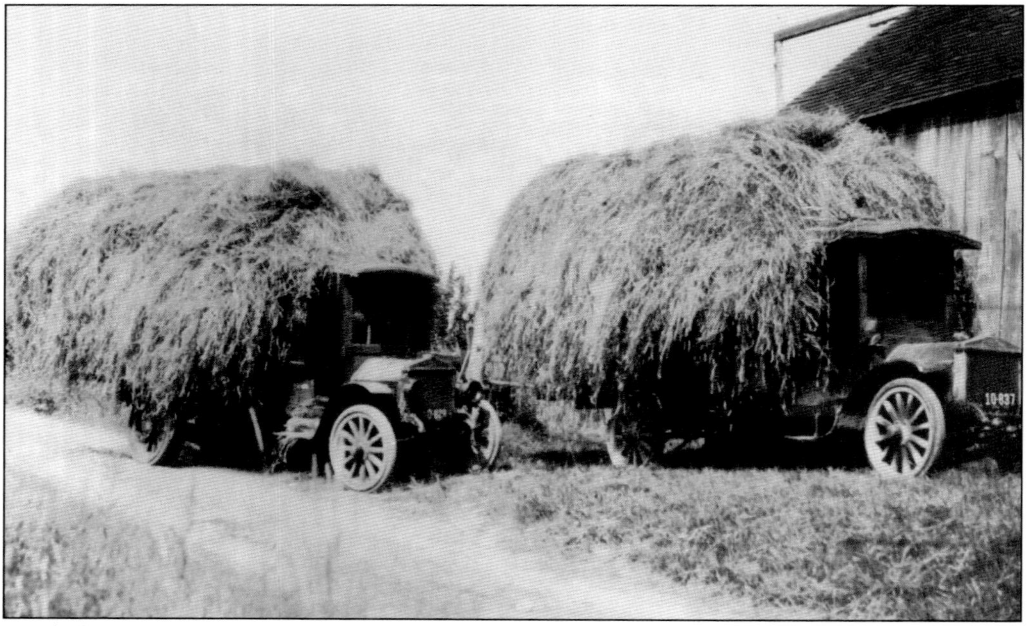

Trucks loaded with hay make a delivery at the Williams' barn on Frenchtown Road. The vehicles, owned by brothers Joe and Lee Williams, are Federal trucks. Founded in Detroit as Bailey Motor Truck in 1910, Federal produced about 160,000 vehicles during its history, with many sold overseas. The company's slogan was "Known in Every Country—Sold on Every Continent."

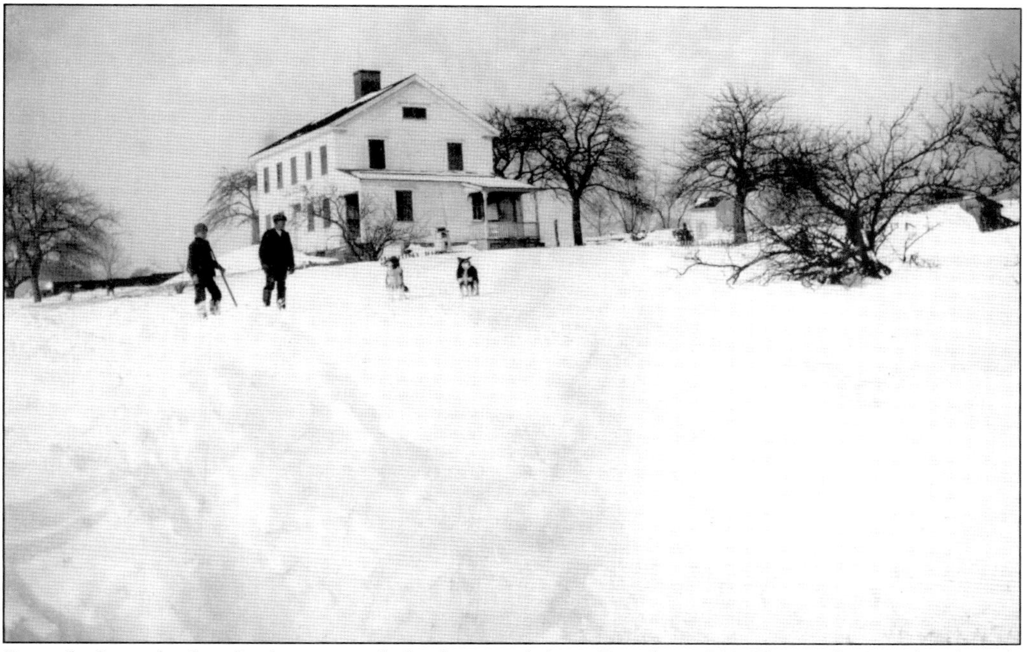

Snowdrifts eight feet high surround the home of Agur Beach at 739 Plattsville Road. Though this photograph is undated, it is likely to have been taken during the extremely harsh winter of 1934.

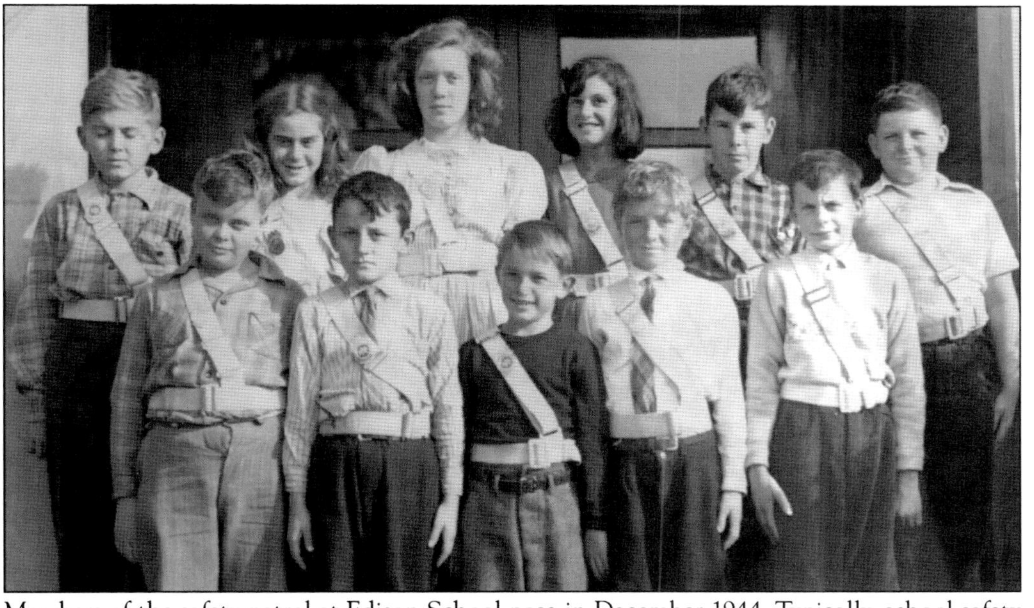

Members of the safety patrol at Edison School pose in December 1944. Typically, school safety patrols were charged with helping guide students across streets on their way to school. Built in 1929 on Edison Road near the intersection of Main Street, the school was attended by many Chestnut Hill children. In its early days, the Chestnut Hill Mother's Club raised money to have a telephone installed for the nurse. Edison School was closed in 1971 and razed in 1980 to make room for Trumbull's new police station.

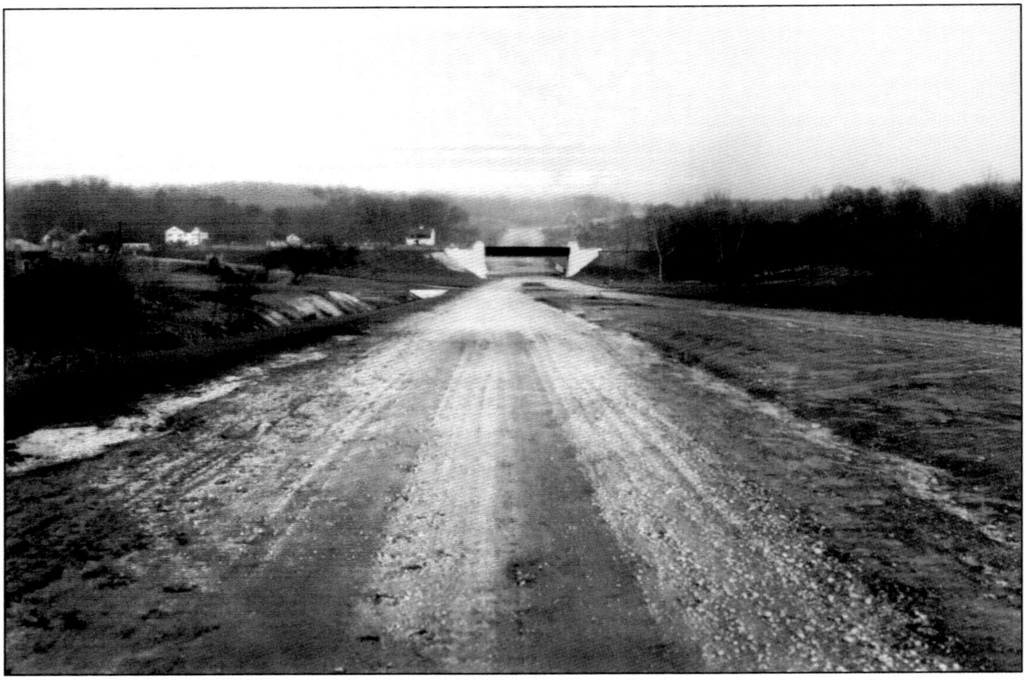

Ground breaking for the Merritt Parkway, named for Stamford congressman Schuyler Merritt, began in 1934. When it officially opened on September 2, 1940, the overpass bridge for Trumbull's Main Street and the railroad bridge at Rocky Hill Road, pictured here, had not yet been completed.

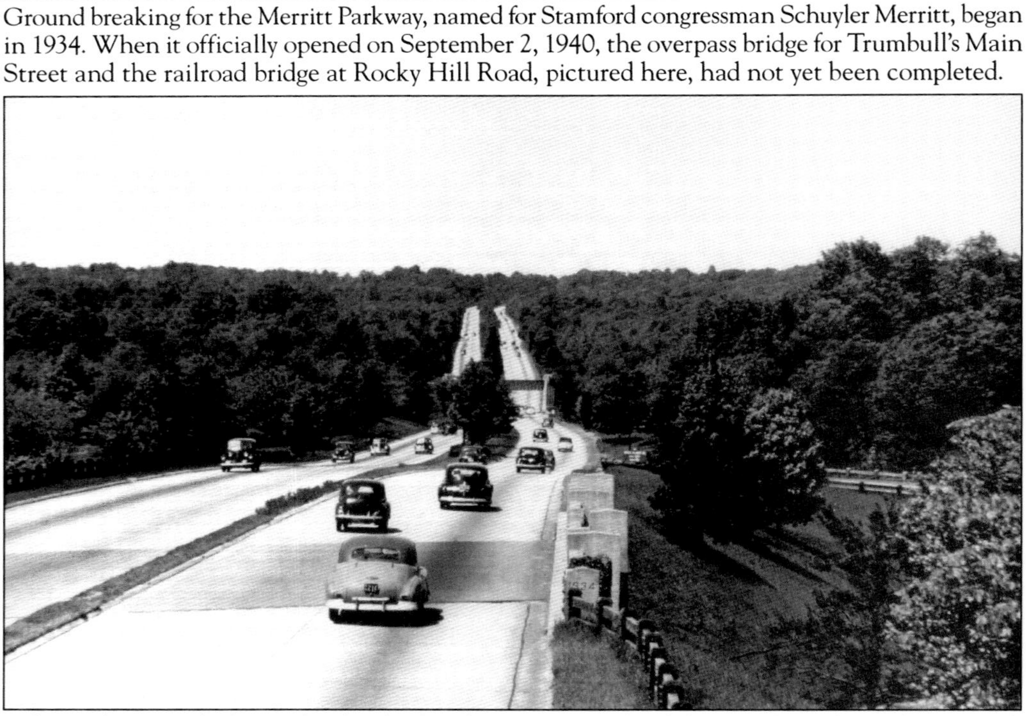

A later photograph shows the finished parkway just north of the exit for White Plains Road. Connecticut's first divided limited-access road, the parkway provided fast automobile access to New York and led to Trumbull's first suburban developments. In 1991, the Merritt Parkway was added to the National Register of Historic Places.

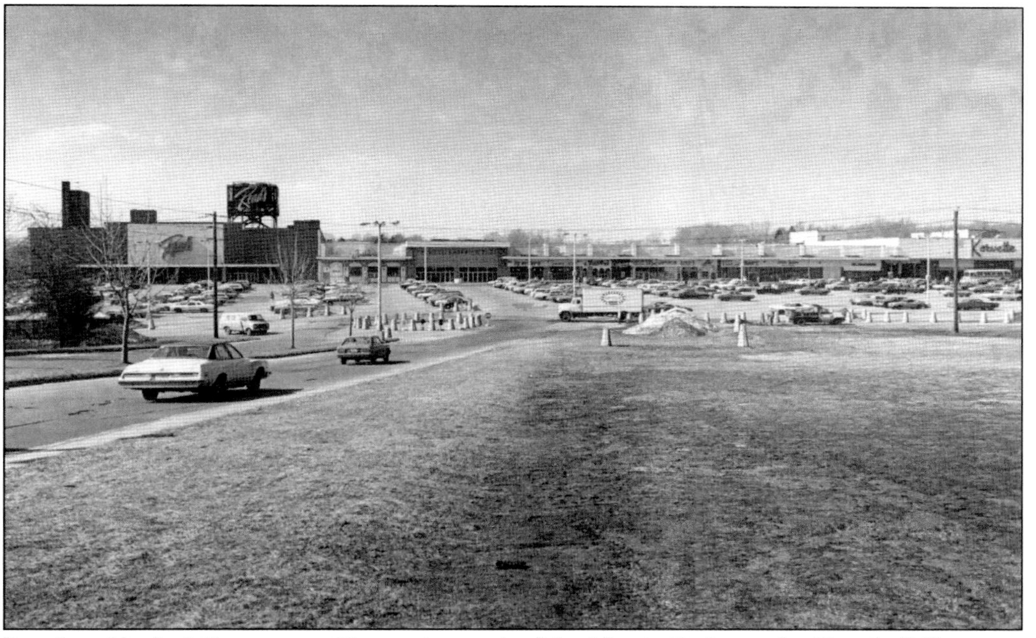

Developed by Jack Frouge on a 66-acre site south of the Merritt Parkway, the Trumbull Shopping Park, pictured in 1977, opened in November 1963. Original anchor stores included discount department store E.J. Korvette, the more upscale D.M. Read department store, and Waldbaum's supermarket. F.W. Woolworth's five-and-dime occupied two floors and featured a lunch counter and coin-operated photograph booth.

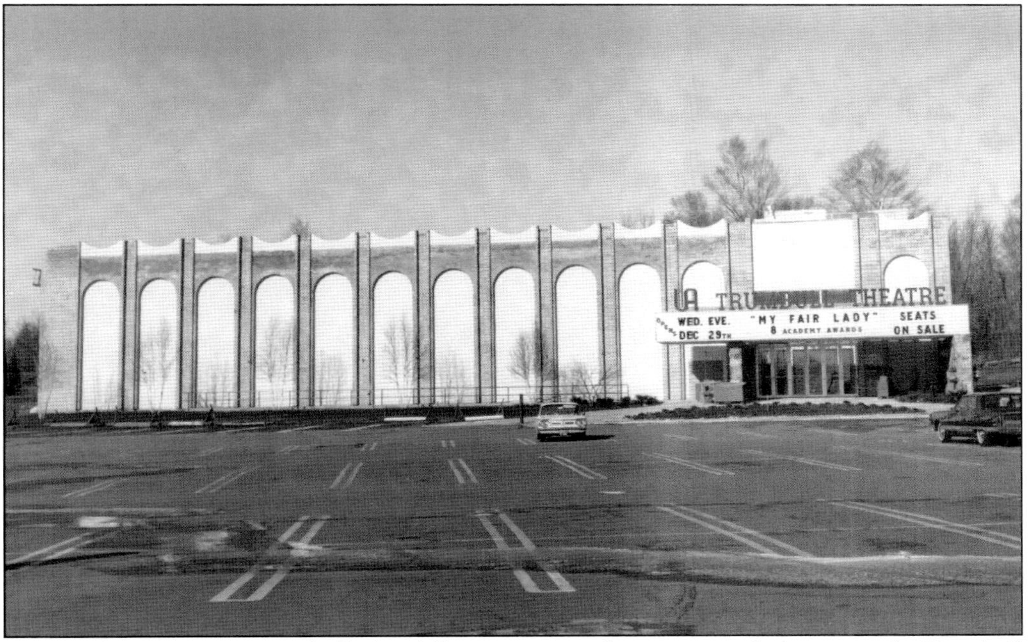

In 1967, the Trans-Lux, Trumbull's first full-screen movie theater, opened adjacent to the Trumbull Shopping Park. It later added a second screen and operated under the United Artists company. The building would later house an appliance store and a gym.

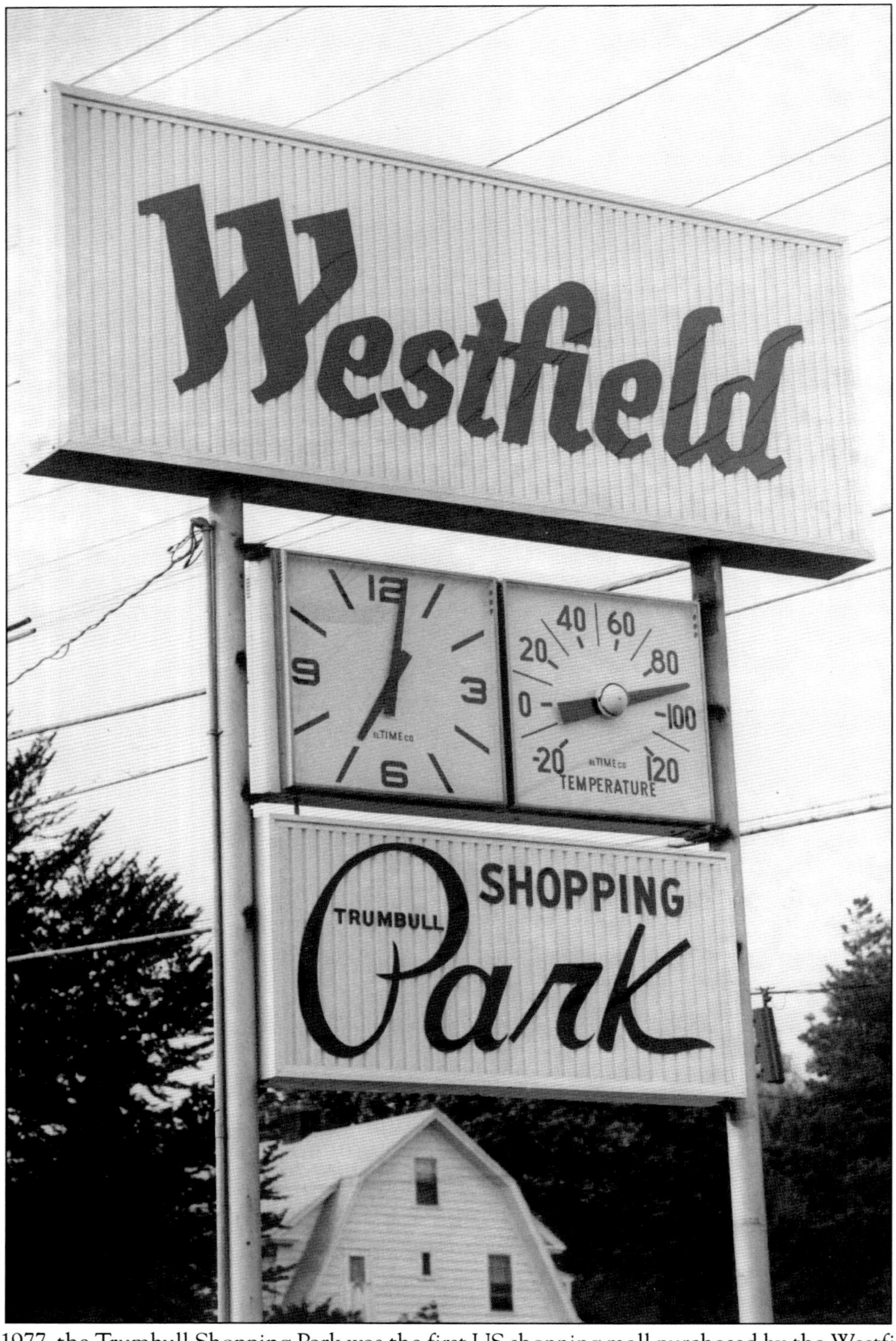

In 1977, the Trumbull Shopping Park was the first US shopping mall purchased by the Westfield Group, an Australian mall operator. It was renamed Westfield Shoppingtown-Trumbull in 1998.

BIBLIOGRAPHY

The following books are available at the Trumbull Historical Society Research Library. Most titles are also available at the museum gift shop.

Beach, E. Merrill. *They Face the Rising Sun*. The Pequot Press, Inc., 1971.

———. *Trumbull Church and Town*. The Trumbull Historical Society, Inc., 1972. Original publication: Church of Christ in Trumbull, 1955.

Seeley, Dorothy M. *Tales of Trumbull's Past*. The Trumbull Historical Society, Inc., 1984.

Trumbull Historical Society. *Trumbull*. Charleston, SC: Arcadia Publishing, 1997.

Wachenheim, Lora M. Freer. *Trumbull, Churches and People*. Bridgeport, CT: Brewer-Borg. Corp., 1964.

——— and Florence Plonsky Majewski. *Trumbull People and Friends*. Bridgeport, CT: Brewer-. Borg Corp., 1965.

Trumbull Board of Education. *Trumbull 200: Portrait of a Connecticut Town*. West Kennebunkport, . ME: Phoenix Publishing, 1997.